MOON HANDBOOKS

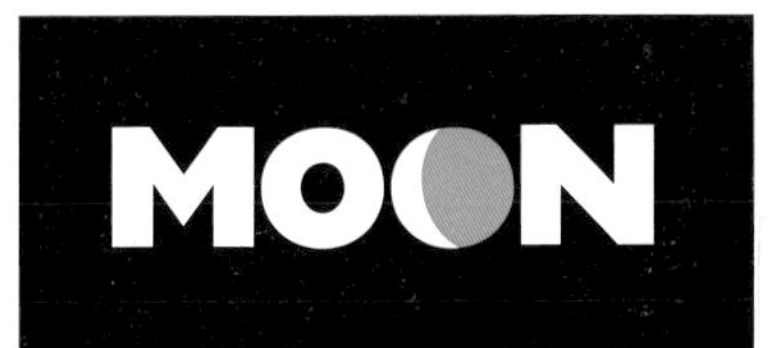

KANSAS CITY

KATY RYAN

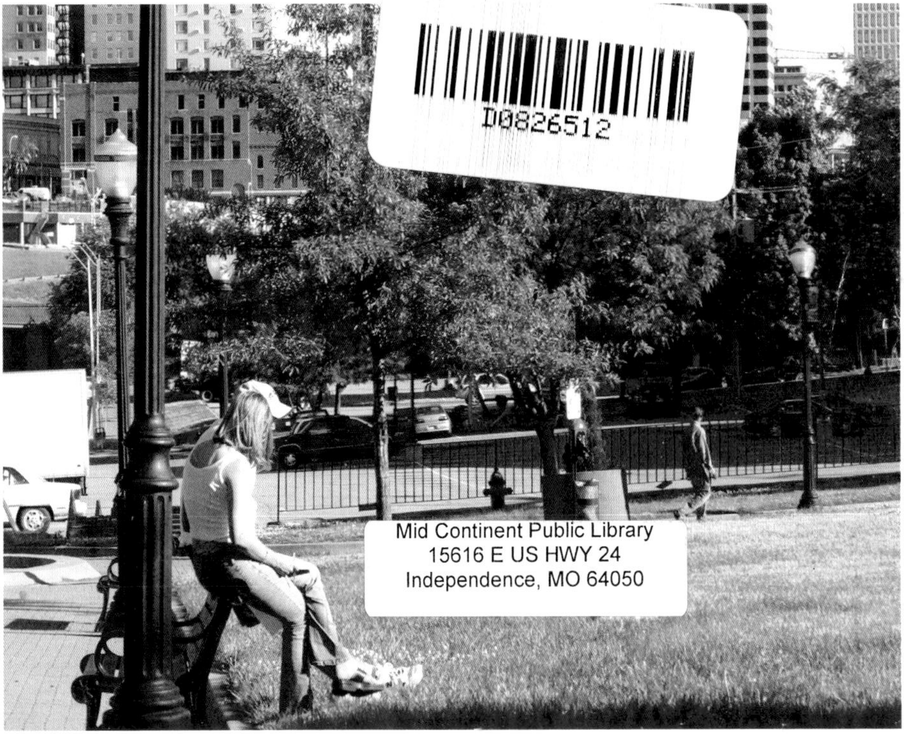

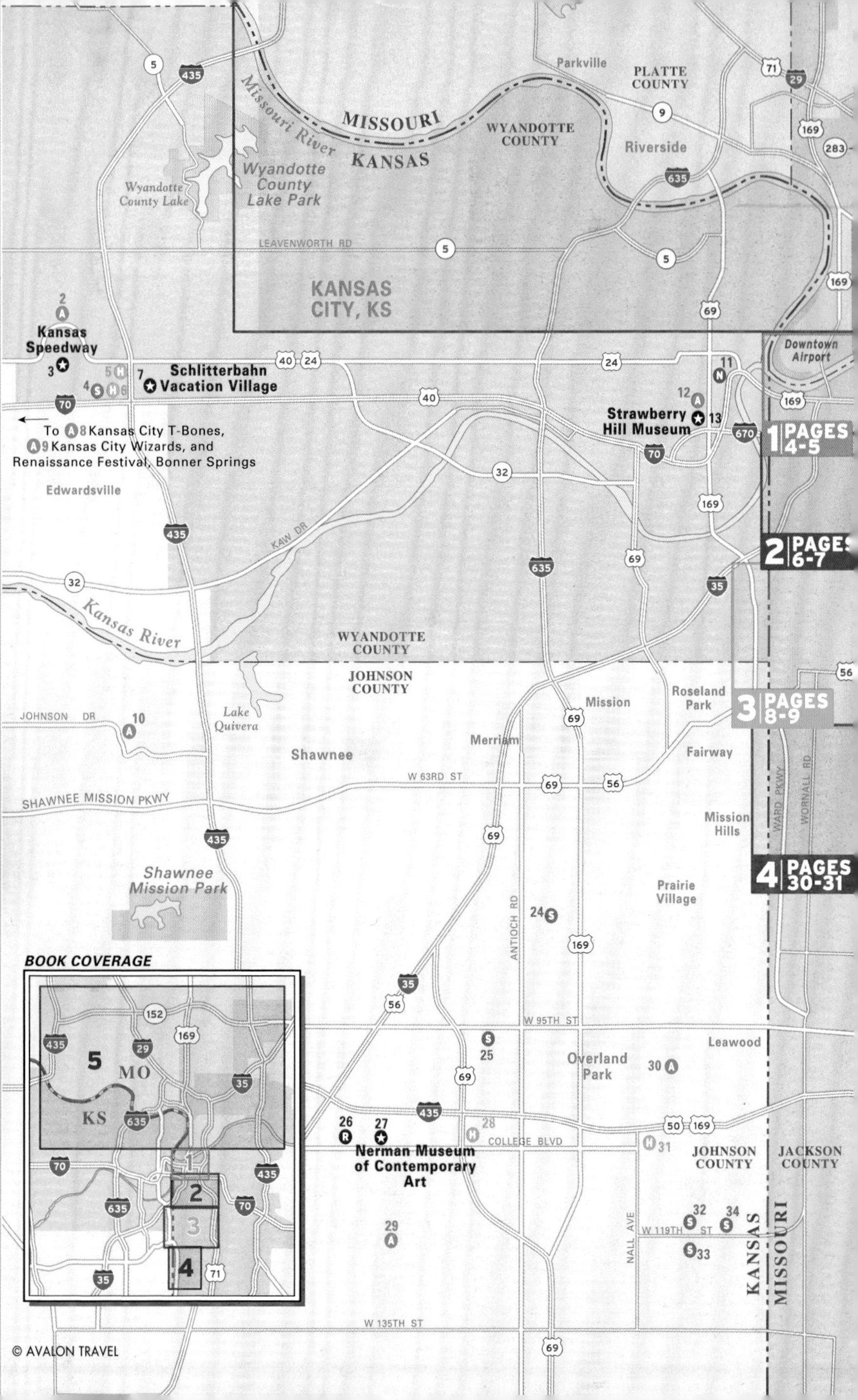

Parkville
PLATTE COUNTY
MISSOURI
Missouri River
KANSAS
WYANDOTTE COUNTY
Riverside
Wyandotte County Lake
Wyandotte County Lake Park
LEAVENWORTH RD
KANSAS CITY, KS
Downtown Airport
2 Kansas Speedway
3 Kansas Speedway
4, 5, 6
7 Schlitterbahn Vacation Village
11
12
Strawberry Hill Museum 13
To 8 Kansas City T-Bones, 9 Kansas City Wizards, and Renaissance Festival, Bonner Springs
Edwardsville
KAW DR
Kansas River
WYANDOTTE COUNTY
JOHNSON COUNTY
JOHNSON DR
10
Lake Quivera
Shawnee
Merriam
Mission
Roseland Park
Fairway
W 63RD ST
SHAWNEE MISSION PKWY
Mission Hills
WARD PKWY
WORNALL RD
Shawnee Mission Park
Prairie Village
ANTIOCH RD
24
W 95TH ST
25
Overland Park
Leawood
30
26
27 Nerman Museum of Contemporary Art
28
COLLEGE BLVD
31
JOHNSON COUNTY
JACKSON COUNTY
29
NALL AVE
32
34
W 119TH ST
33
KANSAS
MISSOURI
W 135TH ST

1 PAGES 4-5
2 PAGES 6-7
3 PAGES 8-9
4 PAGES 30-31

BOOK COVERAGE
5
MO
KS
1
2
3
4

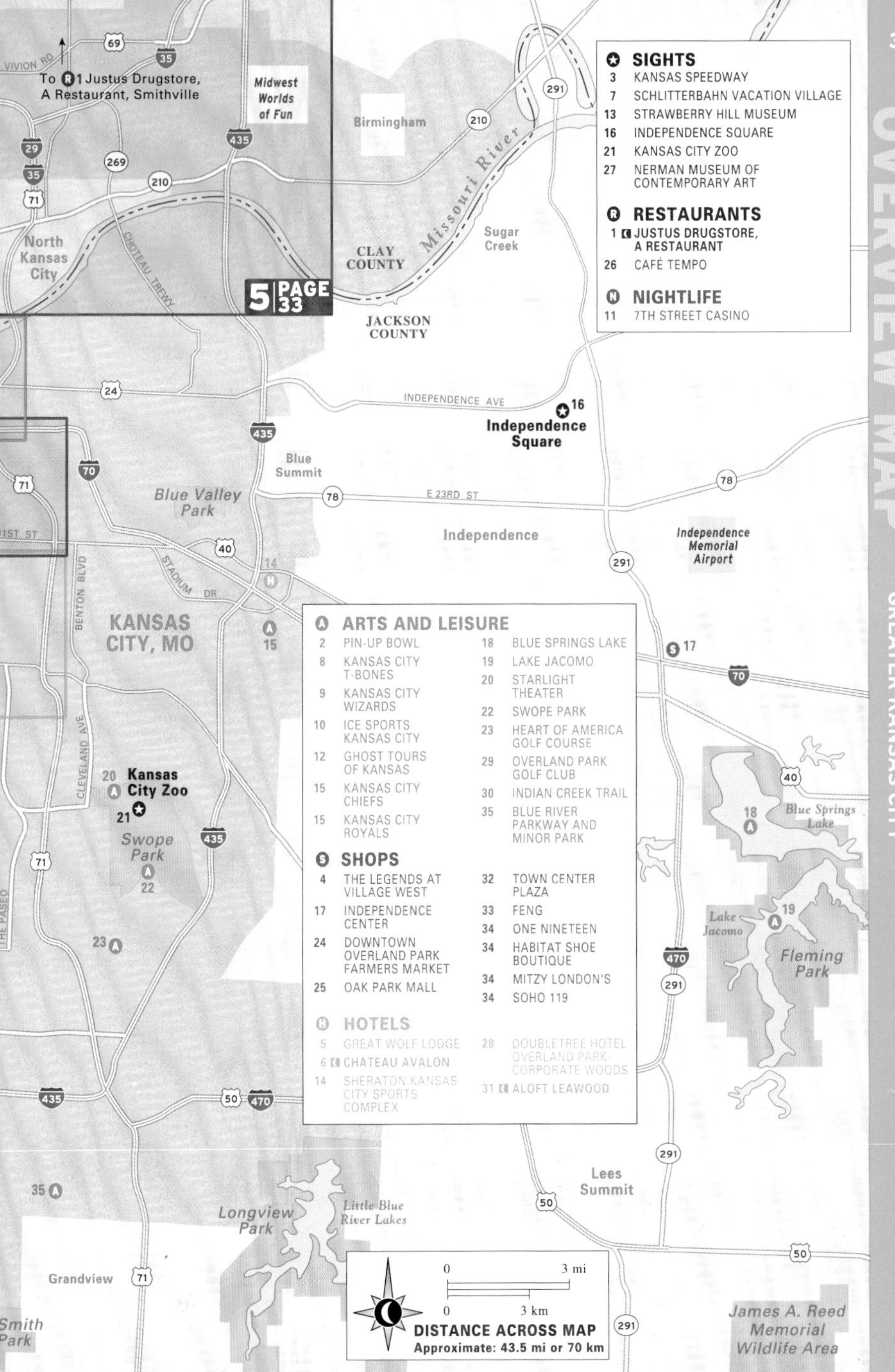

SIGHTS
3 KANSAS SPEEDWAY
7 SCHLITTERBAHN VACATION VILLAGE
13 STRAWBERRY HILL MUSEUM
16 INDEPENDENCE SQUARE
21 KANSAS CITY ZOO
27 NERMAN MUSEUM OF CONTEMPORARY ART
RESTAURANTS
1 JUSTUS DRUGSTORE, A RESTAURANT
26 CAFÉ TEMPO
NIGHTLIFE
11 7TH STREET CASINO
ARTS AND LEISURE
2 PIN-UP BOWL
8 KANSAS CITY T-BONES
9 KANSAS CITY WIZARDS
10 ICE SPORTS KANSAS CITY
12 GHOST TOURS OF KANSAS
15 KANSAS CITY CHIEFS
15 KANSAS CITY ROYALS
18 BLUE SPRINGS LAKE
19 LAKE JACOMO
20 STARLIGHT THEATER
22 SWOPE PARK
23 HEART OF AMERICA GOLF COURSE
29 OVERLAND PARK GOLF CLUB
30 INDIAN CREEK TRAIL
35 BLUE RIVER PARKWAY AND MINOR PARK
SHOPS
4 THE LEGENDS AT VILLAGE WEST
17 INDEPENDENCE CENTER
24 DOWNTOWN OVERLAND PARK FARMERS MARKET
25 OAK PARK MALL
32 TOWN CENTER PLAZA
33 FENG
34 ONE NINETEEN
34 HABITAT SHOE BOUTIQUE
34 MITZY LONDON'S
34 SOHO 119
HOTELS
5 GREAT WOLF LODGE
6 CHATEAU AVALON
14 SHERATON KANSAS CITY SPORTS COMPLEX
28 DOUBLETREE HOTEL OVERLAND PARK-CORPORATE WOODS
31 ALOFT LEAWOOD
VIVION RD
To 1 Justus Drugstore, A Restaurant, Smithville
Midwest Worlds of Fun
Birmingham
Missouri River
North Kansas City
CHOTEAU TRFWY
CLAY COUNTY
Sugar Creek
JACKSON COUNTY
5 PAGE 33
INDEPENDENCE AVE
Independence Square
Blue Summit
Blue Valley Park
E 23RD ST
Independence
Independence Memorial Airport
31ST ST
BENTON BLVD
STADIUM DR
KANSAS CITY, MO
CLEVELAND AVE
Kansas City Zoo
Swope Park
THE PASEO
Blue Springs Lake
Lake Jacomo
Fleming Park
Lees Summit
Longview Park
Little Blue River Lakes
Grandview
Smith Park
James A. Reed Memorial Wildlife Area
DISTANCE ACROSS MAP
Approximate: 43.5 mi or 70 km
0 3 mi
0 3 km

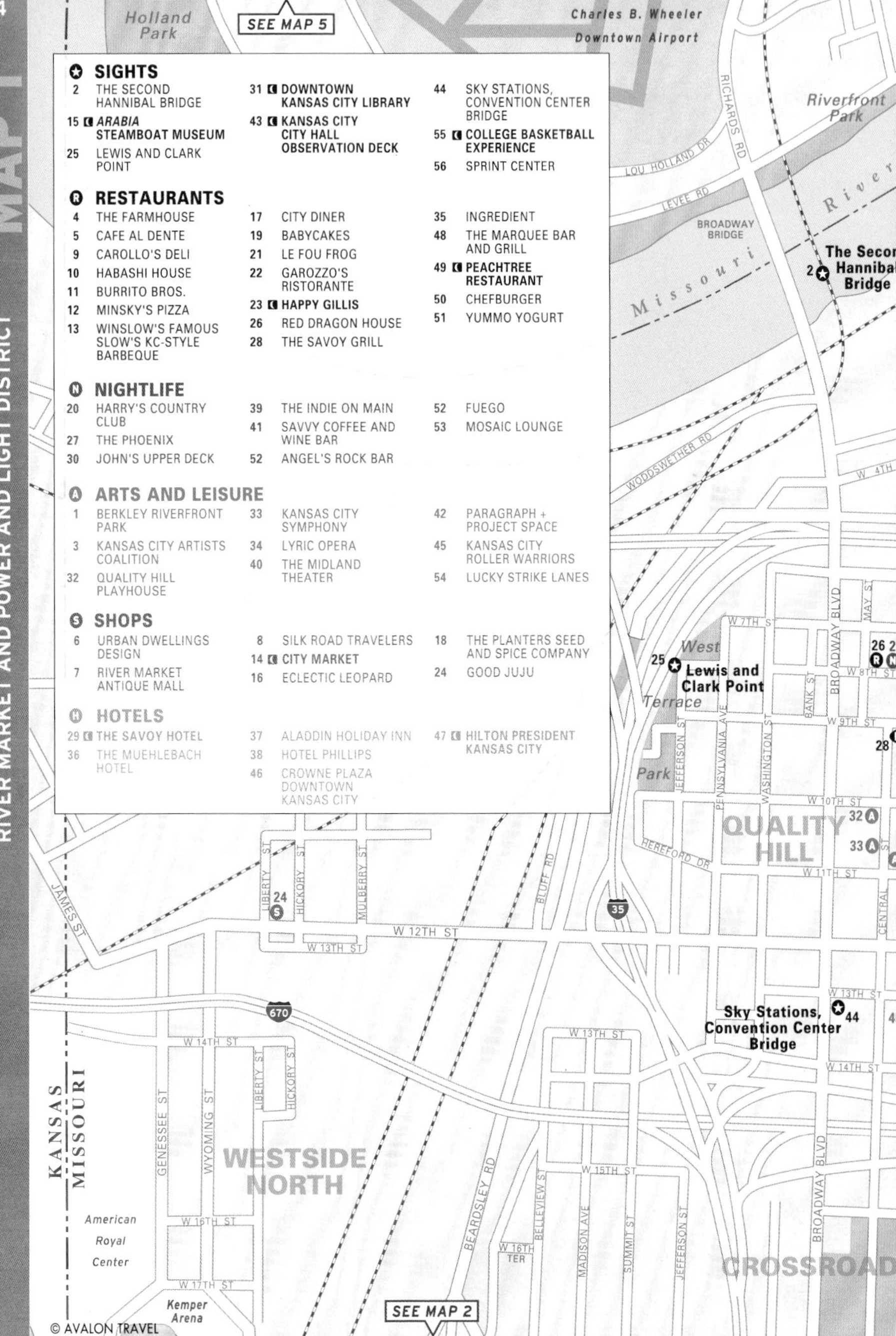
SEE MAP 5
Holland Park
Charles B. Wheeler Downtown Airport
Riverfront Park
SIGHTS
2 THE SECOND HANNIBAL BRIDGE
15 ARABIA STEAMBOAT MUSEUM
25 LEWIS AND CLARK POINT
31 DOWNTOWN KANSAS CITY LIBRARY
43 KANSAS CITY CITY HALL OBSERVATION DECK
44 SKY STATIONS, CONVENTION CENTER BRIDGE
55 COLLEGE BASKETBALL EXPERIENCE
56 SPRINT CENTER
RESTAURANTS
4 THE FARMHOUSE
5 CAFE AL DENTE
9 CAROLLO'S DELI
10 HABASHI HOUSE
11 BURRITO BROS.
12 MINSKY'S PIZZA
13 WINSLOW'S FAMOUS SLOW'S KC-STYLE BARBEQUE
17 CITY DINER
19 BABYCAKES
21 LE FOU FROG
22 GAROZZO'S RISTORANTE
23 HAPPY GILLIS
26 RED DRAGON HOUSE
28 THE SAVOY GRILL
35 INGREDIENT
48 THE MARQUEE BAR AND GRILL
49 PEACHTREE RESTAURANT
50 CHEFBURGER
51 YUMMO YOGURT
NIGHTLIFE
20 HARRY'S COUNTRY CLUB
27 THE PHOENIX
30 JOHN'S UPPER DECK
39 THE INDIE ON MAIN
41 SAVVY COFFEE AND WINE BAR
52 ANGEL'S ROCK BAR
52 FUEGO
53 MOSAIC LOUNGE
ARTS AND LEISURE
1 BERKLEY RIVERFRONT PARK
3 KANSAS CITY ARTISTS COALITION
32 QUALITY HILL PLAYHOUSE
33 KANSAS CITY SYMPHONY
34 LYRIC OPERA
40 THE MIDLAND THEATER
42 PARAGRAPH + PROJECT SPACE
45 KANSAS CITY ROLLER WARRIORS
54 LUCKY STRIKE LANES
SHOPS
6 URBAN DWELLINGS DESIGN
7 RIVER MARKET ANTIQUE MALL
8 SILK ROAD TRAVELERS
14 CITY MARKET
16 ECLECTIC LEOPARD
18 THE PLANTERS SEED AND SPICE COMPANY
24 GOOD JUJU
HOTELS
29 THE SAVOY HOTEL
36 THE MUEHLEBACH HOTEL
37 ALADDIN HOLIDAY INN
38 HOTEL PHILLIPS
46 CROWNE PLAZA DOWNTOWN KANSAS CITY
47 HILTON PRESIDENT KANSAS CITY
RICHARDS RD
LOU HOLLAND DR
LEVEE RD
BROADWAY BRIDGE
Missouri River
The Second Hannibal Bridge
WOODSWETHER RD
W 4TH ST
W 7TH ST
W 8TH ST
W 9TH ST
W 10TH ST
W 11TH ST
W 12TH ST
W 13TH ST
W 14TH ST
W 15TH ST
W 16TH ST
W 16TH TER
W 17TH ST
MAY ST
BROADWAY BLVD
BANK ST
West Terrace Park
Lewis and Clark Point
JEFFERSON ST
PENNSYLVANIA AVE
WASHINGTON ST
HEREFORD DR
CENTRAL
QUALITY HILL
LIBERTY ST
HICKORY ST
MULBERRY ST
BLUFF RD
JAMES ST
35
670
Sky Stations, Convention Center Bridge
KANSAS
MISSOURI
GENESSEE ST
WYOMING ST
WESTSIDE NORTH
BEARDSLEY RD
BELLEVIEW ST
MADISON AVE
SUMMIT ST
CROSSROADS
American Royal Center
Kemper Arena
SEE MAP 2
© AVALON TRAVEL

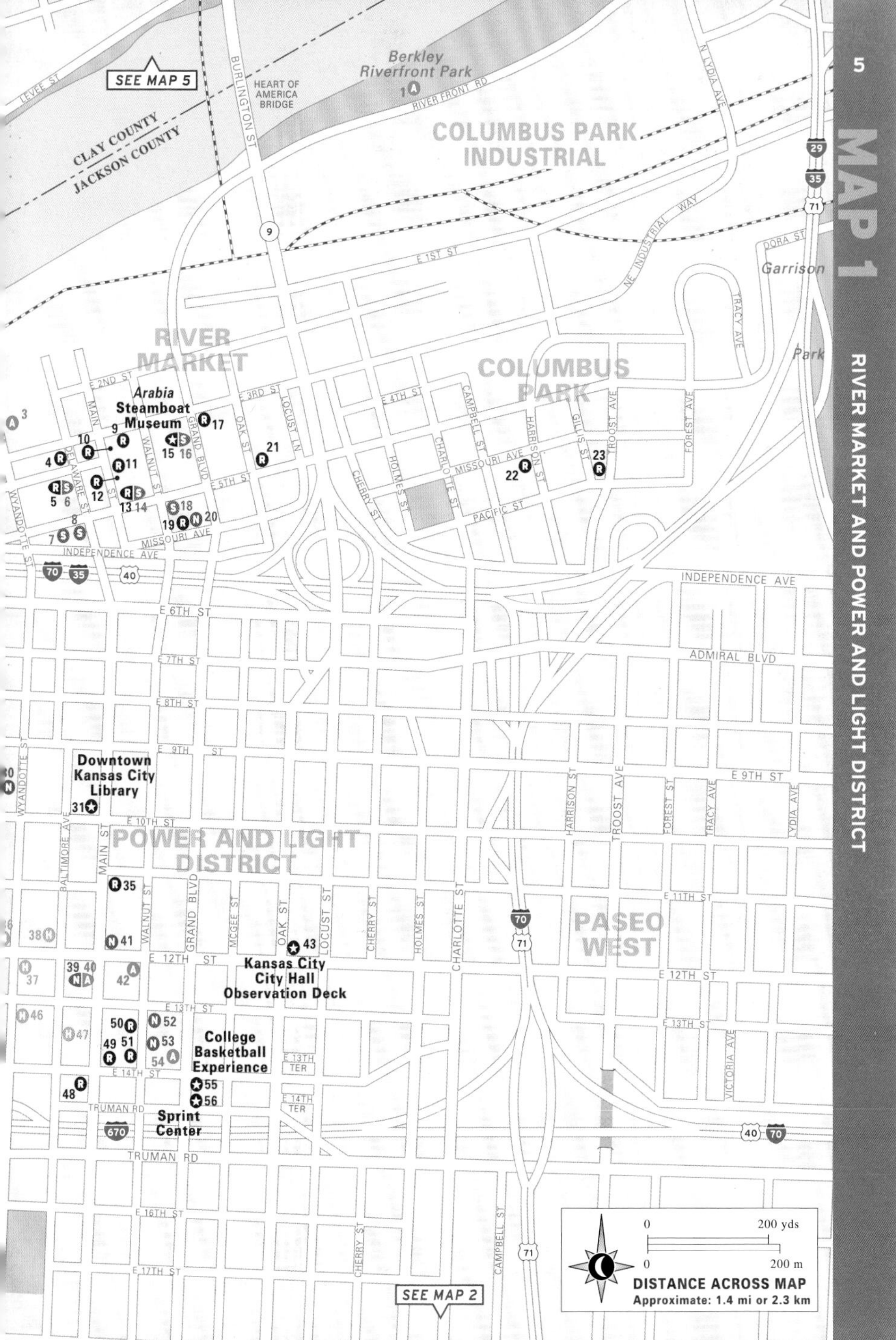
SEE MAP 5
Berkley Riverfront Park
HEART OF AMERICA BRIDGE
COLUMBUS PARK INDUSTRIAL
CLAY COUNTY
JACKSON COUNTY
RIVER MARKET
Arabia Steamboat Museum
COLUMBUS PARK
Garrison
Park
Downtown Kansas City Library
POWER AND LIGHT DISTRICT
PASEO WEST
Kansas City City Hall Observation Deck
College Basketball Experience
Sprint Center
SEE MAP 2
DISTANCE ACROSS MAP
Approximate: 1.4 mi or 2.3 km
0
200 yds
0
200 m

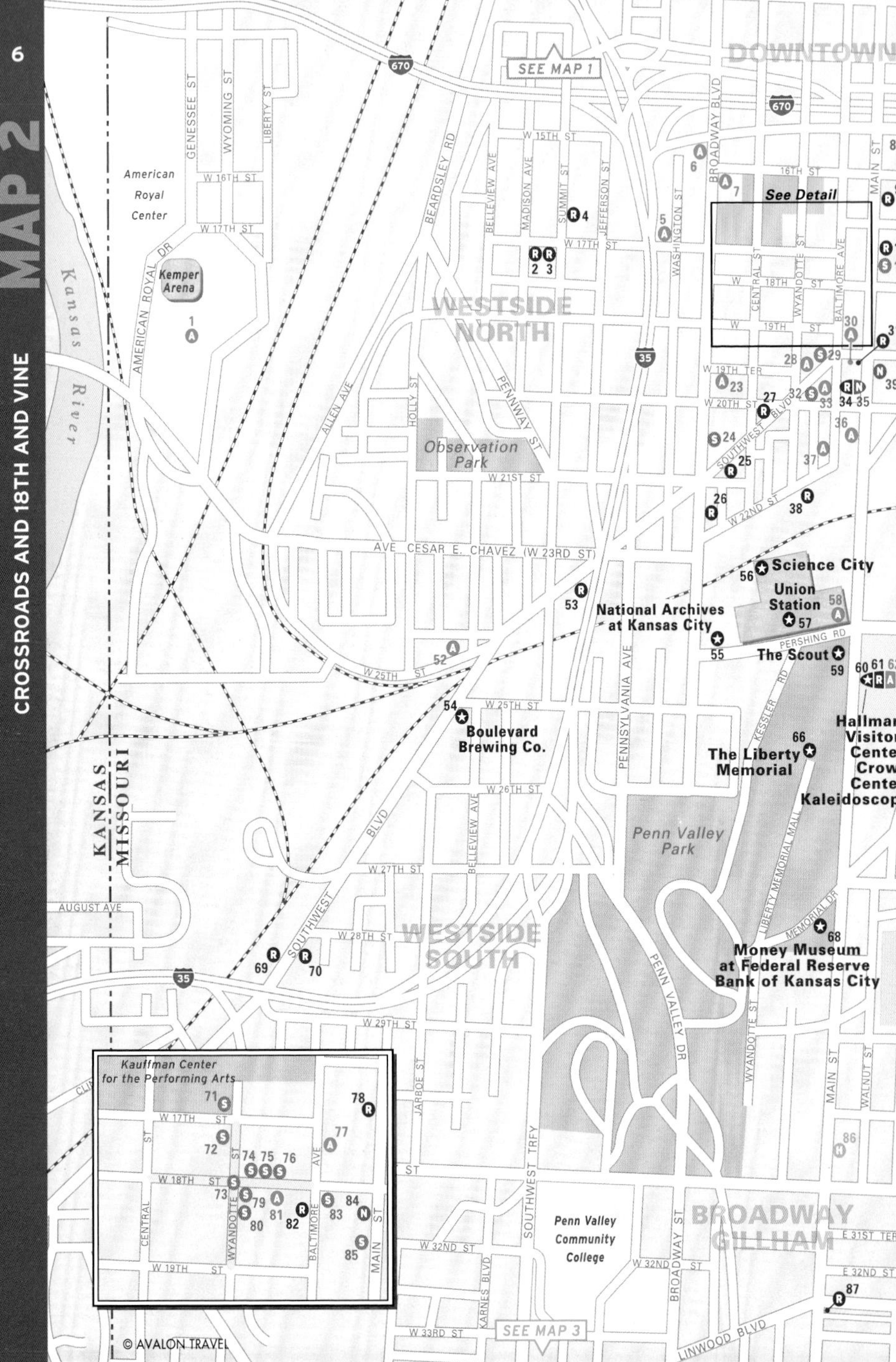

DOWNTOWN
WESTSIDE NORTH
WESTSIDE SOUTH
BROADWAY GILLHAM
SEE MAP 1
SEE MAP 3
See Detail
American Royal Center
Kemper Arena
Kansas River
KANSAS
MISSOURI
Observation Park
Penn Valley Park
Science City
Union Station
National Archives at Kansas City
The Scout
Hallmark Visitors Center, Crown Center, Kaleidoscope
Boulevard Brewing Co.
The Liberty Memorial
Money Museum at Federal Reserve Bank of Kansas City
Penn Valley Community College
Kauffman Center for the Performing Arts
AVE CESAR E. CHAVEZ (W 23RD ST)
PERSHING RD
SOUTHWEST BLVD
BROADWAY BLVD
PENNSYLVANIA AVE
PENN VALLEY DR
LIBERTY MEMORIAL MALL
LINWOOD BLVD

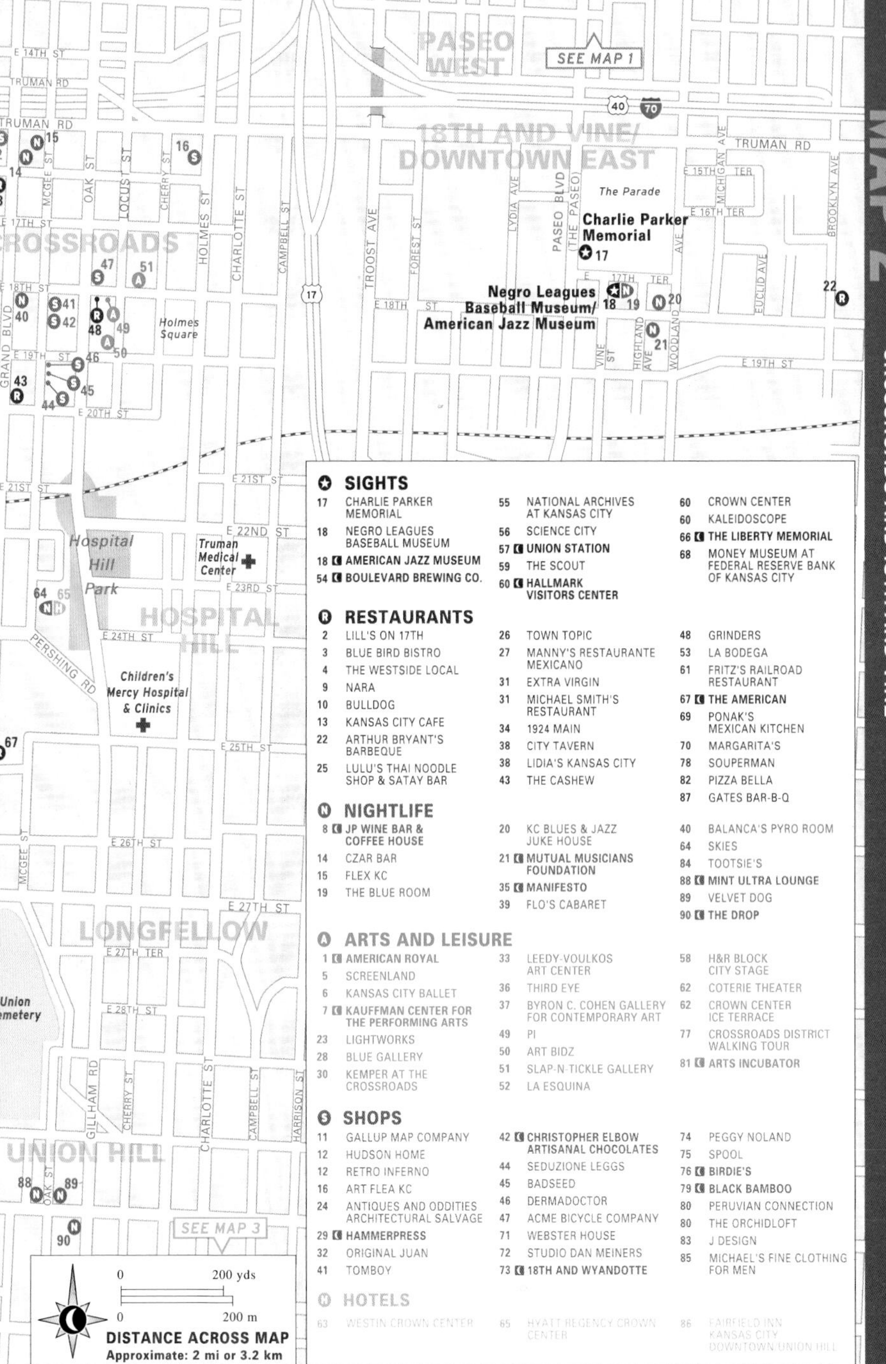
PASEO WEST
SEE MAP 1
18TH AND VINE/ DOWNTOWN EAST
CROSSROADS
HOSPITAL HILL
LONGFELLOW
UNION HILL
SEE MAP 3
E 14TH ST
TRUMAN RD
E 15TH TER
E 16TH TER
E 17TH ST
E 17TH TER
E 18TH ST
E 19TH ST
E 20TH ST
E 21ST ST
E 22ND ST
E 23RD ST
E 24TH ST
E 25TH ST
E 26TH ST
E 27TH ST
E 27TH TER
E 28TH ST
GRAND BLVD
MCGEE ST
OAK ST
LOCUST ST
CHERRY ST
HOLMES ST
CHARLOTTE ST
CAMPBELL ST
TROOST AVE
FOREST ST
LYDIA AVE
PASEO BLVD (THE PASEO)
VINE ST
HIGHLAND AVE
WOODLAND AVE
MICHIGAN AVE
EUCLID AVE
BROOKLYN AVE
PERSHING RD
GILLHAM RD
HARRISON ST
The Parade
Charlie Parker Memorial
Negro Leagues Baseball Museum/ American Jazz Museum
Holmes Square
Hospital Hill Park
Truman Medical Center
Children's Mercy Hospital & Clinics
Union Cemetery
SIGHTS
17 CHARLIE PARKER MEMORIAL
18 NEGRO LEAGUES BASEBALL MUSEUM
18 AMERICAN JAZZ MUSEUM
54 BOULEVARD BREWING CO.
55 NATIONAL ARCHIVES AT KANSAS CITY
56 SCIENCE CITY
57 UNION STATION
59 THE SCOUT
60 HALLMARK VISITORS CENTER
60 CROWN CENTER
60 KALEIDOSCOPE
66 THE LIBERTY MEMORIAL
68 MONEY MUSEUM AT FEDERAL RESERVE BANK OF KANSAS CITY
RESTAURANTS
2 LILL'S ON 17TH
3 BLUE BIRD BISTRO
4 THE WESTSIDE LOCAL
9 NARA
10 BULLDOG
13 KANSAS CITY CAFE
22 ARTHUR BRYANT'S BARBEQUE
25 LULU'S THAI NOODLE SHOP & SATAY BAR
26 TOWN TOPIC
27 MANNY'S RESTAURANTE MEXICANO
31 EXTRA VIRGIN
31 MICHAEL SMITH'S RESTAURANT
34 1924 MAIN
38 CITY TAVERN
38 LIDIA'S KANSAS CITY
43 THE CASHEW
48 GRINDERS
53 LA BODEGA
61 FRITZ'S RAILROAD RESTAURANT
67 THE AMERICAN
69 PONAK'S MEXICAN KITCHEN
70 MARGARITA'S
78 SOUPERMAN
82 PIZZA BELLA
87 GATES BAR-B-Q
NIGHTLIFE
8 JP WINE BAR & COFFEE HOUSE
14 CZAR BAR
15 FLEX KC
19 THE BLUE ROOM
20 KC BLUES & JAZZ JUKE HOUSE
21 MUTUAL MUSICIANS FOUNDATION
35 MANIFESTO
39 FLO'S CABARET
40 BALANCA'S PYRO ROOM
64 SKIES
84 TOOTSIE'S
88 MINT ULTRA LOUNGE
89 VELVET DOG
90 THE DROP
ARTS AND LEISURE
1 AMERICAN ROYAL
5 SCREENLAND
6 KANSAS CITY BALLET
7 KAUFFMAN CENTER FOR THE PERFORMING ARTS
23 LIGHTWORKS
28 BLUE GALLERY
30 KEMPER AT THE CROSSROADS
33 LEEDY-VOULKOS ART CENTER
36 THIRD EYE
37 BYRON C. COHEN GALLERY FOR CONTEMPORARY ART
49 PI
50 ART BIDZ
51 SLAP-N-TICKLE GALLERY
52 LA ESQUINA
58 H&R BLOCK CITY STAGE
62 COTERIE THEATER
62 CROWN CENTER ICE TERRACE
77 CROSSROADS DISTRICT WALKING TOUR
81 ARTS INCUBATOR
SHOPS
11 GALLUP MAP COMPANY
12 HUDSON HOME
12 RETRO INFERNO
16 ART FLEA KC
24 ANTIQUES AND ODDITIES ARCHITECTURAL SALVAGE
29 HAMMERPRESS
32 ORIGINAL JUAN
41 TOMBOY
42 CHRISTOPHER ELBOW ARTISANAL CHOCOLATES
44 SEDUZIONE LEGGS
45 BADSEED
46 DERMADOCTOR
47 ACME BICYCLE COMPANY
71 WEBSTER HOUSE
72 STUDIO DAN MEINERS
73 18TH AND WYANDOTTE
74 PEGGY NOLAND
75 SPOOL
76 BIRDIE'S
79 BLACK BAMBOO
80 PERUVIAN CONNECTION
80 THE ORCHIDLOFT
83 J DESIGN
85 MICHAEL'S FINE CLOTHING FOR MEN
HOTELS
63 WESTIN CROWN CENTER
65 HYATT REGENCY CROWN CENTER
86 FAIRFIELD INN KANSAS CITY DOWNTOWN/UNION HILL
0 200 yds
0 200 m
DISTANCE ACROSS MAP
Approximate: 2 mi or 3.2 km

WESTPORT
DISTANCE ACROSS MAP
Approximate: 2.3 mi or 3.7 km
0 200 yds
0 200 m
SEE MAP 2
SEE MAP 4
ROANOKE
Roanoke Park
Thomas Hart Benton Home and Studio
HANOVER PLACE
OLD WESTPORT
VOLKER
MIDTOWN
State Line Road
University of Kansas Hospital
See WESTPORT Detail
WESTPORT
Harris-Kearney House
WEST PLAZA
ARTS AND ANTIQUES DISTRICT
Vietnam Veterans Memorial
Mill Creek Park
The Cancer Institute
Kemper Museum of Contemporary Art
See THE PLAZA Detail
J.C. Nichols Memorial Fountain
Country Club Plaza
WYANDOTTE COUNTY
JOHNSON COUNTY
Westwood
Westwood Park
Westwood Hills
KANSAS
MISSOURI
Mission Woods
Kansas City Board of Trade
SUNSET HILL
Brush Creek
Jacob L. Loose Park
Mission Hills
To 70 Rainy Day Books
COUNTRYSIDE
SHAWNEE MISSION PKWY
WARD PKWY

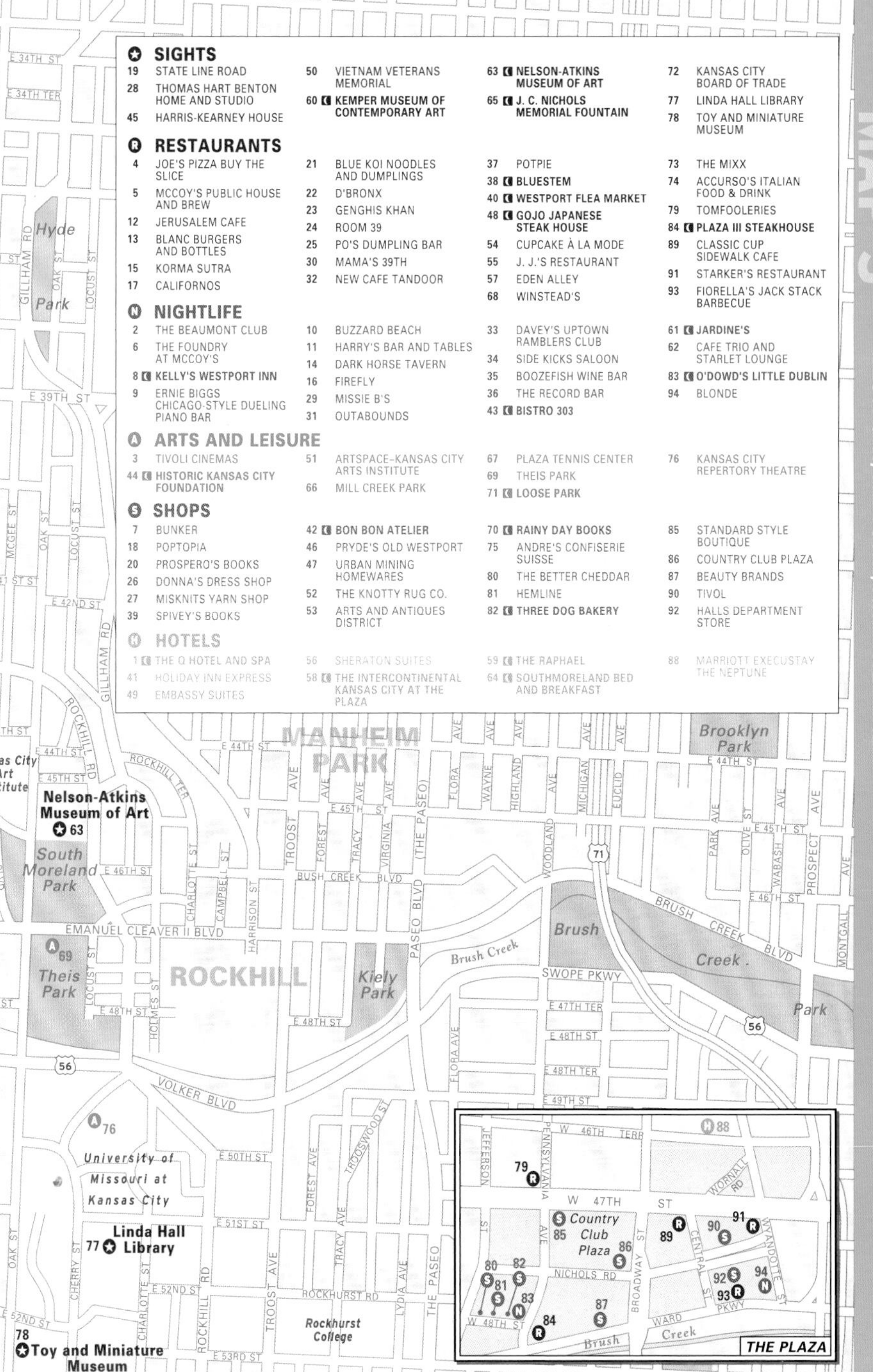
SIGHTS
19 STATE LINE ROAD
28 THOMAS HART BENTON HOME AND STUDIO
45 HARRIS-KEARNEY HOUSE
50 VIETNAM VETERANS MEMORIAL
60 KEMPER MUSEUM OF CONTEMPORARY ART
63 NELSON-ATKINS MUSEUM OF ART
65 J. C. NICHOLS MEMORIAL FOUNTAIN
72 KANSAS CITY BOARD OF TRADE
77 LINDA HALL LIBRARY
78 TOY AND MINIATURE MUSEUM
RESTAURANTS
4 JOE'S PIZZA BUY THE SLICE
5 MCCOY'S PUBLIC HOUSE AND BREW
12 JERUSALEM CAFE
13 BLANC BURGERS AND BOTTLES
15 KORMA SUTRA
17 CALIFORNOS
21 BLUE KOI NOODLES AND DUMPLINGS
22 D'BRONX
23 GENGHIS KHAN
24 ROOM 39
25 PO'S DUMPLING BAR
30 MAMA'S 39TH
32 NEW CAFE TANDOOR
37 POTPIE
38 BLUESTEM
40 WESTPORT FLEA MARKET
48 GOJO JAPANESE STEAK HOUSE
54 CUPCAKE À LA MODE
55 J. J.'S RESTAURANT
57 EDEN ALLEY
68 WINSTEAD'S
73 THE MIXX
74 ACCURSO'S ITALIAN FOOD & DRINK
79 TOMFOOLERIES
84 PLAZA III STEAKHOUSE
89 CLASSIC CUP SIDEWALK CAFE
91 STARKER'S RESTAURANT
93 FIORELLA'S JACK STACK BARBECUE
NIGHTLIFE
2 THE BEAUMONT CLUB
6 THE FOUNDRY AT MCCOY'S
8 KELLY'S WESTPORT INN
9 ERNIE BIGGS CHICAGO-STYLE DUELING PIANO BAR
10 BUZZARD BEACH
11 HARRY'S BAR AND TABLES
14 DARK HORSE TAVERN
16 FIREFLY
29 MISSIE B'S
31 OUTABOUNDS
33 DAVEY'S UPTOWN RAMBLERS CLUB
34 SIDE KICKS SALOON
35 BOOZEFISH WINE BAR
36 THE RECORD BAR
43 BISTRO 303
61 JARDINE'S
62 CAFE TRIO AND STARLET LOUNGE
83 O'DOWD'S LITTLE DUBLIN
94 BLONDE
ARTS AND LEISURE
3 TIVOLI CINEMAS
44 HISTORIC KANSAS CITY FOUNDATION
51 ARTSPACE-KANSAS CITY ARTS INSTITUTE
66 MILL CREEK PARK
67 PLAZA TENNIS CENTER
69 THEIS PARK
71 LOOSE PARK
76 KANSAS CITY REPERTORY THEATRE
SHOPS
7 BUNKER
18 POPTOPIA
20 PROSPERO'S BOOKS
26 DONNA'S DRESS SHOP
27 MISKNITS YARN SHOP
39 SPIVEY'S BOOKS
42 BON BON ATELIER
46 PRYDE'S OLD WESTPORT
47 URBAN MINING HOMEWARES
52 THE KNOTTY RUG CO.
53 ARTS AND ANTIQUES DISTRICT
70 RAINY DAY BOOKS
75 ANDRE'S CONFISERIE SUISSE
80 THE BETTER CHEDDAR
81 HEMLINE
82 THREE DOG BAKERY
85 STANDARD STYLE BOUTIQUE
86 COUNTRY CLUB PLAZA
87 BEAUTY BRANDS
90 TIVOL
92 HALLS DEPARTMENT STORE
HOTELS
1 THE Q HOTEL AND SPA
41 HOLIDAY INN EXPRESS
49 EMBASSY SUITES
56 SHERATON SUITES
58 THE INTERCONTINENTAL KANSAS CITY AT THE PLAZA
59 THE RAPHAEL
64 SOUTHMORELAND BED AND BREAKFAST
88 MARRIOTT EXECUSTAY THE NEPTUNE
Hyde Park
MANHEIM PARK
ROCKHILL
Nelson-Atkins Museum of Art
Kansas City Art Institute
South Moreland Park
Theis Park
Kiely Park
Brush Creek Park
Brooklyn Park
University of Missouri at Kansas City
Linda Hall Library
Toy and Miniature Museum
Rockhurst College
Country Club Plaza
THE PLAZA
E 34TH ST
E 39TH ST
EMANUEL CLEAVER II BLVD
BRUSH CREEK BLVD
VOLKER BLVD
SWOPE PKWY
ROCKHILL RD
GILLHAM RD
TROOST AVE
PASEO BLVD
W 47TH ST
NICHOLS RD
WARD PKWY
BROADWAY
71
56

Contents

Discover Kansas City

Sometimes dismissed with the oft-used moniker "Cowtown," Kansas City has discreetly wiped the barbecue sauce from its chin, and, in an act of quiet defiance, unveiled the fruits of a multibillion-dollar makeover that has elevated the historic stronghold to a place of metropolitan prominence within the Midwest.

To celebrate Kansas City's accomplishments is to pay homage to the singular motto of the city: unity. Kansas City stretches across 18 counties and straddles the state line, creating two adjoining metropolitan areas in two states: Kansas City, Missouri, and Kansas City, Kansas.

The city continues to define itself both in terms of its storied history and in the glimmers of hope for what lies ahead. It's a destination for those who seek the friendliness and familiarity common to the Midwest while discovering the traditions and trademarks that are the city's signatures.

Explore the streets of downtown to absorb the city's rich history. Stroll past iconic displays of art deco and the city's many fountains. Sample the city's unofficial signature cuisine at any number of its delicious barbecue joints, or come during October for the infamous American Royal barbecue festival. The city's flourishing arts community has inspired an impressive number of new galleries and museums and many live-music venues provide access to local musicians and national touring acts.

This "Paris of the Plains" will leave you with memories of a city that truly embraces the definition of a good time. And each time you return, you'll be welcomed with open arms . . . and a plate of barbecue, of course.

Planning Your Trip

▸ WHERE TO GO

River Market and Power and Light District

Idyllic surroundings and plentiful lofts comprise the historic River Market neighborhood, formerly known as the River Quay. Its centerpiece is the City Market, a weekly spectacle of local food and crafts. In the Power and Light District, past meets future in the heart of downtown's developmental renaissance, with the Sprint Center as one of its crown jewels. Numerous restaurants, bars, retail shops, hotels, and easy access to public transportation make this area an ideal starting point from which to explore the city.

Head to the City Market, the region's largest farmers market, for an incredible selection of produce, baked goods, and other edible goodies.

Crossroads and 18th and Vine

Lauded as one of the nation's most concentrated gallery districts, the Crossroads Arts District boasts an eclectic atmosphere and low-key culture with a colorful array of shops, galleries, and restaurants. Home to the wildly popular First Fridays gallery crawl, the Crossroads is synonymous with local art and culture. The museums and music clubs of 18th and Vine preserve the city's rich jazz history, and it was within this vibrantly musical area that Kansas City's nickname Paris of the Plains originated.

Westport, Midtown, and The Plaza

Historic Westport, once the city's cornerstone, has evolved into a must-see bar and restaurant district, home to Kelly's Westport Inn, the oldest building in Kansas City. Mostly residential, Midtown is a foodie's haven along 39th Street, a restaurant corridor that dishes up dumplings, pizza, and everything in between. Considered by many to be Kansas City's number-one crown jewel, shopping mecca Country Club Plaza is an enduring testament to local icon J. C. Nichols.

Brookside and Waldo

Built in 1920 as the city's first suburban shopping area, Brookside sparked the city's outward growth and remains a popular destination comprised of locally owned boutiques, restaurants, and watering holes. With a similar aesthetic, Waldo houses bars, restaurants, and a sprinkling of specialty shops all surrounded by tree-lined streets and stately Cape Cod- and Prairie-style homes. Although both areas are best reached by car, on-foot navigation is the optimal way to explore Brookside and Waldo.

Northland

Loosely defined as any part of Kansas City north of the river, the Northland boasts shopping,

Arrowhead Stadium hosts the Kansas City Chiefs.

dining, entertainment, and ample recreational opportunities, namely the city's two amusement parks, Oceans of Fun and Worlds of Fun, and a wealth of carefully tended parks and green spaces. Northland unites historic towns, such as Parkville, with newly constructed mixed-use districts like Zona Rosa and Briarcliff. Other Northland attractions include the vast majority of the city's casinos, all within minutes of downtown Kansas City.

Greater Kansas City

As a result of suburban growth that began in the 1950s, Kansas City now includes 18 counties in two states, which boast everything from the Kansas City Zoo to Arrowhead and Kauffman sports stadiums and elaborate mixed-use shopping districts. Pockets of locally owned boutiques, restaurants, and bars intermingle with national chains, often housed in the ubiquitous strip mall. And while you'll find ample new construction, the city's outlying area also hosts historic stops such as Independence, home of former president Harry S. Truman, as well as Overland Park and Leawood.

Excursions from Kansas City

A prototypical college town with a significant place in Kansas history, Lawrence beckons with the University of Kansas campus and Massachusetts ("Mass") Street, downtown's main strip of shops, restaurants, coffeehouses, and bars. Escape to historic Rocheport atop the Missouri River bluffs for quaint surroundings, bed-and-breakfasts, and Missouri's beloved Les Bourgeois winery. With the charming, slightly bohemian Old Market District, world-renowned Henry Doorly Zoo, and architecturally significant Bob Kerrey pedestrian bridge, Omaha is a worthwhile drive.

▸ WHEN TO GO

Kansas City is a destination for all seasons, but local events and activities peak in the spring and summer and again throughout the holiday season. Although outdoor dining and festivals are plentiful during summer months, a sweltering combination of high heat and humidity prompt heat advisories and warnings. If you do come in the summer, plan the bulk of your sightseeing during the early-morning or late-afternoon hours to take advantage of milder temperatures. If you plan to see most of the city on foot, opt for the cooler, less-humid spring and fall months. Winter often brings ice, snow, and below-freezing temperatures. Large crowds converge on Kansas City during the NASCAR races, American Royal barbecue and livestock festival in October, and the Plaza Lighting Ceremony held Thanksgiving night. Hotel rooms near these events are at a premium at that time, and some are booked up years in advance.

Explore Kansas City

THE BEST OF KANSAS CITY

Day 1

- As you depart Kansas City International Airport, enjoy your first glimpse of public art (and water features) as you cruise by Keith Sonnier's commissioned Water and Light project. Head downtown, the best location to stay and play if you're in town for a short time. Try The Savoy Hotel for a sumptuous combination of luxury and history or the Hilton President Kansas City for a superbly renovated retreat.

The Hilton President Kansas City made a triumphant comeback in 2006 after being closed for 25 years.

- Once you've checked in, head out to the picturesque River Market for lunch. Once a local Mafia stronghold, River Market is now home to a huge farmers market as well as pint-sized restaurants. Or, just a short drive away, the predominantly Italian neighborhood of Columbus Park hosts one of the city's best-kept secrets: Happy Gillis, a breakfast and sandwich shop that specializes in creative combinations and made-from-scratch soups.

- Shopaholics and museum aficionados alike will find much to explore in downtown Kansas City. Browse the latest fashions nestled in a quirky row of shops along 18th and Wyandotte Streets. A few blocks over, boutiques like Tomboy and Christopher Elbow Artisanal Chocolates await, both favorite stops within the city's gallery-laden Crossroads Arts District.

- Museums are just as plentiful downtown as shops. Adjacent to the Sprint Center, the College Basketball Experience offers a completely interactive, high-energy atmosphere. Once you've finished, head south on Grand Boulevard and east on 18th Street until you hit 18th and Vine, the city's jazz mecca. Purchase a discounted combo ticket to tour both the American Jazz Museum and Negro Leagues Baseball Museum.

- Drive west on 18th Street and turn south on Main Street to take in a couple more significant sights before dinner. Union Station is a grandiose photo opportunity. Across the street, The Liberty Memorial towers over the city, a stunning architectural tribute to those who served during World War I. If time permits, duck below Liberty Memorial to visit the National World War I Museum.

- Stick around downtown for dinner: Go upscale at The American, enjoy authentic soul food at Peachtree Restaurant, or stick to

TOP 10 FOR KIDS

- Amusement park **Worlds of Fun** is great for the whole family. During the summer months, head next door to **Oceans of Fun.**
- The **Kansas City Zoo** never fails to disappoint. Try an animal encounter show or head to the Discovery Barn, an interactive play area.
- Children channel their inner Picasso at **Kaleidoscope.** Make a memorable souvenir using recycled materials and art supplies during Kaleidoscope's family art sessions.
- Kids are mesmerized by the train decor at **Fritz's Railroad Restaurant,** where their food is delivered by model trains.
- Check out the **Hallmark Visitors Center** for a sneak peek at the greeting card production process, complete with a handmade souvenir you'll finish before you go.
- Follow a genuine yellow-brick road at **The Legends at Village West,** an outdoor shopping and dining district dedicated to Kansas legends.
- Pack a picnic and head to the lawn of the **Nelson-Atkins Museum of Art.** Kids will delight in exploring the sculpture garden.
- Test your child's basketball prowess at the **College Basketball Experience,** a nearly 100 percent interactive museum designed to put visitors in the heart of the action.

Lions, tigers, and bears are all found at the Kansas City Zoo, which also hosts a sizable river otter exhibit among other habitats.

- Fireworks, food, fun – a night out at **Kauffman Stadium** cheering on the **Kansas City Royals** is great for kids of all ages.
- Union Station's significant history may not be all that appealing to younger children; instead, let them loose within Union Station's **Science City** to play, explore, and learn in a variety of colorful, interactive exhibits.

a budget at Chefburger. You'll also be near several barbecue institutions, so grab extra napkins at Arthur Bryant's Barbeque or Gates Bar-B-Q and dish your own opinion on the city's favorite food.

▶ Get a glimpse of Kansas City nightlife in the Power and Light District, which hosts everything from rock haven Angel's Rock Bar to uber-hip nightclub Mosaic Lounge. For a relaxed cocktail, order a drink at walk-up bar Fuego and grab a seat in the main open-air gathering area beneath the main block's towering glass roof. Enjoy an unforgettable nightcap at Skies, a restaurant and lounge perched atop the Hyatt Regency Crown Center.

Day 2

▶ Start the day with breakfast at Mama's 39th, which features one of the best breakfast menus in Midtown.

▶ Head south to Country Club Plaza and soak up some culture at the nearby Nelson-Atkins Museum of Art. If you prefer more

KANSAS CITY ON THE CHEAP

If you're traveling on a budget, Kansas City will happily comply with a wealth of sights and attractions free of charge, including:

- **Boulevard Brewing Co.:** Free brewery tours with complimentary end-of-tour tastings.
- **City Hall Observation Deck:** Arguably the greatest view of the city.
- **Money Museum at Federal Reserve Bank:** An interactive look at currency and its history.
- **Hallmark Visitors Center:** Get a behind-the-scenes peek at the Hallmark cards production process, and grab a few extra Kleenex for a retrospective of Hallmark's most heart-wrenching commercials.
- **Kaleidoscope:** A kid-friendly artistic escape that offers creative activities for the whole family, supplies included.

Boulevard Brewing Co.

- **The Nelson-Atkins Museum of Art:** Not only is the museum free, but the collection is so large you could easily fill a day by exploring all the Nelson has to offer. Bring a picnic lunch to enjoy in the adjoining sculpture garden.

modern works of art, try the Kemper Museum of Contemporary Art, located a few blocks from the Nelson.

- Make your way back to the Plaza and lunch at the Classic Cup Sidewalk Cafe for unmatched alfresco dining—and some of the best people-watching in the city. Make sure to pause for a picture at the nearby J. C. Nichols Memorial Fountain.
- Spend the afternoon shopping the Plaza, featuring an enticing mix of locally owned boutiques like Three Dog Bakery and Standard Style Boutique alongside nationally owned retailers.
- It's a bit of a walk, but if you head south on Wornall Road and up the rather daunting hill past The InterContinental Kansas City you'll hit Loose Park, one of the city's most beautiful recreational spots. Spend time relaxing amid the lush foliage and winding trail system that traverses the sizable park.
- Stick to the Plaza or nearby Westport for dinner. For the ultimate splurge—and the best steak in town—head to Plaza III Steakhouse. Or try Westport's Bluestem, a local favorite with the best dessert menu in the city. For the best burger in Cowtown, try Westport Flea Market, a Kansas City institution.
- Dine in Westport and you won't need to go far for after-dinner drinks. Westport has an eclectic mix of bars, but if you have to stop at only one, make it Kelly's Westport Inn, Kansas City's oldest building.

SIGHTS

Missouri's largest metropolitan area, offers an abundant array of sights and attractions for both locals and visitors. Kansas City is an arts mecca, home to the impressive Nelson-Atkins Museum of Art, boasting the world's largest Asian art collection, and abundant public art in the form of outdoor sculptures and fountains. In fact, Kansas City boasts so many fountains that it rivals Rome for most water features.

Downtown Kansas City and its surrounding vicinity host the majority of the city's sights, but appealing destinations are also sprinkled throughout the outlying boundaries of Kansas City as a result of continuing suburban sprawl. Attractions range from significant examples of local architecture, namely art deco and Beaux Arts, to strongholds of history and culture that reflect the city's diversity and roots as a 19th-century metropolis built on agriculture, stockyards, and the unyielding iron of railroad tracks. Modern iconic buildings like the Sprint Center and downtown Kansas City Library represent a sweeping renaissance that's transformed the city's urban core into a bustling mix of shops, restaurants, attractions, and businesses, a long-anticipated contrast to the desolate, empty buildings that were a common sight in earlier decades.

The city's playful side emerges in an energetic mix of water parks, the Kansas City Zoo, and the Kansas Speedway, a high-octane destination that's a must-see for members of the NASCAR nation.

COURTESY OF THE KANSAS CITY CONVENTION AND VISITORS ASSOCIATION

HIGHLIGHTS

LOOK FOR TO FIND RECOMMENDED SIGHTS.

Best Historic Discovery: After a century's worth of various salvage attempts, a local team managed to locate, uncover, and partially reconstruct a doomed steamboat, now housed at the ***Arabia* Steamboat Museum** along with recovered cargo items (page 19).

Best Interactive Museum: Step onto center court at the **College Basketball Experience** – or, if you prefer to be on the sidelines, test your broadcast skills at the ESPNU anchor station (page 19).

Best Public Art: Although the **Downtown Kansas City Library**'s interior is nothing short of majestic, the giant outdoor bookshelf with 25-foot volumes is equally mesmerizing (page 19).

Best View: Perched 30 floors above downtown Kansas City, the **Kansas City City Hall Observation Deck** offers picturesque and panoramic views of downtown and beyond (page 20).

Best Non-Art Museum: Explore Kansas City's melodic jazz history within the colorful, interactive surroundings of the **American Jazz Museum** (page 22).

Best Tour: Sure, a behind-the-scenes look at Kansas City's **Boulevard Brewing Co.** is fascinating, but the best part is the free end-of-tour beer tasting (page 22).

Best Local Export: Get an insiders' look at a multibillion-dollar industry with a visit to the **Hallmark Visitors Center,** complete with a view of the greeting card production process (page 23).

Best Local Monument: The Liberty Memorial is a towering and solemn tribute to those lost during World War I. Be sure to go below the monument to tour the expansive World War I Museum (page 23).

Best Local Landmark: Once the scene of a historic massacre, **Union Station** remains a distinguished monument and still operates as a full-service train station (page 25).

COURTESY OF THE KANSAS CITY CONVENTION AND VISITORS ASSOCIATION

Amercian Jazz Museum

Best Water Feature: Stop for a photo op in front of one of the most recognizable of Kansas City's many fountains, the **J. C. Nichols Memorial Fountain** (page 26).

Best Reason to Skip the Nelson: An astounding collection of contemporary art makes the **Kemper Museum of Contemporary Art** a must-see while you're in Kansas City. Stop at the museum gift shop for books, prints, and other artistic gifts (page 27).

Best Place to Spend a Day: With the world's largest Asian art collection, the **Nelson-Atkins Museum of Art** also offers a staggering collection of paintings, furniture, sculpture, photography, and more. Don't miss the outdoor sculpture garden and the infamous shuttlecock statues (page 27).

River Market and Power and Light District Map 1

ARABIA STEAMBOAT MUSEUM

400 Grand Blvd., 816/471-1856, www.1856.com

HOURS: Mon.-Sat. 10 A.M.-5:30 P.M.

COST: $12.50 adult, $11.50 senior, $4.75 child

As 19th-century expansionists pushed their way through the Midwest, river travel became a popular way to transport people and goods. The steamboat industry flourished and muddy river waters served as a lengthy, and at times treacherous, highway. Prior to her untimely sinking, the steamboat *Arabia* had traveled the Mississippi and Ohio Rivers before changing hands twice. In 1856, the steamboat made nearly 30 trips across Missouri before the hidden trunk of a walnut tree dragged the *Arabia* to a watery grave. Persons aboard were saved by the steamboat's high-level cabins, which remained above water as a single lifeboat transported passengers to safety. Later on, salvage attempts were made, each thwarted by seasonal flooding and frequent deposits of topsoil that mired the wreckage to the river's floor. More than a century later, a salvage crew led by David Hawley located the wreckage and, after a painstaking and incredibly time-consuming process, raised pieces of the *Arabia* from the depths and transported them to what is now the *Arabia* Steamboat Museum. Frequent tours throughout the day inform guests about the steamboat's legacy and excavation, and painstakingly restored items from the ship's cargo hold offer a peek into 19th-century life. Be sure and stop for a picture in front of the steamboat's preserved six-ton stern section, complete with remnants of the ship's original paint.

COLLEGE BASKETBALL EXPERIENCE

1401 Grand Blvd., 816/949-7500, www.collegebasketballexperience.com

HOURS: Wed.-Sat. 10 A.M.-6 P.M., Sun. 11 A.M.-6 P.M.

COST: $10 adult, $7 child

The College Basketball Experience's interactive environment allows visitors to immerse themselves in various stages of a college basketball game, from a pre-game pep talk delivered in the museum's elevator to audio-guided drills such as dribbling, passing, and shooting. Be prepared to sweat as the game continues, and take your chance at a slam dunk. Tune out the sideline hecklers and dribble your way to victory before spending a reflective moment in the National Collegiate Basketball Hall of Fame, dedicated to unforgettable players and nostalgic moments. Those who prefer their action through a television screen can step behind the ESPNU anchor desk and call out the play-by-play for some of college basketball's greatest games. College Basketball Experience's architect, New York City–based ESI Design, also created Cleveland's Rock and Roll Hall of Fame.

DOWNTOWN KANSAS CITY LIBRARY

14 W. 10th St., 816/701-3400, www.kclibrary.org

HOURS: Mon.-Wed. 9 A.M.-9 P.M., Thurs. 9 A.M.-6 P.M., Fri. 9 A.M.-5 P.M., Sat. 10 A.M.-5 P.M., Sun. 1-5 P.M.

A five-story structure originally built in 1904 as a bank underwent a complete renovation in 2005 to become the central branch of Kansas City's public library system. Architecturally significant features such as ceiling plaster, millwork, and numerous chandeliers remain as tributes to the building's history, making the library a popular choice for weddings, gatherings, and other special events. While you're at the library, take the elevator to the fifth floor and go out to the library rooftop, a peaceful oasis that offers breathtaking downtown views.

Umbrella-covered tables are an ideal spot for a picnic, and on select summer evenings the library hosts rooftop movies and other special events. Along the south exterior wall of the library's parking garage, the Community Bookshelf remains a visually striking addition to downtown. The spines of 22 literary classics and regional favorites, each measuring 25 feet by 9 feet and immortalized in signboard mylar, create a sculptural tribute to the written word. For a self-guided tour of the Library District, visit www.kclibrary.org/district-tour.

KANSAS CITY CITY HALL OBSERVATION DECK

414 E. 12th St., 816/513-2778, www.kcmo.org

HOURS: Mon.-Fri. 7 A.M.-3 P.M.

COST: Free

Known as one of the tallest city halls in the country, Kansas City's 30-story City Hall remains a towering example of local architecture. Adorned with Beaux Arts and art deco details, the building was completed in 1937 as part of a three-building construction program. An outdoor frieze on the building's sixth floor is comprised of relief sculptures that depict early city growth. Take the elevator to the 30th-floor observation deck for one of the best views of Kansas City's skyline and prime photo opportunities. As you walk through the main lobby, admire the carefully installed architectural features such as sculpted brass elevator doors that depict Kansas City's four methods of transportation: planes, boats, cars, and trains.

LEWIS AND CLARK POINT

8th and Jefferson Sts., www.moksriverbend.org

As Meriwether Lewis and William Clark wended their way through the country on an expedition ordered by president Thomas

COURTESY OF THE KANSAS CITY CONVENTION AND VISITORS ASSOCIATION

The Sky Station pylon caps are one of several art deco architectural elements found throughout downtown Kansas City.

Jefferson, the duo stopped at several points throughout Missouri, including Kansas City. At what was merely a bluff overlooking the picturesque Missouri River Valley, the two were said to exclaim that the site "offered a commanding situation for a fort." Today, a statue of Lewis and Clark by Eugene Daub stands in tribute to their historical journey through the heart of the city.

THE SECOND HANNIBAL BRIDGE

Adjacent to Broadway Bridge, Broadway Blvd. and Missouri 169

Built in 1869, the original Hannibal Bridge was the first Kansas City bridge built across the Missouri River. After a tornado destroyed much of the bridge, a second Hannibal Bridge was built less than 200 feet upstream. The double-decker bridge served vehicular and railroad traffic until the Broadway Bridge opened to automobile traffic in 1956. Having withstood severe weather, floods, and a four-riverboat collision that tore the swinging span open, the second Hannibal Bridge still serves as a primary railway passage across the Missouri River.

SKY STATIONS, CONVENTION CENTER BRIDGE

301 W. 13th St., www.kcconvention.com

In a nod to the city's art deco heritage, the four stainless-steel Sky Stations sculptures were created to blend Kansas City's past and future. A result of the city's One Percent for Art program to increase public art throughout Kansas City, New York resident R. M. Fischer's 40-foot-by-30-foot Sky Stations are visible from a two-mile radius and, in addition to serving an aesthetic purpose, support the convention center's cable-stayed roof. Because of the sculptures' size and precarious location, the pieces were lowered onto the concrete pylons by helicopter during the installation process.

SPRINT CENTER

1407 Grand Blvd., 816/949-7000, www.sprintcenter.com

Created by the Downtown Arena Design Team, the Sprint Center is one of the crown jewels in downtown Kansas City's renaissance. Poised just north of I-35 in the heart of downtown, the concert and event venue hovers next to Grand Boulevard like a futuristic space craft poised for lift-off. A curved glass exterior and outdoor video display boards combine to make the Sprint Center a true modern marvel amid the city's statuesque skyscrapers, a visual merging of old and new. Since its opening in late 2007 the Sprint Center has welcomed over 200 events, which means you'll have a better chance at seeing a favorite performer while in town.

In late 2009, *Pollstar* magazine ranked the Sprint Center the ninth best arena in the world and the third best in the United States in terms of concert attendance and revenue.

Crossroads and 18th and Vine — Map 2

AMERICAN JAZZ MUSEUM

1616 E. 18th St., 816/474-8463,
www.americanjazzmuseum.com
HOURS: Tues.-Sat. 9 A.M.-6 P.M., Sun. noon-6 P.M.
COST: $8 adult, $3 child; Negro Leagues Museum combo ticket $10 adult, $5 child

Billed as "the premier jazz museum in the United States," the American Jazz Museum is an interactive testament to a musical culture that not only shaped Kansas City, but also lent its significant soundtrack to other major U.S. cities. Opened in 1997, the American Jazz Museum hosts four major exhibits on Louis Armstrong, Duke Ellington, Ella Fitzgerald, and Charlie "Yardbird" Parker. A wealth of memorabilia including rare photos, album covers, recordings, films, and special collections detail "the artistic, historical, and cultural contributions of jazz." Try your hand at sound mixing in The Studio, which includes 16 separate listening and mixing stations that focus on music's three main elements: rhythm, melody, and harmony. After you've finished touring the museum, stop in The Blue Room for live music most evenings or a show at the renovated 500-seat Gem Theater, which hosts the annual Jammin' at the Gem national jazz concert series. When you plan your trip to the American Jazz Museum, consider purchasing a combo ticket that offers reduced admission into the adjacent Negro Leagues Baseball Museum.

BOULEVARD BREWING CO.

2501 Southwest Blvd., 816/474-7095,
www.blvdbeer.com
HOURS: Tour times vary
COST: Free tours

Now one of Missouri's largest locally owned breweries, Boulevard Brewing Company began in 1988 when founder John McDonald began building a brewing facility on Southwest Boulevard, incorporating a vintage Bavarian brewhouse. Boulevard began producing beer in 1989 with a keg of Pale Ale, still a city favorite. The brewery has since expanded to offer several year-round and limited-edition brews, as well as the Smokestack Series, a group of complex, experimental ales including Double-Wide I.P.A. and Long Strange Tripel. Before your trip, visit Boulevard's website to book a brewery tour complete with free post-tour samples.

CHARLIE PARKER MEMORIAL

17th Terrace and The Paseo

The 18-foot bronze sculpture created by Robert Graham is a likeness of Charlie "Yardbird" Parker, a legendary jazz musician who came to Kansas City at the age of seven to study music. Known for his fluid style on the alto sax, Parker also excelled at the tenor sax and clarinet. He's credited for fathering the "be-bop" style of music. Although he was celebrated worldwide as a musical prodigy, a fast and reckless lifestyle filled with substance abuse brought his life to an early close at the age of 37, and he was transported from New York City to Kansas City for burial. The City of Kansas City commissioned Parker's memorial statue, with the proclamation "BIRD LIVES" on its base.

CROWN CENTER

2450 Grand Blvd., 816/274-8444,
www.crowncenter.com
HOURS: Mon.-Wed. 10 A.M.-6 P.M., Thurs.-Fri. 10 A.M.-9 P.M., Sat. 10 A.M.-6 P.M., Sun. noon-5 P.M.

With more than 2.2 million square feet of office space and 300,000 square feet of retail space, the Crown Center is home to a variety of shops and attractions, including the **Crayola Cafe, Kaleidoscope, Fritz's Union Station,** an outdoor fountain play park, and numerous theaters that host both professional and amateur theater troupes. You can also visit the **Hallmark** world headquarters and browse **Halls department store** and **Halls Gold Crown boutique.** Adjacent condominiums have added a residential component to the 85-acre Crown Center, named for the instantly recognizable crown within Hallmark's logo.

HALLMARK VISITORS CENTER

2450 Grand Blvd., 816/274-3613, www.hallmarkvisitorscenter.com

HOURS: Tues.-Fri. 9 A.M.-5 P.M., Sat. 9:30 A.M.-4:30 P.M.

COST: Free

If you're a fan of Hallmark Cards, the Hallmark Visitors Center is a must-see while in Kansas City. Attractions include a virtual tour with Hallmark characters Hoops and YoYo, as well as a viewing station where you can reminisce while watching Hallmark commercials (tissues optional). Visitors can also interact with operators who explain the card-production process. Special exhibits cover a variety of topics from antique cards to the latest artistic techniques. Check the visitors center website and print a coupon for a free gift, which you'll receive at the conclusion of your self-guided tour.

KALEIDOSCOPE

2500 Grand Blvd., 816/274-8300, www.hallmarkkaleidoscope.com

HOURS: Vary

COST: Free

Part of Kansas City's Hallmark experience, Kaleidoscope is a kid-friendly artistic retreat designed to let children and parents unleash their inner artists. Numerous interactive sessions are held throughout the day, including family art, independent art for 5-to-12-year-olds, and preschool art for 3-to-5-year-olds. Explore a variety of topics and create artwork using various art supplies and recycled materials—the messier, the better! For sessions held during the school year, Kaleidoscope requests that reservations be made to ensure enough space and supplies for attendees.

THE LIBERTY MEMORIAL

100 W. 26th St., 816/784-1918, www.theworldwar.org

HOURS: Tues.-Sun. 10 A.M.-5 P.M.

COST: Combo ticket to museum and tower $12 adult, $10 senior, $6 child 6-11

An iconic part of Kansas City's skyline, the Liberty Memorial dates back to the early 1920s when city leaders met and agreed on the creation of a monument to honor those who had served in World War I. A community-based

COURTESY OF THE KANSAS CITY CONVENTION AND VISITORS ASSOCIATION

Built underneath The Liberty Memorial, the National World War I Museum offers a comprehensive look at "the war to end all wars."

fundraising drive raised $2.5 million in a mere 10 days, and the Kansas City Chapter of the American Institute of Architects sponsored a national competition to select the monument's design. Architect H. Van Buren Magonigle's towering monument won, and visitors can now visit the top of the tower as well as the National World War I Museum, an underground structure that spreads beneath the memorial.

MONEY MUSEUM AT FEDERAL RESERVE BANK OF KANSAS CITY

1 Memorial Dr., 816/881-2683, www.kc.frb.org/moneymuseum

HOURS: Mon.-Fri. 8:30 A.M.-4:30 P.M.

COST: Free

Who knew banks could be exciting? At the Money Museum you can explore the history of money, the process of currency making, and even design your own money using museum-provided templates. View the Harry S. Truman coin collection and the cash vault, or test your strength by trying to lift a 400-troy-ounce gold bar cast at the San Francisco Mint in 1959. Today the bar's value is an estimated $400,000. A nearby screen calculates the bar's daily value based on the market price of gold. Museum guests over 18 must bring a photo ID. Hour-long guided tours are available for groups by reservation.

NATIONAL ARCHIVES AT KANSAS CITY

400 W. Pershing Rd., 816/268-8000, www.archives.gov/central-plains/kansas-city

HOURS: Tues.-Sat. 9 A.M.-5 P.M.

COST: Free

If you're envisioning a dusty building filled with teetering stacks of government-compiled papers, think again. A 2009 move to a new facility brought a much-needed expansion to the National Archives at Kansas City, one of 13 regional branches of the National Archives. When you arrive, stop in at the auditorium for a short presentation about the National Archives produced by employees of the Discovery Channel. In addition to research and computer rooms, the National Archives hosts two floors of rotating exhibits that display invaluable pieces of local history. To read more on many of the subjects presented, or pick up a historical memento of your own, stop in at the *Kansas City Star*-operated store on your way out.

NEGRO LEAGUES BASEBALL MUSEUM

1616 E. 18th St., 816/221-1920, www.nlbm.com

HOURS: Tues.-Sat. 9 A.M.-6 P.M., Sun. noon-6 P.M.

COST: $8 adult, $3 child; American Jazz Museum combo ticket $10 adult, $5 child

The result of a collaborative effort between local historians, business leaders, and former baseball players, the Negro Leagues Baseball Museum began with just one room when it opened in the early 1990s. After becoming incorporated, adding a board of directors and staff, and creating a licensing program, the museum expanded to 2,000 square feet and later 10,000 square feet that includes memorabilia and interactive exhibits dedicated to the history of the Negro Leagues, which began in Kansas City's Paseo YMCA in 1920. The Negro Leagues declined in the mid-1940s after African-American players were recruited to Major League teams. Explore Negro Leagues history at multimedia computer stations and pose for photos in a "field" of 12 bronze sculptures, including iconic local baseball player Buck O'Neil. On your way out, stop at the museum store for souvenirs including books, artwork, apparel, collectibles, and DVDs.

COURTESY OF THE KANSAS CITY CONVENTION AND VISITORS ASSOCIATION

Union Station's soaring interior is a breathtaking display of local architecture.

SCIENCE CITY

30 W. Pershing Rd., 816/460-2020, www.sciencecity.com

HOURS: Tues.-Sat. 9:30 A.M.-5:30 P.M., Sun. noon-5:30 P.M.

COST: $9.50

The interactive exhibits at Union Station's Science City are so entertaining that your kids will have a hard time believing they're learning as they explore a variety of science-related topics, including space travel, dinosaurs, astronomy, and more. Dig for fossils, or test your skills at landing a space shuttle using a NASA-style simulator. Children ages three to six can access the Half Pint room, which changes programs monthly to offer a new area of exploration. Guided programs are available on Thursdays, and the room is also open for drop-ins during general hours. Topics include mixtures and solutions, messy science, and how cold is cold.

THE SCOUT

Penn Valley Park, Pershing Rd. and Main St., 816/513-7500, www.kcmo.org

A Sioux on horseback overlooks the city skyline in an infinite vigil from his perch in Penn Valley Park. Created by Cyrus E. Dallin in 1915, the sculpture won a gold medal during San Francisco's Panama Pacific Exposition. In transit to the East Coast, the sculpture was temporarily displayed in this Kansas City park. Residents were so taken by The Scout that they launched the Kids of Kansas City campaign and raised $15,000 in loose change to permanently keep the statue in Kansas City. In 1922, The Scout was dedicated as a permanent memorial to Indian tribes.

UNION STATION

30 W. Pershing Rd., 816/460-2020, www.unionstation.org

HOURS: Daily 6 A.M.-midnight

Union Station was once one of Kansas City's crown jewels, a bustling depot filled with train passengers. After falling into disrepair in the 1980s, the nation's first bi-state tax raised enough funds in the 1990s to renovate the building, and it's now home to **Science City, H&R Block City Stage,** an **Amtrak** train station, restaurants, and traveling exhibits.

Westport, Midtown, and The Plaza Map 3

HARRIS-KEARNEY HOUSE

4000 Baltimore Ave., 816/561-1821, www.westporthistorical.com

HOURS: Call for current hours

Now home to the Westport Historical Society's offices, the Harris-Kearney House was once the home of the Col. John Harris family. Bricks for the Greek Revival mansion were created on-site, and in 1922 the house was moved in two sections to its current location from the southwest corner of Westport Road and Main Street. After the Westport Historical Society acquired the property in 1976, a careful renovation restored the 1855 portion of the house. The home's significance was reaffirmed with placement on the National Register of Historic Places. In addition to office space, the Harris-Kearney House hosts a museum that showcases the rich history of Westport.

J. C. NICHOLS MEMORIAL FOUNTAIN

W. 47th St. btwn. J. C. Nichols Pkwy. and Main St., www.kcfountains.org

The best known and most photographed fountain in Kansas City, the J. C. Nichols Memorial Fountain, is a significant tribute to iconic developer Jesse Clyde Nichols, whose extensive résumé includes the Country Club Plaza. Created in the early 1900s in Paris, the sculptural fountain originally embellished Clarence Mackay's Long Island mansion. After a fire destroyed Mackay's mansion and the fountain's figures were damaged, the pieces were sold for salvage and purchased by the Nichols family. The fountain was later transported to Kansas City, refurbished, and dedicated in 1960. Four statuesque horses surround a multi-tiered pool of water that shoots spray both upward and in arcs across the sizable water feature. At night, the illuminated fountain becomes even more eye-catching.

CITY OF FOUNTAINS

Forget the debate over the city's best barbecue. In Kansas City, the true mystery lies within the watery depths of the city's fountains. Residents and visitors alike have long argued over the number of fountains, which according to the City of Fountains Foundation is more than 200. And yes, the rumor is true – Kansas City has the second-largest number of fountains in the world, after Rome. Some, like the J. C. Nichols Memorial Fountain, are architectural spectacles that command a photograph. Others are more modest, lending a watery trickle to a nearby building or landscaped plot.

The city's fountains offer more than an elegant aesthetic. To commemorate special events, several of the more prominent fountains have their waters dyed in a show of support. The waters turn a vivid blue prior to the Royals' baseball home opener, and in October, pink water cascades freely in a nod to National Breast Cancer Awareness Month. Once the temperatures drop below freezing, all but one of the fountains are silenced. The Northland Fountain flows year-round, creating an eye-catching ice sculpture during the season's most frigid days.

KANSAS CITY BOARD OF TRADE

4800 Main St., Ste. 303, 816/753-7500, www.kcbt.com

HOURS: Tours by appointment

COST: Free

Founded by a group of local merchants in 1856, the Kansas City Board of Trade grew out of a need to create a more organized way of buying and selling grain. The Board of Trade's location in the heart of one of the world's most productive wheat-growing nations has made KCBT an icon in the wheat industry. During a Board of Trade tour, you'll learn the details about wheat, futures, options, and other industry lingo, and you'll also get a view of the high-energy opening or closing of the trade floor. Tour participants must be high school age or older.

KEMPER MUSEUM OF CONTEMPORARY ART

4420 Warwick Blvd., 816/561-0903, www.kemperart.org

HOURS: Tues.-Thurs. 10 A.M.-4 P.M., Fri.-Sat. 10 A.M.-9 P.M., Sun. 11 A.M.-5 P.M.

COST: Free

The Gunnar Birkerts–designed Kemper Museum of Contemporary Art opened in 1994 and has since evolved into one of the region's most comprehensive collections of contemporary art. At the heart of the Kemper's permanent exhibits is the Bebe and Crosby Kemper Collection, donated by the museum's financier and namesake. Jackson Pollock, Robert Rauschenberg, and Georgia O'Keeffe, among others, are represented in this landmark collection. Throughout the year, the Kemper welcomes a revolving display of temporary exhibits highlighting significant trends in and contributions to contemporary art. If you're inspired to start your own collection, don't leave the museum without a visit to the gift shop. Handcrafted jewelry, textiles, pottery, and home accessories make eye-catching souvenirs and memorable conversation pieces.

LINDA HALL LIBRARY

5109 Cherry St., 816/363-4600, www.lindahall.org

HOURS: Mon.-Fri. 9 A.M.-5 P.M.

What started as a gift established by the wills of Herbert and Linda Hall has evolved into the largest independently funded public library of science, engineering, and technology in North America. Extensive collections from the 15th century to the present have made the library a go-to research source for both individuals and companies. Numerous additions throughout the years have added much-needed space to the library. A surrounding arboretum provides a scenic respite for both researchers and visitors. More than 58 genera and 165 species of trees grow within the 14-acre space. Free tours of the library and arboretum are offered.

NELSON-ATKINS MUSEUM OF ART

4525 Oak St., 816/751-1278, www.nelson-atkins.org

HOURS: Wed. 10 A.M.-4 P.M., Thurs.-Fri. 10 A.M.-9 P.M., Sat. 10 A.M.-5 P.M., Sun. noon-5 P.M.

COST: Free

Upon its opening in 1933, the Nelson-Atkins' Beaux Arts facade and intricately detailed interior combined to make the museum a true landmark for the city. The permanent collections feature pieces from a number of styles ranging from African and American Indian to decorative arts and South/Southeast Asian. Among the highlights of the museum's permanent collection are the more than 900 pieces that comprise the European collection, including Caravaggio's "Saint John the Baptist in the Wilderness." A carefully curated Chinese collection has been recognized as one of the best of its kind outside Asia. Additional highlights include a 22-acre sculpture garden and two in-museum restaurants.

STATE LINE ROAD

State Line Rd. btwn. U.S. 56 and Rte. 150

Forget rivers as state borders. Straddle State Line Road, and you're standing in two different states. The north–south thoroughfare

NEW KID ON THE BLOCH

Inspired by a growing need for larger facilities, Nelson-Atkins Museum of Art board members decided to create an iconic addition to the Beaux Arts-style building. Steven Holl Architects accepted the task, and in 2007 the **Bloch Building** opened to accolades calling it a significant work of contemporary architecture. The slender building exists mostly underground along the east side of the Nelson-Atkins' original building. Five freestanding structures jut upward from the above-ground expanse in an architectural triumph that melds building with landscape.

Inside the Bloch Building, floor-to-ceiling windows and sleek corridors create a sense of spacious modernity that lends itself to the numerous exhibits and special events housed within the addition. Several permanent collections, including African art, photography, and contemporary art, were relocated to the Bloch Building. Outside, a sculpture park honoring the works of Isamu Noguchi leads seamlessly to the surrounding Kansas City Sculpture Park. Overall, the Bloch Building represents a successful completion of the original mission: to create an expansion that didn't compromise the original integrity of the building and landscaping. Like its namesake, local businessman and H&R Block co-founder Henry W. Bloch, the Bloch Building triumphs, forever leaving an imprint on the city.

runs from U.S. 56 in Missouri to Route 150 in Kansas, stopping in Kansas City (both Missouri and Kansas), Leawood, Mission Hills, Prairie Village, and Westwood Hills. Stop near a street sign for a prime photo opportunity.

THOMAS HART BENTON HOME AND STUDIO

3616 Belleview Ave., 816/931-5722, www.mostateparks.com/benton.htm

HOURS: Vary

COST: $2.50 adult, $1.50 child 6-12

After studying art in Chicago and Paris, Thomas Hart Benton moved to Kansas City and continued an illustrious career as a painter, sculptor, lecturer, and writer. Accomplished in the American Regionalist school of art, Benton is best known for his vibrant paintings of Midwestern people and landscapes quickly characterized by their cartoon-like figures and vivid colors. Benton also created several series of murals, which can be found in such locations as New York's Whitney Museum of American Art and the Missouri state capitol building. His carefully preserved Victorian home and adjacent studio are open to tour, and several of Benton's paintings and sculptures are on display.

TOY AND MINIATURE MUSEUM

5235 Oak St., 816/333-9328, www.toyandminiaturemuseum.org

HOURS: Wed.-Sat. 10 A.M.-4 P.M., Sun. 1-4 P.M.

COST: $7 adult, $6 senior/student, $5 child 5-12

Explore the colorful world of nostalgic toys, miniatures, and marbles in a 38-room house that features one of the largest collections of toys in the Midwest. The museum opened in 1982 after dollhouse collector Mary Harris Francis formed a partnership with miniatures collector Barbara Marshall. The two were often told they had so many collectibles they should open a museum; after founding a not-for-profit corporation in 1979, they did just that. Museum staff recommends at least an hour for self-guided tours, and photography is not permitted.

VIETNAM VETERANS MEMORIAL

43rd St. and Broadway St., 816/561-8387

Kansas City's prevalence of statuesque fountains led city officials to sponsor a contest for the design of a Vietnam Veterans Memorial fountain. Local artist and Vietnam veteran David Baker created a water feature that symbolized the war through an abstract design. Numerous pools, increasing in size, represent the country's growing involvement in the conflict. Adjoining the fountain, a 10-foot-high wall inscribed with the names of 336 Kansas City–area soldiers listed as killed or missing in action completes the memorial.

Brookside and Waldo

Map 4

ARMOUR HILLS

Btwn. 65th St. and Gregory Blvd., www.waldokc.org/historyofwaldo_armour.html

Armour Hills' 1,608 homes stand as sentries to some of the city's most notable events, and their former residents are among some of the city's most famous. Developed by famed city planner and urban architect J. C. Nichols, Armour Hills stood during Jayhawk raids, the forced evacuation prompted by Order No. 11 and the Civil War's Battle of Westport. Past residents read like a who's who of Kansas City history, including David and Eliza Waldo, the John Wornall family, John C. McCoy, Olive Waldo Hinkle, and Kirkland Armour. The 1920s-era homes still represent some of the best in early residential architecture, and a thorough network of sidewalks encourages leisurely strolls throughout Armour Hills.

COURTESY OF THE KANSAS CITY CONVENTION AND VISITORS ASSOCIATION

Stately homes, an array of bars and restaurants, and numerous locally owned boutiques make Brookside and Waldo must-visit neighborhoods.

THE JOHN WORNALL HOUSE MUSEUM

6115 Wornall Rd., 816/444-1858, www.wornallhouse.org

HOURS: Tues.-Sat. 10 A.M.-4 P.M., Sun. 1-4 P.M.

COST: $6 adult, $5 student/senior

Once the centerpiece of a 500-acre farm, the statuesque John Wornall House Museum is an enduring tribute to one of the most successful farmers in Kansas City. By selling horses, mules, corn, and wheat to travelers headed west, the Wornall family paid for the farm just one year after its purchase. After nearly two decades, the Wornalls built the mansion now known as The John Wornall House Museum, purchased by the Jackson County Historical Society in 1964. Tour the carefully preserved home for a look at wealthy farm life of the 19th century, and learn about the home's other uses, including as a hospital during the Civil War.

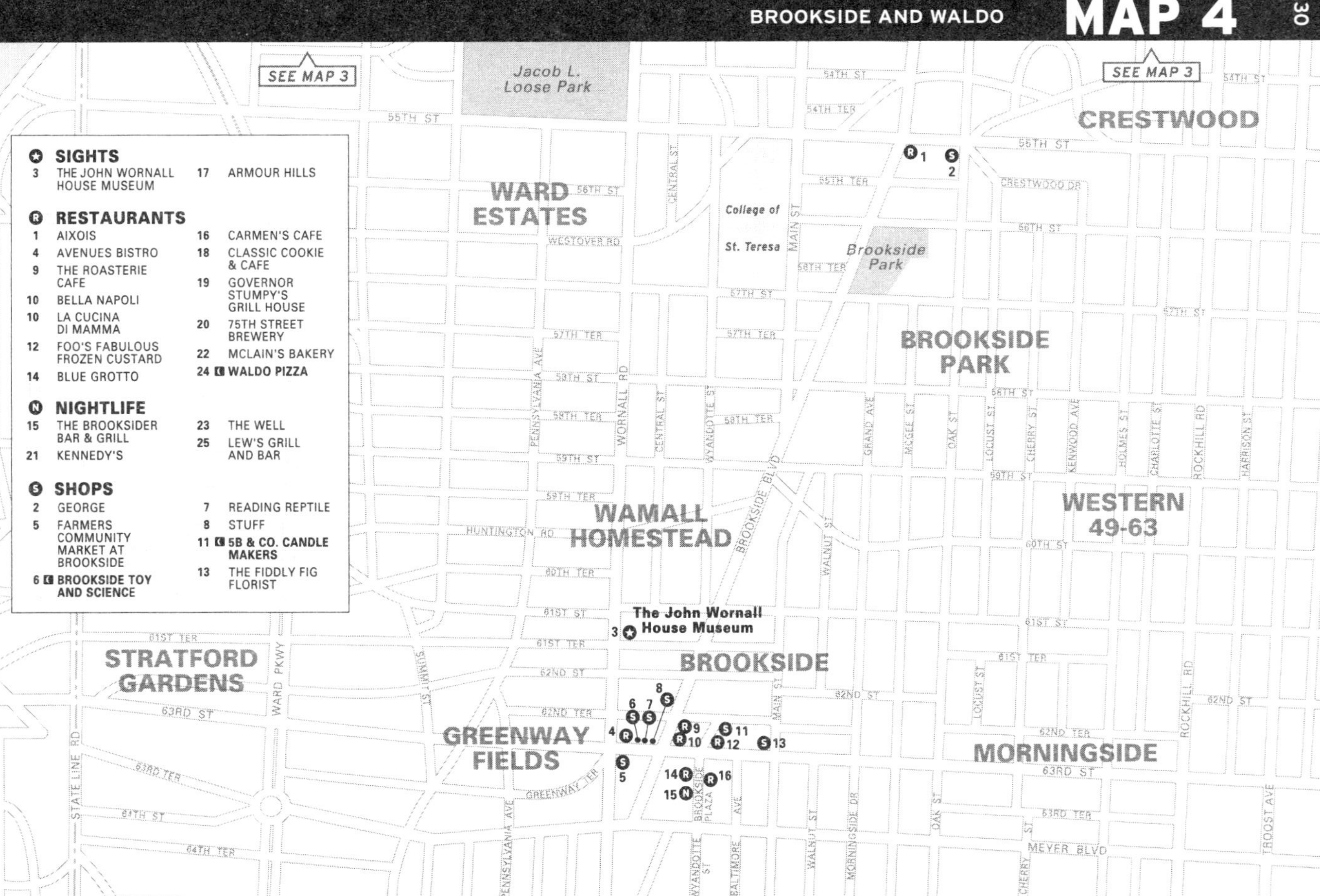

SIGHTS

3 THE JOHN WORNALL HOUSE MUSEUM
17 ARMOUR HILLS

RESTAURANTS

1 AIXOIS
4 AVENUES BISTRO
9 THE ROASTERIE CAFE
10 BELLA NAPOLI
10 LA CUCINA DI MAMMA
12 FOO'S FABULOUS FROZEN CUSTARD
14 BLUE GROTTO
16 CARMEN'S CAFE
18 CLASSIC COOKIE & CAFE
19 GOVERNOR STUMPY'S GRILL HOUSE
20 75TH STREET BREWERY
22 MCLAIN'S BAKERY
24 **WALDO PIZZA**

NIGHTLIFE

15 THE BROOKSIDER BAR & GRILL
21 KENNEDY'S
23 THE WELL
25 LEW'S GRILL AND BAR

SHOPS

2 GEORGE
5 FARMERS COMMUNITY MARKET AT BROOKSIDE
6 **BROOKSIDE TOY AND SCIENCE**
7 READING REPTILE
8 STUFF
11 **5B & CO. CANDLE MAKERS**
13 THE FIDDLY FIG FLORIST

DISTANCE ACROSS MAP
Approximate: 1.4 mi or 2.3 km
0 200 yds
0 200 m
HOLMES PARK
OAK MEYER GARDENS
ARMOUR HILLS
ARMOUR FIELDS
TOWER HOMES
WALDO
WARD PARKWAY
Forest Hill Cemetery
Rose Hill Cemetery
Holmes Park
Tower Park
Arbor Villa Park
Armour Hills
MISSOURI
KANSAS
GREGORY BLVD
WARD PKWY
WORNALL RD
BROOKSIDE RD
STATE LINE RD
TROOST AVE
HOLMES ST
ROCKHILL RD
MAIN ST
PENNSYLVANIA AVE
© AVALON TRAVEL

Northland

Map 5

AIRLINE HISTORY MUSEUM

201 NW Lou Holland Dr., 816/421-3401, www.ahmhangar.com

HOURS: Mon.-Sat. 10 A.M.-4 P.M., Sun. noon-4 P.M.

COST: $8 adult, $7 senior, $4 child 6-12

Step back in time at the downtown airport, where photographs, artifacts, printed materials, and audiovisual displays showcase earlier eras of air travel. The Airline History Museum also boasts an outstanding aircraft collection that includes the Lockheed L1049 "Super G" Constellation, a Martin 404, and a Douglas DC-3 that just completed an extensive renovation. Check the museum's calendar prior to your trip; your Kansas City visit may coincide with a museum-hosted special event, including an air show.

Greater Kansas City

Overview Map

INDEPENDENCE SQUARE

112 W. Lexington St., Independence, 816/461-0065, www.theindependencesquare.com

Travel to Harry S. Truman's hometown, Independence, and spend a day on the Square, a historic district home to boutiques, art galleries, and restaurants. Civil War enthusiasts must stop in the **Blue & Grey Book Shoppe,** a local bookstore dedicated to Civil War and local and U.S. history. Browse the plush colorful yarns at **Knitcraft Yarn Shop,** or visit the **Uptown Boutique,** a boutique owned by a mother and daughter that specializes in stylish apparel and accessories. When you're in need of refreshment, stop at **Clinton's Soda Fountain** for an old-fashioned soda phosphate. A young Harry Truman worked behind the counter, making Clinton's an integral part of Independence history. Dine at **Ophelia's,** an inviting restaurant that specializes in modern American cuisine. Stay for live jazz on the weekends, and if you'd prefer to stay on the Square, book a room at **The Inn at Ophelia's.** The Square's picturesque surroundings make it an ideal setting for year-round events, including ghost tours, a Halloween parade and trick-or-treating, and the holiday-themed Winterfest.

KANSAS CITY ZOO

6800 Zoo Dr., 816/513-5700, www.kansascityzoo.org

HOURS: Daily 9:30 A.M.-4 P.M.

COST: $10.50 adult, $9.50 senior, $7 child; discounted admission on Tues.

An aggressive renovation at the Kansas City Zoo in May 2008 added a North American river otter exhibit, a zoo learning center, and reconstructed parking lots and admission gates to the 202-acre facility. The zoo's four largest sections—Africa, Australia, KidZone, and Tiger Trail—offer an up-close look at native species, habitat information, and more. The zoo also hosts one of North America's largest chimpanzee environments, as well as a Discovery Barn filled with exotic species like meerkats and lemurs. Explore the zoo with several transportation options including boats, trains, and trams, as well as tours by golf cart or Segway. Three restaurants and six snack bars offer ample options for on-site dining and refreshments, and picnic areas are available if you'd prefer to pack a meal. Zoo officials recommend arriving before 10 A.M. or after 2 P.M. to avoid the largest crowds.

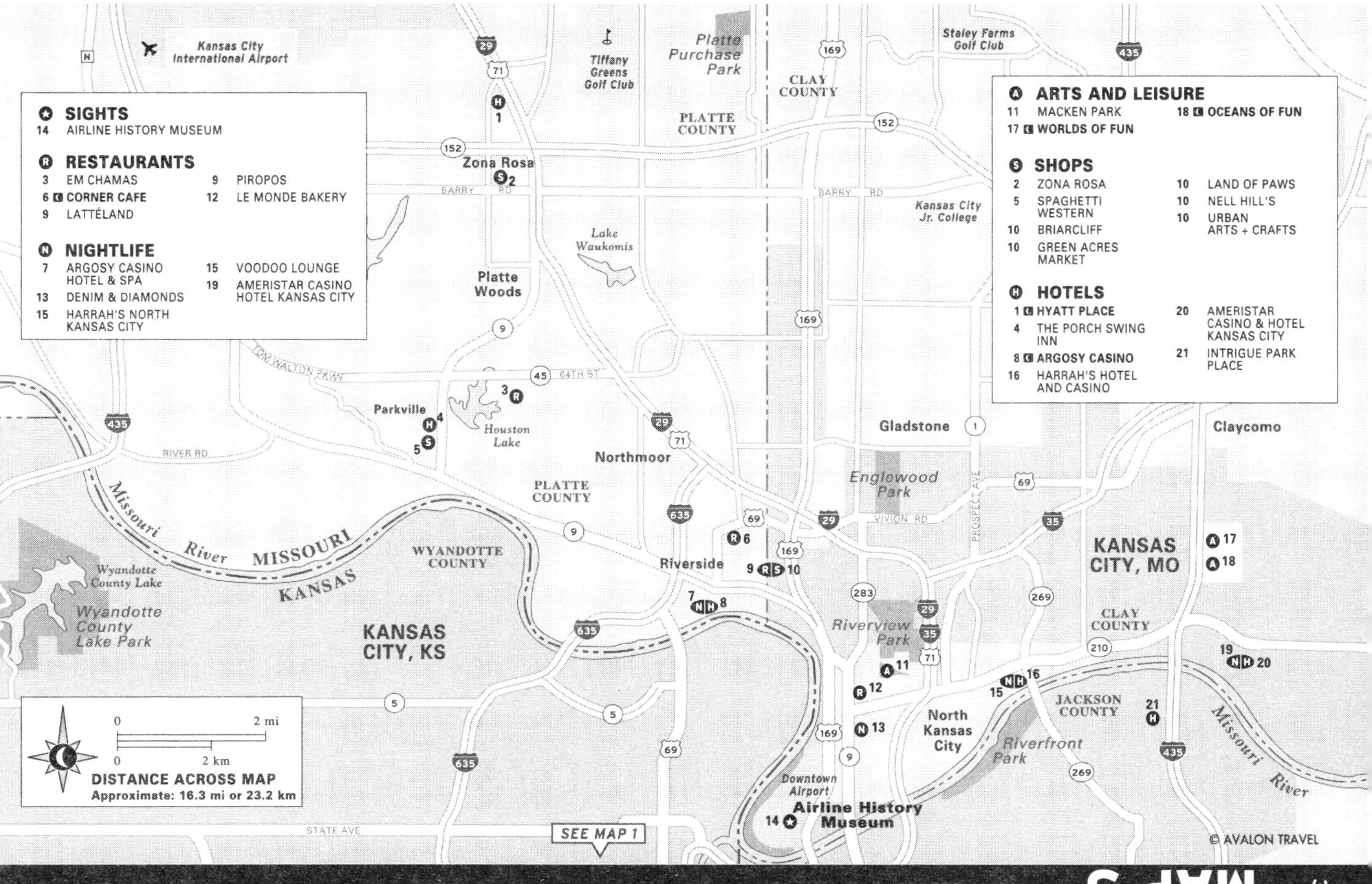
SIGHTS
14 AIRLINE HISTORY MUSEUM
RESTAURANTS
3 EM CHAMAS
6 CORNER CAFE
9 LATTÉLAND
9 PIROPOS
12 LE MONDE BAKERY
NIGHTLIFE
7 ARGOSY CASINO HOTEL & SPA
13 DENIM & DIAMONDS
15 HARRAH'S NORTH KANSAS CITY
15 VOODOO LOUNGE
19 AMERISTAR CASINO HOTEL KANSAS CITY
ARTS AND LEISURE
11 MACKEN PARK
17 WORLDS OF FUN
18 OCEANS OF FUN
SHOPS
2 ZONA ROSA
5 SPAGHETTI WESTERN
10 BRIARCLIFF
10 GREEN ACRES MARKET
10 LAND OF PAWS
10 NELL HILL'S
10 URBAN ARTS + CRAFTS
HOTELS
1 HYATT PLACE
4 THE PORCH SWING INN
8 ARGOSY CASINO
16 HARRAH'S HOTEL AND CASINO
20 AMERISTAR CASINO & HOTEL KANSAS CITY
21 INTRIGUE PARK PLACE
Kansas City International Airport
Tiffany Greens Golf Club
Platte Purchase Park
CLAY COUNTY
PLATTE COUNTY
Staley Farms Golf Club
Zona Rosa
BARRY RD
Kansas City Jr. College
Lake Waukomis
Platte Woods
TOM WALTON PKWY
64TH ST
Parkville
Houston Lake
Gladstone
Claycomo
RIVER RD
Northmoor
Englewood Park
PROSPECT AVE
VIVION RD
PLATTE COUNTY
Missouri River
MISSOURI
KANSAS
WYANDOTTE COUNTY
Riverside
KANSAS CITY, MO
Wyandotte County Lake
Wyandotte County Lake Park
KANSAS CITY, KS
Riverview Park
CLAY COUNTY
JACKSON COUNTY
North Kansas City
Riverfront Park
Missouri River
Downtown Airport
Airline History Museum
0 2 mi
0 2 km
DISTANCE ACROSS MAP
Approximate: 16.3 mi or 23.2 km
STATE AVE
SEE MAP 1
© AVALON TRAVEL

KANSAS SPEEDWAY

400 Speedway Blvd., Kansas City, Kansas, 913/328-3300, www.kansasspeedway.com

HOURS: Vary

COST: $10-300 race tickets

NASCAR came speeding through Kansas City in 2001 with the completion of Kansas Speedway, a 1.5-mile tri-oval track that hosts the NEXTEL Cup Series, IndyCar Series, the NASCAR Busch and Craftsman Truck Series, and ARCA's RE/MAX Series. Speedway statistics indicate that most season ticket–holders come from a six-state region. The track is one of several projects that fueled a development boom in western Wyandotte County. If you're planning to stay in this part of the city, check the NASCAR schedule before you go; hotels fill up quickly for races and heavy traffic makes navigation difficult on the highways surrounding the speedway.

COURTESY OF THE KANSAS CITY CONVENTION AND VISITORS ASSOCIATION

Feel your heart race at Kansas Speedway, a cornerstone of development in western Wyandotte County.

NERMAN MUSEUM OF CONTEMPORARY ART

12345 College Blvd., Shawnee Mission, 913/469-3000, www.nermanmuseum.org

HOURS: Tues.-Thurs. 10 A.M.-5 P.M., Fri. 10 A.M.-9 P.M., Sat. 10 A.M.-5 P.M., Sun. noon-5 P.M.

COST: Free

A mix of permanent and temporary collections highlights various styles of contemporary art within the Kansas limestone–clad exterior of the Nerman Museum, designed by architect Kyu Sung Woo. The 41,000-square-foot contemporary art museum, the largest in a four-state region, is adjacent to Johnson County Community College. Permanent collections focus on several areas: painting, sculpture, works on paper, clay, photography, and indigenous American art. In addition, 14 temporary exhibits are displayed throughout the year, showcasing the work of international, national, and regional artists. Free guided tours are available, or pick up a visitors guide for a self-paced tour.

SCHLITTERBAHN VACATION VILLAGE

1709 N. 98th St., Kansas City, Kansas, 913/334-5200, www.schlitterbahn.com

HOURS: Vary

COST: $32.99 adult, $24.99 child/senior

From the award-winning Schlitterbahn family, based in New Braunfels, Texas, comes Schlitterbahn Vacation Village, one of the newer jewels in western Wyandotte County's crown. The sprawling development features a water park complete with the latest in splash-soaked entertainment like the Kristal River, Raging River Tube Chute, Bahnzai Pipeline Tube Slide, and Kristal Beach. Outside the water park, a

COURTESY OF THE KANSAS CITY CONVENTION AND VISITORS ASSOCIATION

This rendering depicts the Schlitterbahn Vacation Village, one of the newer additions to western Wyandotte County.

3,000-foot Riverwalk connects visitors to a lush shopping, dining, and entertainment district. Book a room at Schlitterbahn's on-site hotel and choose from a waterfront cabin or a Treehaus, an elevated pod that connects to the park's river system through an individual waterslide.

STRAWBERRY HILL MUSEUM

720 N. 4th St., Kansas City, Kansas, 913/371-3264, www.strawberryhillmuseum.org

HOURS: Sat.-Sun. noon-5 P.M.

COST: $5

The interior of a restored 1887 Victorian house features a museum dedicated to local history with an emphasis on Croatian and Slavic cultures, two of the predominant ethnic groups that helped found Kansas City, Kansas. In addition to permanent exhibits, the Strawberry Hill Museum hosts monthly events dedicated to various cultures with a display of clothing, artifacts, and other culturally significant memorabilia. During the holiday season, lavish decorations make the Strawberry Hill Museum a picturesque retreat. While you're at the museum, stop at the on-site tea room for refreshments and snacks.

RESTAURANTS

Kansas City may be the Midwest's barbecue stronghold, but that's not all that you'll find on offer: Local restaurateurs are busy serving up a mouthwatering array of dishes that range from contemporary American and Asian fusion to Argentinean, Brazilian, and Indian.

National food experts are slowly turning their sights to Kansas City in celebration of its truly innovative restaurants that have attracted the accolades of James Beard and Zagat. Places like Bluebird Bistro, Justus Drugstore: A Restaurant, and Bluestem have perfected the art of using seasonal, local ingredients in inventive dishes that transform a typical meal into a memorable dining experience.

The city's large Italian population has left a lasting imprint on its culinary scene, and restaurants like Garozzo's and La Cucina di Mamma are popular choices for those who like a lot of garlic served with a heaping side of tradition.

For a meal in a pinch, street vendors set up shop in Westport and throughout downtown's high-traffic areas to dish out fast, flavorful, and filling meals. With options from gyros and pizza to hot dogs and gourmet snow cones, local street vendors are a great option if you're on the go—and an even better choice if you're traveling on a budget.

And while you're here, be sure to sample two

© KATY RYAN

HIGHLIGHTS

LOOK FOR TO FIND RECOMMENDED RESTAURANTS.

Best Reason to Not Diet: To resist the crispy fried chicken or authentic Mississippi fried catfish at **Peachtree Restaurant,** complete with whipped mashed potatoes and homemade macaroni and cheese, is futile. And when you're asked about dessert, nod, smile, and say "Yes, please!" (page 40).

Best Biscuits and Gravy: Happy Gillis dishes up a savory combination of biscuits and seasoned gravy peppered with large chunks of sausage that leaves your belly happy, not leaden (page 41).

Best Splurge: Whether you're spellbound by a plate that resembles a work of art or the breathtaking view of downtown Kansas City, **The American** delivers in more ways than one (page 44).

Best Dining Experience: Towering flames, flying shrimp, and expert chefs are highlights of **Gojo Japanese Steak House**, a restaurant that's big on flavor, portions, and mealtime theatrics (page 53).

Best Burger: It's all about the burger in **Westport Flea Market**'s no-fuss interior, complete with a stocked toppings bar. Yes, you really can have it your way (page 55).

Best Dessert: Locally grown ingredients become the ultimate indulgence at **Bluestem,** with a sumptuous dessert menu created by pastry chef and co-owner Megan Garrelts (page 56).

Best Steak: The great steak debate is a favorite local pastime, yet it's always **Plaza III Steakhouse** that marches to triumph on a bed of juicy, perfectly aged beef (page 61).

Best Deal: Write your own coupon (within reason) to redeem at **Waldo Pizza** for an affordable meal that gives customers the power to determine their discounts, and rewards them with some of the best pizza in the city (page 65).

© KATY RYAN

Best Breakfast: Corner Cafe's extensive breakfast menu features oversized omelets and giant cinnamon rolls (page 66).

Best Reason to Dine Outside of the City: Critically acclaimed food made from locally produced ingredients and served in a low-key, leisurely setting is well worth the 35-minute drive to **Justus Drugstore, A Restaurant** (page 68).

PRICE KEY

$ Most entrées less than $10
$$ Most entrées $10-20
$$$ Most entrées more than $20

of the city's unofficial beverages: Boulevard Brewing Co. beer and The Roasterie coffee. Both were created by owners that have a palpable passion for their trades, and the results are rich, flavorful brews that have each become staples in local restaurants, bars, and coffee shops.

River Market and Power and Light District Map 1

AMERICAN

CHEFBURGER $

1350 Walnut St., 816/842-2747, www.chefburgerkc.com

HOURS: Mon.-Sat. 11 A.M.-10 P.M.

Don't be fooled by Chefburger's casual atmosphere and walk-up ordering system. An inspiring array of gourmet burgers awaits, offering combinations like the heart-stopping Widowmaker (cheddar, bacon, fried egg, black bean chili). Or try a hot dog with toppings inspired by nationwide frankfurter capitals like New York, Chicago, and, of course, Kansas City: barbecue sauce, onion, pickle, bacon, and blue cheese. Complete the experience with a side of parsley and garlic-topped waffle fries. And if you're of legal age, don't leave without a spiked shake, a union of ice cream and alcohol that just might prove to be life-changing.

CITY DINER $

301 Grand Blvd., 816/471-5121

HOURS: Daily 6 A.M.-2 P.M.

Step inside the City Diner and transport yourself to a simpler time when hearty, well-made food could solve all the world's problems. Breakfast is a favorite meal at the diner; if you're feeling extra-hungry, try to make your way through a stack of the diner's gigantic pancakes. While you wait for your food, gaze around at the extensive memorabilia collection, a makeshift gallery dedicated to local history. And before you go, here are a couple tips: The diner is cash only, and if you're eating solo, it's best to head straight for the white Formica counter. Grab a stool, a newspaper, and you might just leave with new friends—and a full stomach, of course.

THE FARMHOUSE $

300 Delaware St., 816/569-6032, www.eatatthefarmhouse.com

HOURS: Mon.-Wed. 11 A.M.-2 P.M., Thurs.-Fri. 11 A.M.-11 P.M., Sat. 9 A.M.-11 P.M.

The Farmhouse uses fresh, locally grown food to create flavorful, uncomplicated dishes that let the ingredients shine. The emphasis is on produce, meats, bread, and dairy sourced from area farmers in an effort to promote a farm-to-table eatery. Try the fried green tomato sandwich for a truly inventive spin on the tangy fruit. Subtle touches of farmhouse flair create a welcoming atmosphere, from water served in green glass bottles to waitresses that effortlessly meander through the dining area in cowboy boots. When the weather cooperates, dining on the restaurant's patio is a must—bring your camera to snap pictures of the surrounding River Market loft buildings.

INGREDIENT $

1111 Main St., 816/994-3350, www.ingredientrestaurant.com

HOURS: Mon.-Fri. 6:30 A.M.-7 P.M.

As the name implies, it's the ingredients that

BEER BOULEVARD

To drink anything other than Boulevard beer in Kansas City is akin to treason. John McDonald's local brewery operation produces flavorful year-round and seasonal brews like Boulevard Wheat, Pale Ale, Irish Ale, and Pilsner that have become mainstays on bar taps and in restaurant refrigerators throughout the city and surrounding Midwest region.

Boulevard relies on a vintage Bavarian brewhouse to create distinctive flavors found only in its carefully brewed beers, which are extensively taste-tested to ensure quality results. In 2007, Boulevard expanded to an artisanal line of beers known as the Smokestack Series, offering potent brews with a sophisticated flavor profile in decorative bottles that are as attractive empty as they are full.

Boulevard Brewing Co. tours are a popular Kansas City activity for residents and visitors alike. Tours are held Wednesday through Sunday at various times, but make your reservations as soon as you can: They often fill up weeks in advance. While you're on the tour you'll hear about the history of the company, watch a video detailing the beer-making process, take a walking tour of the plant, and, when you're finished, sample various Boulevard beers. The tour is free; reservations can be made by calling 816/474-7095.

COURTESY OF THE KANSAS CITY CONVENTION AND VISITORS ASSOCIATION

Boulevard Brewing Co. is a favorite hometown brewer.

take center stage at this casual eatery that attracts a diverse crowd looking for a quick, yet flavorful meal. Create a hearty salad from a lengthy list of lettuces, vegetables, meats, fruits, and crunchy toppings, or choose a favorite sauce and toppings for a customized pizza. Grilled sandwiches, wraps, salads, and gourmet pizzas complete the menu. And don't be taken aback by the chef-owned restaurant's philosophy on tipping—or, rather, non-tipping. Employees prefer that customers instead perform a random act of kindness. Good karma and a full belly? Now those are magical ingredients.

THE MARQUEE BAR AND GRILL $

1400 Main St., 816/474-4545, www.themarqueekc.com

HOURS: Sun.-Thurs. 11 A.M.-10 P.M., Fri.-Sat. 11 A.M.-5 A.M.

Nestled within the renovated interior of downtown's AMC Mainstreet Theater, The Marquee Bar and Grill takes the "dinner and a movie" concept to a whole new level. Forget traditional movie concessions and instead enjoy a sumptuous menu as classy as the restaurant's sleek interior. Start (or end) your movie-going experience with The Walnut, an open-faced sandwich piled with roast turkey, melted brie, and caramelized onions, or the Marquee meatloaf, a house specialty. Late-night cravings? The kitchen rolls out culinary blockbusters until 5 A.M.

PEACHTREE RESTAURANT $$

31 E. 14th St., 816/886-9800, www.peachtreerestaurants.com

HOURS: Tues.-Thurs. 11 A.M.-2:30 P.M. and 5-9 P.M., Fri. 11 A.M.-10 P.M., Sat. noon-10 P.M., Sun. noon-7 P.M.

The words "Southern cooking" bring to mind fried chicken, mashed potatoes, fluffy biscuits, and cornbread that walks a fine line between cake-like and crumbly. At Peachtree Restaurant, you'll find all of this and more in an upscale, elegant interior inspired by the elegance of Kansas City's jazz era. The Peachtree is one of the P&L District's few locally owned tenants, making it a favorite gathering spot for a hearty lunch or even larger dinner. Come hungry—really hungry—and don't leave without sampling the sweet potato–studded cornbread, Mississippi fried catfish, and the restaurant's signature dessert: the Peach Tree cobbler served by a wait staff that is as friendly as it is knowledgeable.

THE SAVOY GRILL $$$

219 W. 9th St., 816/842-3890, www.savoygrill.net

HOURS: Mon.-Thurs. 11 A.M.-11 P.M., Fri.-Sat. 11 A.M.-midnight, Sun. 4-10 P.M.

Channel Kansas City's historic elegance at The Savoy Grill, part of the legendary Savoy Hotel. Reputed to be the oldest restaurant in Kansas City, The Savoy Grill serves classic steak house recipes perfected since its 1903 opening. Oysters on the half shell or Alaskan King Crab cocktail delight the palate in preparation for a whole Maine lobster or juicy Savoy T-bone steak; to close, an indulgent dessert menu beckons with the restaurant's trademark strawberry-topped cheesecake, among others. For a flavorful experience that's a bit easier on the wallet, visit The Savoy Grill for lunch, for a business meeting or a leisurely respite after a morning of downtown exploration.

WINSLOW'S FAMOUS SLOW'S KC-STYLE BARBEQUE $

20 E. 5th St., 816/471-7427, www.kc-bbq.com

HOURS: Mon.-Tues. 11 A.M.-3 P.M., Wed. 11 A.M.-close, Thurs. 11 A.M.-8 P.M., Fri.-Sat. 11 A.M.-1 A.M., Sun. 11 A.M.-8 P.M.

Every barbecue master has a specific technique, and at Winslow's the secret is slow smoking over green hickory to produce a tangy flavor that streams over the tongue like liquid smoke. Choose from sandwiches or smoked meats; for the full experience opt for a platter piled high with several meats and accompanied by a side dish. While Winslow's chefs make music in the kitchen, the restaurant often hosts live music on its sizable outdoor patio. Frequent drink specials make Winslow's a popular gathering place, and patrons can drink and dine outdoors year-round on the heated patio. Because the noise level is high when there's live music, opt for a no-performance evening—or better yet, come for lunch—if you'd prefer conversation with your barbecue. Winslow's attracts a mixed, friendly crowd and is one of several Kansas City restaurants that don't require patrons to dress to impress.

ASIAN

RED DRAGON HOUSE $$

312 W. 8th St., 816/221-1388

HOURS: Mon.-Thurs. 11 A.M.-10 P.M., Fri. 11 A.M.-11 P.M., Sat. 11:30 A.M.-11 P.M., Sun. 11:30 A.M.-9 P.M.

Admittedly, Red Dragon House is a bit off the beaten path. Tucked on a quiet side street near the picturesque Quality Hill neighborhood, the traditional Asian restaurant is as welcoming as the hearty favorites listed on the menu. From cashew and sweet and sour chicken to lo mein and fried rice, Red Dragon House embodies tasty, affordable Asian cuisine. Crab rangoons and egg rolls are a must, of course, and try a bowl of the egg drop soup, especially during the colder months. The service is speedy, but while you're waiting on your food to arrive, consult your paper placemat for an enlightening look into the Chinese zodiac—if you keep it clean the placemat makes a portable souvenir that doesn't require refrigeration.

CAFÉS

HAPPY GILLIS $

549 Gillis St., 816/471-3663, www.happysoupeater.com

HOURS: Tues.-Fri. 8 A.M.-5 P.M., Sat. 8 A.M.-4 P.M., Sun. 9 A.M.-2 P.M.

Born out of Todd Schulte's soup delivery service, Happy Soup Eater, Happy Gillis is a charming neighborhood café that brings freshly made sandwiches, soups, and breakfast items to hungry Kansas Citians. Soup selections are rotated throughout the week while a small team of dedicated and knowledgeable

RESTAURANTS

© KATY RYAN

Enjoy soup, sandwiches, and the city's best biscuits and gravy within the quirky, cheerful interior of Happy Gillis.

chefs construct sandwiches that stand alone or make a hearty accompaniment to a bowl of soup. Artisan breads and savory fillings merge to create combinations such as the Vietnamese-inspired *bahn mi* (cilantro lovers, this is for you!). Early birds can fuel up at breakfast with egg sandwiches, a bialy with cream cheese, or an order of biscuits and gravy, hailed by many as the best in town.

LE FOU FROG $$

400 E. 5th St., 816/474-6060, www.lefoufrog.com

HOURS: Tues.-Thurs. 5:30-10 P.M., Fri.-Sat. 5-11 P.M., Sun. 5-9 P.M.

Kansas City native Barbara Rafael and her husband, Mano, opened Le Fou Frog after working at a New York City restaurant owned by Mano and his brother. Le Fou Frog, which can be translated as The Crazy Frog, channels the signature atmosphere and fare of traditional French bistros. The restaurant is a favorite for both couples and groups of friends, but the high prices and upscale interior aren't incredibly family-friendly. Foie gras, coquilles St. Jacques, and escargots all appear under "hors d'oeuvres chauds," or hot appetizers. Entrées include several seafood dishes, steak au poivre, and duck infused with a lavender honey glaze. And because a French restaurant is nothing without a decadent dessert menu, Le Fou Frog wholeheartedly embraces chocolate and pastry, the unofficial fifth French food group. Bon appetit, indeed.

DESSERT

BABYCAKES $

108 Missouri Ave., 816/841-1048, www.babycakeskc.com

HOURS: Tues.-Fri. 10 A.M.-6 P.M., Sat. 10 A.M.-4 P.M.

Stroll down Missouri Avenue and you can't miss the brown and blue BabyCakes awning. In 2006, cupcake queen and chocolatier Laura Caron introduced her sweets boutique to the area and it remains a popular spot, especially with Saturday-morning marketgoers. The strictly to-go menu features concoctions such as vanilla with chocolate fluff, lemon with lemon icing, and red velvet with cream cheese icing are baked daily. Caron also offers Frou Frou Sweets, a line of handmade, hand-dipped chocolates in combinations like raspberry and dark chocolate, dark chocolate toffee, and the Holy Grail: peanut butter and milk chocolate.

YUMMO YOGURT $

1360 Walnut St., 816/994-3799

HOURS: Mon.-Sat. 11 A.M.-8 P.M.

Pinkberry may be all the rage in L.A., but on Missouri's west coast the word is Yummo. The brainchild of superhuman Kansas City restaurateur Rob Dalzell, Yummo operates via a self-service layout that allows customers to mix and match various fro-yo flavors and toppings to create their own frozen masterpiece. Priced by the ounce, Yummo's frozen yogurt ranges from predictable (chocolate, vanilla) to insane (green tea, gingerbread). Toppings run a similar gamut, from fruit and nuts to sauces, candy bits, and dried cereal. There is limited seating available inside, but if the weather permits, grab your yogurt and head to the nearby patios to enjoy your yogurt al fresco.

ITALIAN

CAFE AL DENTE $

412 Delaware St., 816/472-9444

HOURS: Mon.-Thurs. 11 A.M.-9 P.M., Fri.-Sat. 11 A.M.-10 P.M.

The family-owned Cafe Al Dente specializes in simple, hearty Italian fare filled with flavor. The no-fuss, laid-back interior offers plenty of window-side booths with picturesque views of the River Market's Delaware Street. For more romantic surroundings, step out on the patio and enjoy the view of the downtown skyline. Try the lasagna or opt for the Quarterback Sneak, a hearty sandwich stacked with handmade meatballs, cheese, and a heaping helping of marinara sauce. Cafe Al Dente also hosts a fully stocked bar and a mouthwatering martini menu, the perfect way to start—or end—your meal.

CAROLLO'S DELI $

9 E. 3rd St., 816/474-1860

HOURS: Mon.-Fri. 10 A.M.-5:30 P.M., Sat. 7:30 A.M.-4:30 P.M., Sun. 9 A.M.-4 P.M.

Stop at the counter and place your order for an Italian-style sandwich stuffed with meats, veggies, and a healthy dose of olive oil. Much of Carollo's meats, including the Italian sausage, are made in-house, and impart a subtly spiced flavor to the sandwiches. Service is brisk and efficient here, which is useful when crowds form during the lunch hour and on farmer's market weekends. There are a few tables inside the deli, but it's best to grab your sandwich, bag of chips, and a bottled soda and head outside to the adjoining park. Once you've finished, head back in for dessert—you can't go wrong with handmade cannoli, Italian lemon cream cake, or homemade gelato.

GAROZZO'S RISTORANTE $$

526 Harrison St., 816/221-2455, www.garozzos.com

HOURS: Mon.-Thurs. 11 A.M.-10 P.M., Fri. 11 A.M.-11 P.M., Sat. 4-11 P.M., Sun. 5-9 P.M.

Mention Garozzo's to a Kansas Citian and be prepared to hear a five-minute sermon on the restaurant's signature chicken spiedini. Sure, the traditional family-owned Italian restaurant offers a menu of pasta favorites like eggplant and chicken parmesan and lasagna, but to try anything other than the speidini on your first visit is criminal. Head to Garozzo's for dinner on your birthday and show your ID to receive a free speidini entrée. The service is top-notch at Garozzo's, with attentive servers that circulate often enough to make you feel important, yet not so much that you're annoyed by their presence.

MINSKY'S PIZZA $

427 Main St., 816/421-1122, www.minskys.com

HOURS: Sun.-Thurs. 11 A.M.-10 P.M., Fri.-Sat. 11 A.M.-11 P.M.

Chicago may be the undisputed home of pizza, but a visit to Minsky's leaves you feeling that Kansas City just might be a close second. A staggering array of gourmet pies, along with traditionally topped classics, are the highlights of Minsky's extensive menu that also includes appetizers, sandwiches, and salads. You can't go wrong with the honey-wheat crust, a substantial dough with a mere hint of sweetness. The carryout service is speedy if you'd prefer to eat elsewhere, but sports fanatics will love Minsky's interior, complete with three jumbo-sized screens and several smaller televisions broadcasting multiple sporting events.

MEXICAN

BURRITO BROS. $

407 Main St., 816/842-0152, www.burritobrotherskc.com

HOURS: Mon.-Fri. 11 A.M.-7 P.M., Sat.-Sun 11 A.M.-3 P.M.

This casual taqueria serves up freshly made burritos, quesadillas, and tacos filled with your choice of meat (including shrimp), veggies, several kinds of salsa, and freshly made guacamole. All entrées come with a generous handful of chips, perfect for scooping up excess burrito fillings. The restaurant's small interior can be crowded, especially during City Market hours, but numerous covered outdoor tables allow for overflow seating in the heart of the market.

MIDDLE EASTERN

HABASHI HOUSE $

309 Main St., 816/421-0414, www.habashihouse.com

HOURS: Sun.-Fri. 10:30 A.M.-2 P.M., Sat. 9:30 A.M.-5 P.M.

A dine-in restaurant, with an adjacent Middle Eastern specialty store, Habashi House is a double-edged culinary sword poised to strike with pungent spices, pillowy pita bread, and some of the best falafel in the city. Cheap prices and ample indoor and outdoor seating make Habashi House a great lunch spot after a morning spent exploring City Market. Try the gyro or its Middle Eastern counterpart, a shawarma. For a more thorough sampling of Habashi House's exemplary cooking, try the house combo platter, available with or without gyro meat. Complimentary tea is available in the back of the restaurant, and while you dine, you can watch Middle Eastern music videos shown on the restaurant's in-house TV screen. After lunch, pick up a piece (or more) of baklava, the perfect sugary afternoon pick-me-up.

Crossroads and 18th and Vine

Map 2

AMERICAN

THE AMERICAN $$$

200 E. 25th St., 816/545-8001,
www.theamericankc.com

HOURS: Mon.-Sat. 5:30-10 P.M.

Located atop Crown Center's Halls department store, The American offers memorable meals set against a panoramic downtown backdrop. With a culinary concept developed by icon James Beard, The American features an indulgent seasonal menu well worth the financial splurge. Caviar, foie gras, beef, and diver-caught sea scallops represent a sampling of The American's dishes. Formal dress is advised here, where the ornately decorated ceiling and plush banquettes provide an elegant atmosphere. Check The American's website for an updated schedule of tasting dinners and other special events.

BLUE BIRD BISTRO $$

1700 Summit St., 816/221-7559,
www.bluebirdbistro.com

HOURS: Mon.-Sat. 7 A.M.-10 P.M., Sun. 10 A.M.-2 P.M.

Settle in at one of Blue Bird's cozy tables scattered throughout an eclectic, modern interior and prepare for a sustainable, organic feast that explodes with flavor and color. Locally produced ingredients from 40 area family farms are a priority at Blue Bird, and the brunch, lunch, and dinner seasonal menus offer an array of small plates, salads, and entrées. Start your day with Summit Street Benedict, named for Blue Bird's address. For dinner, try wild-caught American shrimp or house-made herb ravioli. Because Blue Bird Bistro is small and a city favorite, consider making a reservation for dinner.

BULLDOG $$

1715 Main St., 816/421-4799, www.kcbulldog.com

HOURS: Mon.-Fri. 11 A.M.-1:30 A.M.,
Sat.-Sun. 5 P.M.-1:30 A.M.

Part restaurant, part bar, and part live-entertainment venue, Bulldog specializes in contemporary American fare in a contemporary dining room. Indulgent fried brie, country-fried steak, and a K.C. strip steak rubbed with a 12-pepper blend are just a few of the menu offerings, along with pasta, sandwiches, pizza, and entrée-sized salads. Bulldog caters to a younger crowd, especially during the evening hours, when patrons come to eat first, and drink later. In the late evening there is an expansive drink menu and live entertainment including a DJ and Thursday-night brodioke, where costumed participants perform over-the-top imitations of rock stars.

THE CASHEW $

2000 Grand Blvd., 816/221-5858,
www.thecashew.com

HOURS: Mon.-Sat. 11 A.M.-1:30 A.M., Sun. 11 A.M.-midnight

A modern, upscale version of Kansas City's The Peanut, The Cashew serves simple fare including appetizers, salads, quesadillas, and sandwiches in a spacious, minimalist interior made even more open when the restaurant's garage door–like windows are thrown open in the warmer months. Restaurant by day and popular watering hole at night, The Cashew is a great place to convene before or after the Crossroads' First Fridays gallery crawl. While you wait for your meal to arrive, snack on the restaurant's signature starter—a bowl of perfectly salted cashews.

CITY TAVERN $$$

101 W. 22nd St., Ste. 200, 816/421-3696,
www.citytavern.net

HOURS: Mon.-Thurs. 11 A.M.-2 P.M. and 5-9 P.M.,
Fri. 11 A.M.-2 P.M. and 5-10 P.M., Sat. 5-10 P.M.

Originally celebrated for its fresh coldwater oysters, City Tavern has recently become a front-runner in Kansas City's battle for the best steak. Located in the historic Freight House district, which formerly served as a cargo pick-up area, City Tavern is a popular spot for business lunches and special-occasion dinners. The restaurant's interior evokes an age-old aesthetic with exposed brick walls, a heavy timber ceiling, and hardwood floors. The menu is slightly more modern, uniting oysters and mussels with pancetta-wrapped diver scallops or an aged filet mignon. End your meal with an artisan cheese plate, buttermilk panna cotta, or an old-fashioned root beer float made with Sioux City sasparilla and Poppy's vanilla bean ice cream.

FRITZ'S RAILROAD RESTAURANT $

2450 Grand Blvd., 816/474-4004,
www.crowncenter.com

HOURS: Daily 10:30 A.M.-8 P.M.

Kids and adults alike delight in the Fritz's family-friendly dining experience. Dedicated to trains, the city's original form of transportation, Fritz's delivers tasty hamburgers, fries, chicken tenders, and more via a model train system that winds throughout the restaurant. Pick up the phone at your booth and place your food order with the "operator." After a brief wait, the food is deposited at your table by several train cars. On your way out, pose for a picture at the restaurant's train-themed entrance—don't forget to pick up a cardboard conductor's hat.

KANSAS CITY CAFE $

1532 Grand Blvd., 816/471-7111,
www.kansascitycafe.net

HOURS: Mon.-Fri. 11 A.M.-3 P.M.

Thanks to cheerful yellow awnings, the contemporary, yet casual Kansas City Cafe is a visible and favorite lunch spot for the downtown crowd looking for a quick bite. You'll find typical café fare such as soups, salads, and sandwiches on the menu, but be prepared for unexpected flavor twists like chilled watermelon-chipotle soup or a Pale Ale BBQ portobello. Kansas City Cafe is also open for dinner before select Sprint Center shows, so check the website for the current schedule.

MICHAEL SMITH'S RESTAURANT $$$

1900 Main St., 816/842-2202,
www.michaelsmithkc.com

HOURS: Tues.-Thurs. 11:30 A.M.-2 P.M., Fri. 11:30 A.M.-2 P.M. and 5-10 P.M., Sat. 5-10 P.M.

James Beard Award–winner Michael Smith knows how to pack a punch on a plate. Ingredients both traditional and inventive unite to produce flavorful, memorable meals, such as the signature eight-hour pork roast or the Campo Lindo Farms chicken breast served with a dollop of bacon-bread pudding. For lunch, indulge in the Dungeness crab ravioli topped with pancetta, almond *gremolata,* and celery broth or the roasted sweet breads served alongside wood-fired artichokes, fig tapenade, and a puff-pastry crouton. The restaurant's eye-catching contemporary decor is the ideal backdrop for Smith's contemporary cuisine, and the upscale ambience makes it a popular choice for weekday lunch meetings for nearby businesspeople. Dressier attire is recommended, and reservations are recommended for Friday and Saturday night (especially the first Friday of the month).

1924 MAIN $$

1924 Main St., 816/472-1924, www.1924main.com

HOURS: Tues.-Fri. 11 A.M.-2 P.M. and 5 P.M.-close, Sat. 5 P.M.-close, happy hour Tues.-Fri. 4-7 P.M.

The stylish, minimal interior of 1924 Main is an ideal backdrop for the restaurant's contemporary American cuisine. Settle into one of the cushy black banquette seats with a pre-dinner classic cocktail, then try some of the inventive dishes that feature seasonal, local ingredients, such as blackened fish tacos with green tomato salsa and chipotle cream, or the watermelon salad with feta, mint, and basil. Although the dishes tend to be pricey here, a prix fixe menu at lunch and dinner provides a satisfying dining experience at

© KATY RYAN

Lightly fried rock shrimp piled atop chipotle aioli is one of several delicious lunch items available at 1924 Main.

a reasonable price. Servers are quick to answer any questions about the menu and the bartenders are very efficient, which is especially helpful during the busier evening hours.

SOUPERMAN $

1724 Main St., 816/421-7687, www.soupkc.com

HOURS: Mon.-Fri. 10 A.M.-3 P.M.

The good news? Souperman is delicious. The bad news? The soup and sandwich eatery is open for weekday lunch only. Decorated with pictures of soup-slurping superheroes, Souperman offers a cheeky take on the superhero-ruled worlds found within the pages of comic books. Yet there's nothing comical about the flavorful, hearty soups that have made Souperman a favorite downtown dining destination. There are several flavors daily, but I've never been able to stray from the Thai coconut chicken. Souperman also serves sandittos, pressed sandwiches enfolded in grilled tortillas. Food is placed on gunmetal-colored trays, a chic upgrade from the cafeteria mainstay. The restaurant's small interior is often crowded during the lunch rush, yet several outdoor tables allow for overflow seating and a prime view of the Crossroads District. The eatery is very popular with business professionals from nearby offices because of the friendly yet efficient service during the lunch rush. After ordering at the counter, patrons don't typically wait more than a couple of minutes for their orders.

TOWN TOPIC $

2021 Broadway Blvd., 816/471-2020

HOURS: Daily 24 hours

Instantly recognizable by its slightly battered blue and red sign with white lettering, Town Topic is nothing short of a local institution. The burgers, debated as the best in town, are often described as larger versions of White

Town Topic is a local favorite for greasy, inexpensive burgers and late-night service.

Castle burgers, piled on doughy buns with plenty of grease and onions. The best seating option within the cramped, worn interior is at the counter, a mandatory feature of diners and greasy spoons everywhere. Town Topic is one of a few late-night eateries in downtown Kansas City, making it a prime choice for night owls eager for sustenance after an evening of drinking.

THE WESTSIDE LOCAL $

1663 Summit St., 816/997-9089, www.thewestsidelocal.com

HOURS: Tues.-Thurs. and Sun. 11 A.M.-11 P.M., Fri.-Sat. 11 A.M.-midnight

This upscale tavern is one of a growing number of local restaurant pioneers dedicated to the farm-to-table culinary concept. Seasonal, locally grown ingredients comprise a menu that includes "localities," snacks, large plates, sandwiches, and desserts. Try the Westside roast beef, deviled eggs, or mussels. The Westside Local's historic exterior makes way for a modern interior that's befitting a restaurant described by the owners as having the "social setting of a tavern with the flavors of upscale dining." Service can be slow here, so be prepared for a leisurely meal and you won't be disappointed. In back of the restaurant, a large beer garden has communal rustic wood tables that encourage conversation while visitors make their way through an extensive beer list complete with American IPAs, wheats, Belgians, and more. Wine and cocktails are also served.

ASIAN

LULU'S THAI NOODLE SHOP & SATAY BAR $

333 Southwest Blvd., 816/474-8424, www.lulusnoodles.com

HOURS: Mon.-Fri. 11 A.M.-3 P.M. and 5-10 P.M., Sat. noon-10 P.M.

Thai food is the star at Lulu's Noodles, and it's best to opt for the deliciously flavorful *satay,* skewers of grilled meat, shrimp, or tofu available as an individual portion or on a *satay* plate accompanied with soft jasmine rice. Lulu's large menu also includes curries, fried rice, soups, and Lulu's "no-brainers," traditional favorites like *ma po* noodles and pepper beef basil. A sizable lunch and dinner crowd keeps Lulu's a fun, boisterous place to enjoy Thai cuisine. Despite the large number of diners, especially during lunch, service is fast and no-fuss. Arrive early to secure a table, but once seated, you won't wait too long for your food.

NARA $$

1617 Main St., 816/221-6272, www.narakc.com

HOURS: Mon.-Thurs. 11 A.M.-midnight, Fri. 11 A.M.-1 A.M., Sat. 4 P.M.-1 A.M.

Named for an ancient Japanese city famed for its tranquility, Nara is equal parts hip nightspot and Japanese *robata,* where a traditional open-flame grilling method is used. Try the drunken duck or stir-fried beef sirloin, or, if you're in the mood for sushi, something from the extensive sushi menu complete with traditional favorites like California roll and house specialties like the Sexy Mama roll. With an extensive cocktail menu as well, Nara is a stylish eatery perfect for lunch, happy hour, dinner, and everything in between.

BARBECUE

ARTHUR BRYANT'S BARBEQUE $

1727 Brooklyn Ave., 816/231-1123, www.arthurbryantsbbq.com

HOURS: Mon.-Thurs. 10 A.M.-9:30 P.M., Fri.-Sat. 10 A.M.-10 P.M., Sun. 11 A.M.-8 P.M.

New Yorker columnist Calvin Trillin once declared Arthur Bryant's "the single best restaurant in the world." Judge for yourself when you visit one of Kansas City's iconic barbecue joints, known for its one-of-a-kind sauce that adds a rich blend of tangy flavor to any of Arthur Bryant's smoked meats. The restaurant's no-fuss interior hasn't changed much in the decades since it opened, and when you place your order at the counter you'll get a bird's-eye view of the kitchen action. The food is the main attraction, but before you leave take a moment to browse the restaurant's walls lined with memorabilia, including signed pictures from visiting celebrities.

GATES BAR-B-Q $$

3205 Main St., 816/753-0828, www.gatesbbq.com

HOURS: Daily 10 A.M.-midnight

If you're seeking some of Kansas City's best barbecue, you've got to head to Gates. To make your first visit less overwhelming, follow these tips. You'll immediately be greeted with the restaurant employees' signature opener: "Hi, may

FEELING SAUCY?

It's not an accident that the unofficial cuisine of Kansas City, a city born out of the stockyards, is barbecue – saucy, smoky, and infused with a signature flavor found only in Cowtown. The phenomenon began in the 1920s when the city's first grill master, Henry Perry, set up shop inside a streetcar barn at 19th and Highland Streets and began grilling slabs of barbecue ribs in an outdoor pit. Wrapped in newspaper, the tangy cuts of meat were wildly popular, and in time, some of the city's founding fathers of barbecue like Charlie and Arthur Bryant, George Gates, Otis Boyd, John Harris, and Sherman Thompson learned Perry's technique before branching out to create their own carefully nuanced lines of sauces and rubs.

The only real problem is deciding where to go – with barbecue restaurants seemingly around every corner, choosing just one is a difficult task. Start at **Arthur Bryant's** (18th and Brooklyn Sts., 816/231-1123), proclaimed by many to be the best barbecue in Kansas City. Or try **Gates Bar-B-Q** (3205 Main St., 816/753-0828), where you'll be greeted with the restaurant's signature "May I help you?" as soon as you walk in the door. If you don't mind a short drive, head to the state line – 47th Street and Mission Road, to be exact – to **Oklahoma Joe's** (913/722-3366), a local favorite that serves plates of steaming-hot barbecue out of a gas station. The line to order is often out the door, an indication of just how much people in Kansas City love barbecue. And in October, the granddaddy of all barbecue events, the **American Royal,** washes a wave of hickory smoke over the city as barbecue competitors come from around the country to take home the grand prize in a number of categories. For the mere barbecue enthusiast, the American Royal is a weekend-long buffet filled with tender pork, sauce-slathered ribs, and other delicacies that, together, combine to create one of Kansas City's best traditions. Grab a napkin and dive in!

RESTAURANTS

COURTESY OF THE KANSAS CITY CONVENTION AND VISITORS ASSOCIATION

Once served from streetside carts, Kansas City's unofficial cuisine is now served at many of the city's restaurants.

COURTESY OF THE KANSAS CITY CONVENTION AND VISITORS ASSOCIATION

Gates Bar-B-Q's coveted sauce recipe that dates back to 1946 has made it a local favorite restaurant.

I help you?" You probably won't know what to order, so smile, make eye contact and signal for an extra minute. The best bet is a sandwich with your favorite meat, served with a heaping helping of fries. If you're with a larger group, try the mixed plate for a sampling of Gates' tender meats and a heaping dollop of the restaurant's famous sauce. The dining room retains a traditional, old-fashioned feel thanks to a rich color scheme, leather booths, and vintage, belt-powered ceiling fans. It's a fitting atmosphere for one of Kansas City's first families of barbecue, and a perfect example of an old adage: "If it ain't broke, don't fix it."

ITALIAN

LIDIA'S KANSAS CITY $$

101 W. 22nd St., 816/221-3722, www.lidias-kc.com

HOURS: Sun.-Thurs. 11 A.M.-2 P.M. and 5-9 P.M., Fri.-Sat. 11 A.M.-2 P.M. and 5-10 P.M.

The namesake of Italian cooking legend Lidia Bastianich, Lidia's Kansas City brings the best in Italian cooking to the Midwest. Lidia and her husband, Joseph, offer a daily tasting of three homemade pastas, a service modeled after the Bastianichs' New York–based restaurant, Bucco. Or try the rich seafood-studded *zuppa di pesce,* a seafood soup with Sardinian couscous. Lidia's also offers a market brunch on Saturday and Sunday, as well as daily lunch service and happy hours complete with drink and food specials, all served in a spacious Italian farmhouse–inspired interior. Servers are friendly, professional, and knowledgeable about the menu and its changing, seasonal offerings.

MEXICAN

MANNY'S RESTAURANTE MEXICANO $

207 Southwest Blvd., 816/474-7696, www.mannyskc.com

HOURS: Mon.-Sat. 11 A.M.-10 P.M.

Family-owned Manny's is a favorite local spot

for addictive salsa and a menu filled with traditional favorites like fajitas, burritos, and tacos. Try the favorite Monterey burrito, a filling concoction of pork, ground beef, or chicken combined with chile sauce and beans and slathered with a healthy dollop of Manny's signature Monterey Jack cheese spread. On your way out, pick up a jar of Familia Lopez salsa and bring the taste of Manny's home with you. If you head to Manny's during First Fridays, be prepared to wait: The favorite gathering spot often has a line out the door. The wait staff at Manny's is a well-oiled machine that is used to the large crowds that seem to form throughout the day, especially on First Fridays. If you're meeting a large party, ensure that your guests arrive promptly; you typically will not be seated unless your entire party is present. The large interior is dimly lit, yet the pace remains hectic as servers rush by with food carts.

MARGARITA'S $

2829 Southwest Blvd., 816/931-4849,
www.margaritaskansascity.com
HOURS: Mon.-Thurs. 11 A.M.-10:30 P.M.,
Fri.-Sat. 11 A.M.-11 P.M., Sun. noon-10 P.M.

Before you even decide what to order, request a bowl of the popular Margarita Dip, an indulgent blend of white pepper cheese and secret ingredients. That and an icy margarita just might be the perfect meal, but if you're in need of something more substantial you'll find something on Margarita's expansive menu that fits the bill. A hard-working staff prepares almost everything in-house, including the perfectly salted chips and aromatic salsa, so popular it's available by the jar in most Kansas City grocery stores. The restaurant is often busy, especially during lunch, when parking can be difficult.

PONAK'S MEXICAN KITCHEN $

2856 Southwest Blvd., 816/753-0775,
www.ponaksmexicankitchen.com
HOURS: Mon.-Sat. 11 A.M.-10 P.M.,
Sun. 11 A.M.-9 P.M.

Frequently recognized as one of the city's best Mexican restaurants, Ponak's serves food inspired by Mexico's Sonora region. Try a house burrito topped with a fried egg or the sweetly indulgent chicken mole, simmered in a spicy, chocolaty sauce and served alongside a heaping helping of rice and beans. Ponak's talented bartenders mix up the city's best margaritas, made with a healthy splash of Cuervo Gold tequila. Order an original margarita on the rocks for the true Ponak's experience.

PIZZA

GRINDERS $

4175 E. 18th St., 816/472-5454,
www.grinderspizza.com
HOURS: Mon.-Sat. 11 A.M.-1:30 A.M.,
Sun. noon-11 P.M.

The creation of celebrated local sculptor and artist Stretch, Grinders is a funky, colorful eatery that's part bar, part pizza shop, and part live-music venue—concerts are frequently held in the restaurant's "backyard." Giant New York–style pizza slices, authentic Philly cheesesteak sandwiches, tater tots, and "death wings" are local favorites, washed down with a large selection of craft and specialty beers. Head to the bathroom for the express purpose of reading the multitude of rejection letters Stretch has collected over the years from arts organizations around the country. Spiky-haired Food Network star Guy Fieri stopped at Grinders for a taping of *Diners, Drive-Ins and Dives,* forever cementing Grinders' status as a purposefully divey—and delicious—local haunt.

PIZZA BELLA $$

1810 Baltimore Ave., 816/421-7492, www.pizzabellakc.com

HOURS: Mon.-Thurs. 11 A.M.-9 P.M, Fri.-Sat. 11 A.M.-close

Named for owner Rob Dalzell's daughter and pizza connoisseur, Isabella, Pizza Bella is a casual eatery dedicated to the art of wood-fired pizza. In fact, you'll only find antipasto, pizza, and a small array of desserts on the menu, a culinary streamlining that allows the focus to remain on the restaurant's namesake. Closely positioned tables make for a communal atmosphere, and crunchy breadsticks are piled in glass jars on each table. Pizza Bella boasts one of the better patios in Kansas City, so opt to enjoy your meal alfresco, weather permitting. Service can be slow during the lunch rush and weekend evenings, but servers are affable and quick to recommend wine pairings.

SPANISH

EXTRA VIRGIN $$

1900 Main St., 816/842-2205, www.extravirginkc.com

HOURS: Mon.-Thurs. 11:30 A.M.-10 P.M., Fri. 11:30 A.M.-11 P.M., Sat. 5-11 P.M.

At Extra Virgin, celebrated Kansas City chef Michael Smith combines a fresh, funky atmosphere with an inventive array of Mediterranean tapas. Order two or three plates for a filling meal, or if you're with a group, order several and share. If you're feeling especially daring, choose from an array of adventurous tapas including crispy pig ear salad, grilled beef tongue, and fried duck gizzards served with a homemade hot sauce. Sautéed tiger shrimp, a stuffed whole artichoke, or crab-stuffed piquillo peppers make for a more conventional meal. The abundant minimalist wood-and-metal and high-top tables accommodate hungry patrons. If you plan to try Extra Virgin during afternoon happy hour, arrive early to ensure a good seat, especially during the monthly First Fridays gallery crawl.

LA BODEGA $$

703 Southwest Blvd., 816/472-8272, www.labodegakc.com

HOURS: Mon.-Sat. 11 A.M.-11 P.M., Sun. 4-10 P.M.

In the tradition of the tapas of northern Spain, La Bodega serves small plates that encourage sharing and thereby foster camaraderie and leisurely dining. The restaurant's Spanish-inspired decor, featuring elaborately tiled floors, vibrant colors, and white-tiled tables, compliments the extensive tapas menu. Must-try tapas include the *tortilla Española,* a Spanish–style omelet; *albondigas caseras,* meatballs garnished with a spicy garlic cream sauce; and the *papas fritas con ajo,* a savory blend of refried, roasted potatoes with garlic, parsley, and garlic-cumin aioli. One of the best ways to spend a summer afternoon in Kansas City is at La Bodega's happy hour. Grab an outdoor table for prime views of Southwest Boulevard and order several tapas and a pitcher of the restaurant's expertly mixed sangria for a relaxed dining experience that could stretch into the late evening hours in the blink of an eye.

LILL'S ON 17TH $$

815 W. 17th St., 816/421-4441, www.lillson17th.com

HOURS: Wed.-Thurs. 11 A.M.-2 P.M. and 5-9 P.M., Fri.-Sat. 11 A.M.-2 P.M. and 5:30-10 P.M.

If dining within the quiet luxury of Lill's on 17th makes you feel as if you're in someone's house, well, that's because you are in someone's house. A converted house, to be exact, whose various dimly-lit rooms create cozy dining spaces perfect for group meals or more intimate gatherings. Servers at Lill's are unhurried yet attentive, allowing guests to leisurely enjoy flavorful tapas or larger dishes. Start your meal with a savory array of tapas from grilled garlicky shrimp to sumptuous bacon-wrapped dates. Then move on to the steak or seafood dishes, all perfectly seasoned and cooked. The restaurant's front and back patios are some of the best al fresco options in the city. If you happen to be traveling with a pet, four-legged friends are welcome on the two patios.

Westport, Midtown, and The Plaza Map 3

ASIAN

BLUE KOI NOODLES AND DUMPLINGS $$

1803 W. 39th St., 816/561-5003, www.bluekoi.net

HOURS: Mon.-Thurs. 11 A.M.-9:30 P.M., Fri. 11 A.M.-10:30 P.M., Sat. noon-10:30 P.M.

The Chang family, known locally as the minds behind Genghis Khan Mongolian barbecue, extended their Kansas City empire with Blue Koi. The menu combines traditional Asian favorites with innovative dishes such as Ants on a Tree, cellophane noodles tossed with small clumps of delicately spiced pork and bits of cabbage. Handmade northern Chinese dumplings make for a savory, comforting meal, enhanced with one of Blue Koi's signature bubble teas: Non-dairy milk, ice, and tea are combined with tapioca pearls to create an oddly refreshing concoction that is quickly becoming a standard offering in Asian restaurants.

GENGHIS KHAN $$

3906 Bell St., 816/753-3600, www.genghiskhankc.com

HOURS: Mon.-Thurs. 11 A.M.-9:30 P.M., Fri.-Sat. 11 A.M.-10:30 P.M., Sun. 11 A.M.-9 P.M.

The power is in your hands at Genghis Khan, the city's only locally owned Mongolian grill. Two bars of noodles, meats, vegetables, and sauces inspire nearly limitless possibilities. Once your bowl is heaping, head over to the massive, circular grill station where speedy chefs sauté each concoction to steaming perfection. The chefs' speed and skill is a sight worth watching, and if you agree, drop a buck or two into a countertop tip jar as you make your way back to the table. Traditional Asian entrées such as general Tso's chicken and egg-studded fried rice, as well as various vegetable and meat combinations simmered and served in clay pots, are also on the menu.

GOJO JAPANESE STEAK HOUSE $$

4163 Broadway St., 816/561-2501

HOURS: Mon.-Thurs. 5-9 P.M., Sat. 4:30-10:30 P.M., Sun. 4:30-8:30 P.M.

Don't be fooled by Gojo's unassuming exterior. Inside, a true dining spectacle awaits, as carefully trained chefs staff tableside grills to prepare feasts of freshly sautéed vegetables and meats. The chefs are personable and talkative, and some have a great sense of humor that adds to the theatrical feel of the evening. Bring your appetite, as each meal begins with several appetizers including grilled shrimp, rice doused with spinach and hollandaise sauce, and a small portion of grilled vegetables. Before dinner, test your reflexes as the chef flips grilled shrimp into the mouths of hungry patrons. A creamy bowl of sherbet concludes the experience, and it's not uncommon to need a box for leftover food. Because of Gojo's popularity, reservations are recommended. Arrive early and relax with one of the restaurant's signature cocktails.

STREET EATS

Although street vendors are located sparingly throughout the city, stumbling upon one of the food-laden carts guarantees a quick, cheap, and tasty meal. Street fare extends beyond deli sandwiches and chips. On a good day, you'll find barbecue, Mexican, even fried fish. In Westport, one of the city's most popular bar districts, several street vendors set up shop around 7 P.M. on weekends, ready to serve tipsy crowds clamoring for a late-night snack. Visit Westport several times, and **Jerusalem Cafe's** white truck, faithfully parked outside Harry's Bar and Tables at Westport Road and Pennsylvania Street, becomes a familiar sight. If you're in need of refueling while browsing the Crossroads Arts District's galleries during First Fridays, head to the curb outside Hammerpress Studios (110 Southwest Blvd.) for **Fresher than Fresh Snowcones.** Lindsay Laricks, the creative director at Barkley Evergreen & Partners Inc., whips up all-natural concoctions using homegrown ingredients, resulting in flavors like lemon prickly pear and espresso with Mexican cane sugar. Eating curbside may not be the height of glamour, but it's a meal your taste buds – and your wallet – won't forget.

KORMA SUTRA $$

4113 Pennsylvania Ave., 816/931-7775

HOURS: Tues.-Sun. 11 A.M.-2:30 P.M. and 5-9 P.M.

Whether you opt for the economical lunch buffet or a leisurely sit-down dinner, Korma Sutra specializes in "the sensuous cuisine of India." Creamy spices tinged with pungent spice mixtures accompany naan (Indian flatbread) that is simultaneously soft and crispy. Dinner is truly an experience, complete with appetizer and dessert samples and an elaborate hand-washing ritual. When in doubt, opt for the Korma Sutra Korma, a decadent cream sauce that envelops a bouquet of mixed vegetables spiked with nuts and raisins. And no Indian meal is complete without a fragrant mug of chai—Korma Sutra's sweet, milky blend is one of the best in the city.

NEW CAFE TANDOOR $

3623 Broadway St., 816/261-6531,

www.newcafetandoor.com

HOURS: Daily 11 A.M.-3 P.M. and 5-9:30 P.M.

An extensive menu offers the best of Indian and Pakistani cuisine. Traditional favorites such as tandoori chicken and *saag paneer* (spinach and cheese) meet less common delicacies that include goat *mughlai* and shrimp *dopiazza*. As in most of Kansas City's Indian restaurants, a lunch buffet is available for those who prefer to sample a variety of dishes at once. New Cafe Tandoor's dessert menu is more extensive than other restaurants, and includes *kheer* (rice pudding), mango custard, and an assortment of fresh cream pastries.

PO'S DUMPLING BAR $

1715 W. 39th St., 816/931-5991,

http://posdumplingbar.com

HOURS: Daily 11 A.M.-9:30 P.M.

Look for the large, white dumpling printed on a black awning to find Po's Dumpling Bar. If the restaurant isn't terribly crowded, opt for one of the premium window seats. Although the traditional Asian entrées are quite tasty, instead opt for an order of Po's savory, pillowy dumplings that just might be the ultimate in comfort food. Chef and co-owner Rita Hwang also prepares a range of flavorful soups, including Po's wonton soup and chicken velvet corn soup, that instantly make this a meal to remember.

BARBECUE

FIORELLA'S JACK STACK BARBECUE $$

4747 Wyandotte St., 816/531-7427,
www.jackstackbbq.com

HOURS: Mon.-Thurs. 11 A.M.-10 P.M.,
Fri.-Sat. 11 A.M.-10:30 P.M., Sun. 11 A.M.-9 P.M.

In the echelons of Kansas City barbecue, Jack Stack is a more sophisticated alternative, complete with large, plush booths and ornate fixtures that channel a touch of Old World glamour. The exemplary wait staff serves a diverse crowd in crisp white shirts, black pants, and long white aprons. Despite the somewhat formal feel of the dining room, dressy attire isn't required. The smell of smoke permeates the air, a constant byproduct of the restaurant's signature hickory-fired brick ovens that churn out immense piles of tender, flavorful meat. The side dishes nearly eclipse the barbecue, whether you pick the tangy, melt-in-your-mouth baked beans or the indulgent cheesy corn bake. You may find yourself smelling of smoke when you leave, but consider it a souvenir of Kansas City's barbecue heritage.

BREAKFAST AND BRUNCH

MAMA'S 39TH $

3906 Waddell Ave., 816/531-6422

HOURS: Mon.-Tues. 6:30 A.M.-10 P.M.,
Wed.-Thurs. 6:30 A.M.-10:30 P.M., Fri. 6:30 A.M.-3 P.M.,
Sat. 7 A.M.-10:30 P.M., Sun. 8 A.M.-3 P.M.

In 2008, Jan Imber and Ira Auerbach moved their Midtown diner, Bell Street Mama's, into the former home of Nichols Lunch. Homestyle breakfast and lunch favorites rule the menu, with more than 60 omelet combinations that run the gamut from traditional (ham and cheese) to the just plain bizarre (peanut butter, jelly, and banana). Loosen your belt and make room for one of Mama's sky-high slices of cake. Chocolate devotees should choose the German chocolate; more adventurous palates will enjoy the fruity sweetness of banana split cake.

BURGER JOINTS

WESTPORT FLEA MARKET $

817 Westport Rd., 816/931-1986,
www.westportfleamarket.com

HOURS: Daily 11 A.M.-1 A.M.

Those of the monstrous appetite, look no further than Westport Flea Market's burger joint's mammoth 10-ounce burger. Or opt for the Mini-Market, a 5.5-ounce version topped with your choice of cheese. After you've placed your burger order at the counter, grab a table and ogle the merchandise displays at the flea-market booths that line the restaurant's perimeter. Your freshly cooked burger will arrive nestled in a red plastic basket. You can personalize it at the Flea Market's stocked toppings bar, and wash down your meal with any of the 23 beers on tap. Daily specials range from steak night and Two for Tuesday to beer-battered catfish and a market taco trio.

WINSTEAD'S $

101 Emanuel Cleaver II Blvd., 816/753-2244

HOURS: Mon.-Thurs. 6:30 A.M.-midnight,
Fri.-Sat. 6:30 A.M.-1 A.M., Sun. 6:30 A.M.-midnight

In the world of Kansas City diners, Winstead's ranks near the top. A nostalgic '50s-style interior complete with a sizable lunch counter and waitresses that roam the restaurant in pink-skirted uniforms create a quintessential, family-friendly diner atmosphere, made even more appealing by Winstead's signature steak burgers. Enhance your meal with a 50/50 side of french fries and onion rings. And no Winstead's meal is complete without a handmade shake, available in classic flavors like strawberry, vanilla, and chocolate, as well as not-so-traditional flavors like peanut butter and banana. There is also a drive-through window if you just want take-out.

CONTEMPORARY AND NEW AMERICAN

BLANC BURGERS AND BOTTLES $$

419 Westport Rd., 816/931-6200,
www.blancburgers.com

HOURS: Mon. 11 A.M.-10 P.M., Tues.-Sat. 11 A.M.-11 P.M., Sun. 11 A.M.-9 P.M.

The French word for "white," Blanc's name is somewhat misleading. The restaurant's interior is a sleek, trendy homage to the pristine hue, but the colorful flavors of Blanc's gourmet burgers are a stark contrast to the monochromatic theme. Even the classic is kicked up with aged New York white cheddar, homemade pickles, and a sesame brioche bun. À la carte sides roll alongside burgers in miniature shopping carts, and indulgent alcohol-spiked adult milkshakes are also on offer. If you're still thirsty, sample one of the 120 beer, 55 wine, or 40 soda selections, all served in the restaurant's other namesake: glass bottles. Blanc's contemporary decor and menu attracts a largely 20- and 30-something crowd eager to indulge in truffle fries or sample brews from the restaurant's extensive beer menu.

BLUESTEM $$$

900 Westport Rd., 816/561-1101,
www.kansascitymenus.com/bluestem

HOURS: Tues.-Sat. 5:30 P.M.-9:30 P.M., Sun. 10:30 A.M.-2:30 P.M.

Since its opening in March 2004, Bluestem has been a constant critic and customer favorite. The restaurant's list of accolades is nearly as long as its menu and includes chef Colby Garrelts' being nominated Best Chef Midwest by the James Beard Foundation for three consecutive years. In the kitchen, Garrelts and his wife, Megan, prepare an expansive monthly menu influenced by seasonal flavors and local ingredients. For the best value, consider one of Bluestem's four tasting menus that offer 3 to 12 courses plus dessert. If you're traveling on a budget, stop in for Bluestem's happy hour complete with snacks, small plates, and an extensive wine list. Service is top-notch here, which, along with the inventive and flavorful dishes, easily justifies the higher price point. The modern yet intimate interior, complete with plush lounge seating, hardwood floors, pendant-light fixtures, and brick walls, is an ideal location for a romantic date.

CALIFORNOS $$

4124 Pennsylvania Ave., 816/531-7878,
www.californos.com

HOURS: Mon.-Thurs. 11 A.M.-3 P.M. and 5-10 P.M., Fri. 11 A.M.-3 P.M. and 5-11 P.M., Sat. noon-3 P.M. and 5-11 P.M.

This somewhat secluded bistro exudes a European vibe that pairs perfectly with an extensive wine list and menu that changes seasonally, with comfort food like the rosemary-encrusted lamb chop or the grilled steak sandwich with herbed cream cheese. The dim, cozy interior spreads into several rooms, and the bistro's unconventional layout has made it a favorite spot for weddings, business meetings, and other events. Head to the restaurant's back patio and deck, a sizable outdoor space that often hosts local and regional musicians. If you want to experience Westport but prefer an alternative to the bustling bar scene, Californos is a relaxed yet stylish alternative for lunch, dinner, and happy hour.

CLASSIC CUP SIDEWALK CAFE $$

301 W. 47th St., 816/753-1840, www.classiccup.com

HOURS: Mon.-Thurs. 7 A.M.-10:30 A.M., 11 A.M.-4 P.M., and 5-10 P.M., Fri. 7 A.M.-11 P.M., Sat. 8 A.M.-10:30 A.M., 11 A.M.-4 P.M., and 5-11 P.M., Sun. 9 A.M.-3 P.M. and 5-10 P.M.

Forget for a moment the light, contemporary fare served in a casually elegant setting. The fact is Classic Cup Sidewalk Cafe may have one of the best patios in the city, and if you can snag an outdoor table along 47th Street, you're perfectly poised for people-watching along the Plaza's main thoroughfare. While you soak in the view, order from the café's extensive menu that features delicious sandwiches and fresh salads. The Classic Cup Sidewalk Cafe serves breakfast, lunch, and dinner, making it an ideal stop throughout the day for business executives and shoppers eager for fuel before continuing the day's adventures. In a true testament to the café's quality, the Classic Cup Sidewalk Cafe has enjoyed a decade of notoriety as the recipient of the Plaza Art Fair's Best Food Award.

EDEN ALLEY $

707 W. 47th St., 816/561-5415, www.edenalley.com

HOURS: Mon.-Tues. 11 A.M.-2:30 P.M., Wed.-Sat. 11 A.M.-9 P.M.

Built below the Unity Temple, Eden Alley is truly a retreat for Plaza visitors eager for vegetarian or vegan specialties. Meat eaters, don't despair—the diverse menu offers something for everyone, including vegetarian takes on classic meals like the spinach and mushroom loaf, an all-vegetable version of meatloaf. The expansive interior is dotted with cozy tables, and vibrant local artwork injects splashes of color on the restaurant's mostly white walls. After you pay at the register, cross the room to the adjoining Unity Temple gift shop, and don't leave without one of Eden Alley's freshly baked cookies—they're simultaneously sinful and healthy.

MCCOY'S PUBLIC HOUSE AND BREW $$

4057 Pennsylvania Ave., 816/960-0866, www.mccoyspublichouse.com

HOURS: Mon.-Sat. 11 A.M.-3 A.M., Sun. 11 A.M.-midnight

Burgers, sandwiches, brick-oven pizzas, and good old-fashioned comfort food take center

© KATY RYAN

Stop at the Classic Cup Sidewalk Cafe to fuel up while shopping on the Country Club Plaza.

stage at one of Westport's signature restaurants, which later turns into a favorite nightspot. Ditch the diet and indulge in a bowl of Mom's macaroni and cheese, a rich concoction of four cheeses and noodles topped with garlicky breadcrumbs. For those who prefer to drink their meals, McCoy's offers an astounding array of ales, lagers, wines, and scotch. Opt for the six-pack sampler and taste an assortment of hand-crafted beers currently on tap. Once you've found a favorite, take home a 30-ounce flip-top bottle filled with beer or freshly brewed root beer. McCoy's vibe is laidback yet exuberant and is a favorite meeting spot for happy-hour celebrants and those eager to start the evening with a house-made brew. Service is sometimes on the slow side, but the wait staff is personable and accommodating. One of McCoy's best traits is its diverse clientele, which is comprised of older couples, young artists, and everyone in between.

THE MIXX $$

4855 Main St., 816/756-2300, www.mixxingitup.com

HOURS: Mon.-Fri. 7 A.M.-10 P.M., Sat.-Sun. 11 A.M.-10 P.M.

When you walk into The Mixx, grab a menu from one of the wall holders and start your search for the perfect meal. Although the soups and sandwiches are tasty, your best bet is to order the restaurant's signature salad and namesake, which allows you to pick your lettuce, dressing, up to five mix-ins, and a topping of meat or tofu. Chefs whip your salad into a tossed frenzy before your eyes, then you proceed to the counter to pay. The restaurant's bustling interior is complete with sleek chairs and banquette seating beneath large light fixtures that appear to be handspun with colorful string. The Mixx is often crowded during the lunch hour, but because you receive your food at the counter with a minimal wait, diners move in and out at a relatively consistent pace. It's a popular spot for those who work in the numerous offices nearby, but it also attracts a younger crowd drawn to the restaurant's contemporary decor.

POTPIE $$

904 Westport Rd., 816/561-2702, www.kcpotpie.com

HOURS: Tues.-Thurs. 11 A.M.-10 P.M., Fri. 11 A.M.-11 P.M., Sat. 5-11 P.M.

Long celebrated as a quintessential comfort food, potpie is the star at this intimate restaurant. Although the menu changes often, chicken and beef and mushroom potpie are restaurant staples, each a hearty (and steaming-hot) helping of tender meat and succulent gravy nestled in a buttery homemade crust. Continue your glorious carb fest with chocolate chip bread pudding or berry cobbler topped with a healthy dollop of homemade ice cream. Don't be fooled by Potpie's somewhat non-descript exterior. The small, cozy dining room is the perfect atmosphere in which to enjoy hearty food. The large archway allows you to glimpse the open kitchen, a favorite feature of many diners.

ROOM 39 $$

1719 W. 39th St., 816/753-3939, www.rm39.com

HOURS: Mon.-Sat. 7 A.M.-3 P.M. and 5:30-10 P.M.

In November 2004, Andrew Sloan and Ted Habiger opened Room 39, a bistro-like eatery that serves breakfast, lunch, and dinner. Start the day with a fresh-squeezed mimosa and a smoked salmon scramble, or come at lunch for gently seared scallops or an herb-studded chicken salad sandwich. If you head to Room 39 for dinner, choose the restaurant's $39 tasting menu, an impeccable value that imparts regional flavors through local ingredients. Room 39 staff members are known for their expert knowledge of the menu, so expect great service when you go. Limited seating means there is a wait during busy hours, but the well-prepared food is worth it.

STARKER'S RESTAURANT $$$

201 W. 47th St., 816/753-3565,
www.starkersrestaurant.com

HOURS: Mon.-Fri. 11:30 A.M.-2 P.M. and 5:30-10 P.M., Sat. 5:30-10 P.M.

At first glance, Starker's Restaurant isn't visible amid the bustling streetscape of the Plaza. Look again, however, and you'll spy a discreet sign that marks the entrance. Located above Restoration Hardware, Starker's is considered one of the city's best-kept secrets. The second-floor location makes for stunning views of the surrounding Plaza skyline; once you've finished ogling the scenery, turn your attention to a carefully crafted menu that features classics like almond-crusted rainbow trout, roast Campo Lindo chicken, and grilled rack of lamb. Because Starker's cozy interior accommodates only 40 diners, reservations are suggested for both lunch and dinner.

TOMFOOLERIES $$

612 W. 47th St., 816/753-0555, www.tomfooleries.com

HOURS: Mon.-Wed. 11 A.M.-2 A.M., Thurs.-Sat. 11 A.M.-3 A.M., Sun. 9:30 A.M.-2 A.M.

Acknowledging the importance of first impressions, Tomfooleries' door handles—a giant whisk and serving spoon—hint at the merriment inside. The tongue-in-cheek restaurant and bar serves up burgers, sandwiches, pastas, pizzas, and salads, both of the usual—and not-so-usual—variety, such as a bacon cheeseburger topped with a scoop of peanut butter. Save room for gooey s'mores served atop a circular piece of wood. Stay for late-night live music, and come back on Sunday morning for the mother of all brunch buffets: The feast is never-ending with cold pizza, eggs, biscuits, pasta, potatoes, and a dessert-laden table, plus a Bloody Mary bar. Combine the restaurant's dim lighting and high booths and you've got a surprisingly intimate atmosphere that belies the restaurant's upbeat, sometimes raucous atmosphere, especially during the late-night hours. A sizable happy-hour crowd comes from nearby office buildings, and at night, 20-something patrons congregate at the bar for drinks and live music.

DESSERT

CUPCAKE À LA MODE $

1209 W. 47th St., 816/960-1900,
www.cupcakealamode.com

HOURS: Tues.-Fri. 9 A.M.-6 P.M., Sat. 10 A.M.-6 P.M.

Near the crest of a steep hill just west of the Plaza, Cupcake à la Mode awaits in a small shop that exudes charm—not to mention the intoxicating aroma of freshly baked cupcakes. Run by executive pastry chef Lisa Clark and her husband, Daniel, Cupcake à la Mode boasts 20 mouthwatering varieties of cupcakes. Chocoholics can't go wrong with the chocolate obsession, but the vanilla cupcakes are equally tempting with flavors such as Let It Snow (white chocolate cream cheese icing, shredded coconut, and a maraschino cherry). Wash down your cupcake with a custom coffee drink or bottled Izze soda.

ITALIAN

ACCURSO'S ITALIAN FOOD & DRINK $$

4980 Main St., 816/753-0810, www.accursos.com

HOURS: Mon. 10 A.M.-5 P.M., Tues.-Thurs. 10 A.M.-10 P.M., Fri. 10 A.M.-11 P.M., Sat. 5-11 P.M.

As long as the weather cooperates, make a beeline straight for Accurso's scenic patio that offers prime views of Brookside's Main Street. Once you're settled, order a glass of wine and peruse a menu filled with Italian classics like bruschetta, lasagna, eggplant parmesan, and chicken spadini. If you end up inside, don't fret—an expansive interior with glass-paneled walls and polished concrete floors is a modern contrast to the traditional Italian entrée you'll soon be enjoying.

MIDDLE EASTERN

JERUSALEM CAFE $

431 Westport Rd., 816/756-2770

HOURS: Mon.-Sat. 11 A.M.-10 P.M., Sun. 11 A.M.-8 P.M.

Stuffed gyros dripping with tangy tzatziki sauce, subtly seasoned hummus, and fragrant rice are a sampling of the Middle Eastern and Mediterranean specialties available at Jerusalem Cafe. Both vegetarian and meat entrées are plentiful, giving diners a wide selection from which to choose. And if your meal isn't already accompanied by a side salad, make sure to add one to your order. The heartily seasoned dressing kick-starts the taste buds in preparation for the rest of the meal. A young, artsy crowd tends to congregate at Jerusalem Cafe, where the relaxed atmosphere is appropriate for leisurely meals. The efficient service also makes this an ideal stop for diners on a time crunch. After your meal, head upstairs to the on-site hookah bar to experience smoking flavored tobaccos through a Turkish tobacco pipe.

PIZZA

D'BRONX $

3904 Bell St., 816/531-0550, www.dbronxkc.com

HOURS: Mon.-Thurs. 10:30 A.M.-9 P.M., Fri.-Sat. 10:30 A.M.-11 P.M., Sun. noon-8 P.M.

For an authentic taste of New York in the heart of the Midwest, look no further than d'Bronx. Although the menu boasts an array of sandwiches, hot subs, and salads, the main draw is the pizza, available by the giant slice or whole pie. If the weather cooperates, grab a slice and a soda to go and head outside for prime people-watching at one of the restaurant's streetside picnic tables, an airy alternative to the restaurant's bustling interior.

JOE'S PIZZA BUY THE SLICE $

4058 Pennsylvania Ave., 816/931-2777, www.kellyswestportinn.com

HOURS: Mon.-Sat. 11 A.M.-3 A.M., Sun. noon-3 A.M.

Whether you fuel up before a night out or are in need of a late-night snack, Joe's Pizza Buy the Slice offers several varieties of pizza sold, well, by the slice! Visit during peak hours and you may find the restaurant's cramped quarters a little too close for comfort. Instead, grab your slice and a soda and head to the sidewalk. The long-established watering hole, Kelly's Westport Inn, is adjacent to the restaurant if you're interested in having a cheap drink with your slice.

STEAK HOUSES

J. J.'S RESTAURANT $$

910 W. 48th St., 816/561-7136, www.jjs-restaurant.com

HOURS: Mon.-Fri. 11 A.M.-4 P.M. and 5-10 P.M., Sat.-Sun. 5 P.M.-10 P.M.

For more than two decades restaurateur Jimmy Frantze has held court at J. J.'s, one of the city's top restaurants. Chef Linda Duerr uses local, organically grown ingredients to produce lunch and dinner menus bursting with flavor and freshness. For lunch sample wild boar ragu, an exotic, meaty dish enhanced with a burgundy wine sauce flavored with pancetta and mirepoix. Dinner is just as delightful, and to make the meal truly memorable, J. J.'s offers one of the city's most extensive wine lists and a cellar filled with more than 40,000 bottles. J.J.'s off-

Plaza location puts it somewhat off the beaten path, a plus if you enjoy dining with mostly locals for a true Kansas City experience.

PLAZA III STEAKHOUSE $$$

4749 Pennsylvania Ave., 816/753-0000, www.plazaiiisteakhouse.com

HOURS: Mon.-Sat. 11:30 A.M.-2:30 P.M. and 5-10 P.M., Sun. 5-10 P.M.

Affectionately called Cowtown because of its prominent place in the cattle industry, Kansas City takes its beef seriously. Plaza III has earned a reputation as one of the city's top steak houses thanks to expertly prepared, tender cuts of prime USDA beef aged in a specially designed cooler to maximize flavor. Traditional sides such as creamed spinach and baked potatoes complement the savory flavor of the steak. Non-beef eaters are treated to equally tasty choices such as lobster or delicately grilled chicken. If you crave a soundtrack with your meal, opt to eat downstairs and treat your ears to a buffet of sensuous jazz. Multiple seating areas are available here, including the main dining room that is sumptuously decorated in dark wood tones and the spacious wine cellar dining area. Servers are professional, efficient, and happy to make recommendations, especially if you prefer something other than steak. Dressy attire is encouraged and valet parking is available outside the restaurant.

Brookside and Waldo

Map 4

BAR AND GRILL

GOVERNOR STUMPY'S GRILL HOUSE $

321 E. Gregory Blvd., 816/444-2252, www.governorstumpys.com

HOURS: Mon.-Tues. 11 A.M.-9:30 P.M., Wed.-Sat. 11 A.M.-10 P.M.

Put on the spot during a local concert, Kansas City native Edward E. Stine declared himself "Governor Stumpy," ex-governor of Tennessee. The name stuck, and in the lighthearted spirit of the Waldo "dignitary," Stine's family named the restaurant Governor Stumpy's. Owned by Kevin and Tanya Ryan who are often on-site, Governor Stumpy's is a casual, family-friendly bar and grill that specializes in all things super-sized from cheeseburgers to steaks. Try the 42-ounce pitcher of beer or The Reubenator, a monstrous 3.5-pound Reuben sandwich heaped with a pound of corned beef and a half-pound of sauerkraut on six slices of rye bread.

BREWPUBS

75TH STREET BREWERY $$

520 W. 75th St., 816/523-4677, www.75thstreet.com

HOURS: Mon.-Thurs. 11 A.M.-1 A.M., Fri.-Sat. 11 A.M.-1:30 A.M., Sun. 11 A.M.-midnight

Hand-crafted ales and lagers take center stage at 75th Street Brewery, commonly referred to simply as 75th Street. Part of the K. C. Hopps family of restaurants and breweries that also includes O'Dowd's Little Dublin and others, 75th Street serves up classic pub fare including fish-and-chips, pizza, and sandwiches. And if you decide to visit Kansas City often, or even relocate, join 75th Street's esteemed Mug Club that includes discounted 22-ounce beers, a free growler, and invitations to special events and parties throughout the year. During the day, 75th Street Brewery is busy yet low-key, an ideal lunch spot for executives and students alike. At night the bar and restaurant morph into a louder, more boisterous venue.

CAFÉS

CLASSIC COOKIE & CAFE $

409 W. Gregory Blvd., 816/444-1933,
www.theclassiccookie.com

HOURS: Mon.-Sat. 7 A.M.-3 P.M., Sun. 8 A.M.-1:30 P.M.

Whether for breakfast, lunch, or to satisfy a sweet-tooth craving, the Classic Cookie & Cafe delivers tasty breakfast and lunch entrées with featured monthly specials. During the summer months, beat the heat with the café's signature egg salad sandwich, as well as an array of cold soups. And during the frigid winter months, the Classic Cookie specializes in hearty, flavorful soups like vegetable beef barley and artichoke mushroom to warm the soul. Before you leave, stock up on the café's namesake—freshly baked cookies in flavors ranging from classic chocolate chip to chewy oatmeal scotchies and snickerdoodles.

THE ROASTERIE CAFE $

6223 Brookside Blvd., 816/333-9700,
www.theroasterie.com

HOURS: Mon.-Thurs. 6 A.M.-10 P.M., Fri. 6 A.M.-11 P.M., Sat. 7 A.M.-11 P.M., Sun. 7 A.M.-10 P.M.

You won't find much in the way of substantial fare at The Roasterie Cafe, unless your idea of the perfect meal is a freshly brewed espresso drink served alongside a chewy, icing-filled macaroon. Kansas City's hometown coffee company specializes in fresh, flavorful coffees culled from around the world. Espresso concoctions change seasonally and include sumptuous ingredients like chocolate, marshmallow, and peppermint to create richly distinctive drinks. The Roasterie Cafe also offers boxes from local chocolatier Christopher Elbow. Students from the nearby University of Missouri–Kansas City and young professionals stake out tables on which to perch their drinks, snacks, laptops, and reading material. Bring your computer if you're in need of Wi-Fi, or grab one of several local publications scattered throughout the café and enjoy a true taste of the city.

DESSERT

FOO'S FABULOUS FROZEN CUSTARD $

6235 Brookside Plaza, 816/523-2520,
www.foosfabulousfrozencustard.com

HOURS: Sun.-Mon. 1-9 P.M., Tues.-Thurs. 11:30 A.M.-9 P.M., Fri.-Sat. 11:30 A.M.-10 P.M.

Everything you need to know about Foo's can be found in the name: It is, undoubtedly, some fabulous frozen custard. Walk in and your nose is immediately assaulted with yummy smells like candy, sugar, and the freshly made custard that oozes out of the machine directly behind the prep counter. Take some time to process Foo's extensive menu, a colorful mass of descriptions scrawled on an oversized chalkboard. Indulge your adventurous side with one of Foo's signature creations like the Jay-Z inspired "Can I Get A," vanilla custard blended with peanut butter and Oreo cookies. Seating is extremely limited within the tiny shop, so grab your dessert and head to a bench outside, or enjoy it while strolling the streets of the surrounding Brookside neighborhood.

MCLAIN'S BAKERY $

7422 Wornall Rd., 816/333-6562,
www.mclainsbakery.com

HOURS: Tues.-Fri. 7 A.M.-2 P.M., Sat.-Sun. 7 A.M.-noon

For more than six decades, the skilled bakers at McLain's have perfected the art of cookies, pastries, cakes, and other indulgent baked goods. Start the day with sumptuous breakfast rolls, a cream-filled éclair, or miniature croissants. The cookie menu is extensive and includes favorites like chocolate chip, sugar, and oatmeal raisin, as well as Mexican wedding cookies, macaroons, and brownies. The chocolate cup cookies, supposedly

THE ROASTERIE – THE CITY'S OTHER FAVORITE BREW

It was a day he'll remember forever: November 22, 1978, when The Roasterie founder Danny O'Neill picked his first coffee bean while studying in Costa Rica. He channeled his passion for the fragrant brew into a coffee business born in his basement, in what O'Neill calls "one of Kansas City's great neighborhoods: Brookside."

Since then, The Roasterie has grown into a local coffee favorite with both a coffee plant (1204 W. 27th St., 816/931-4000) and a Brookside café (6223 Brookside Blvd., 816/333-9700) that focus on small specialty farmers and their global communities. O'Neill emphasizes quality, freshness, and education, and has perfected a signature air-roasting process that preserves the bean's original flavor while bringing out previously undetected nuances that add depth and life to each cup of coffee.

Head to The Roasterie (coffee plant) at 9 A.M. Saturdays for a free tour of the coffee-making process, as well as other behind-the-scenes glimpses of O'Neill's addictive enterprise.

© KATY RYAN

The Roasterie Cafe's signature coffee concoctions taste even better when accompanied by a sweet treat.

RESTAURANTS

created from a recipe that originated in a Pennsylvania bakery, are a local favorite. Snap a picture of McLain's eye-catching window display to preserve the mouthwatering memory, and take your treats to go or grab one of the few tables within the bakery's sparsely decorated interior.

FRENCH

AIXOIS $$

2159 E. 55th St., 816/333-3305, www.aixois.com

HOURS: Coffee bar Mon.-Fri. 7 A.M.-10 P.M., Sat. 7:30 A.M.-10 P.M., Sun. 8 A.M.-4 P.M.; bistro Mon.-Sat. 11:30 A.M.-2 P.M. and 5:30-10 P.M.

After training in Marseille and working at

restaurants in France and the United States, chef Emmanuel Langlade moved to Kansas City and opened Aixois, a tribute to chef Langlade's home, Aix-en-Provence, in 2001 with his wife, Megan. Part coffee bar, part bistro, Aixois offers the best in traditional French fare, including crepes, quiche, and escargots. For the full experience on a tighter time schedule, grab a table in the coffee bar and sip a steaming mug of café au lait accompanied by a buttery croissant or *pain au chocolat.* On Monday evenings, Aixois offers family-style dinners with a choice of crepes, chicken, fish, or steak served with your choice of sides. Servers are attentive, yet they allow guests to enjoy the sort of relaxed, leisurely dining experience that's a routine part of French life.

AVENUES BISTRO $$

338 W. 63rd St., 816/333-5700,
www.avenuesbistro.com
HOURS: Mon.-Thurs. 11 A.M.-9 P.M.,
Fri.-Sat. 11 A.M.-10 P.M., Sun. 9 A.M.-8 P.M.

It would be a disservice to singularly classify Avenues Bistro's cuisine as French, although France's influence appears throughout the menu from the daily quiche special to the sumptuous *gateau au chocolat.* With a menu described more generally as European, Avenues Bistro is a comfy culinary escape inspired by traditional Spanish tapas, Italian prosciutto, and an extensive wine list that celebrates the best of all European flavors. Avenues Bistro serves brunch, lunch, and dinner, each with extensive menus sure to please even the most discerning of palates. For a sure bet, order from the Avenues Favorites, a compilation of the bistro's five top-sellers. Head to Avenues Bistro during the midday hours, and you'll find yourself dining with a mix of business people and "ladies who lunch." In the evening, a hungry dinner crowd is comprised mostly of couples and small groups.

ITALIAN

BELLA NAPOLI $$

6229 Brookside Blvd., 816/444-5041,
www.kcbellanapoli.com
HOURS: Mon. 10 A.M.-3 P.M., Tues.-Fri. 10 A.M.-6 P.M.,
Sat. 9 A.M.-5 P.M., Sun. 11 A.M.-3 P.M.

In 2001, Jake Imperiale opened the doors to Bella Napoli to provide authentic Italian groceries and baked goods to Kansas City. Browse a savory assortment of premium meats like prosciutto *di parma,* imported *bresaola,* pepperoni, and pancetta. A large cheese selection includes *parmigiano reggiano,* mozzarella, pecorino *pepato, taleggio,* and mascarpone. Bella Napoli also stocks several barrels of fresh olives and a sumptuous dessert counter that includes Italian classics like cream-stuffed cannoli.

CARMEN'S CAFE $$

6307 Brookside Plaza, 816/333-4048,
www.carmenscafekc.com
HOURS: Mon.-Thurs. 11 A.M.-10 P.M., Fri. 11 A.M.-11 P.M., Sat. 4-11 P.M., Sun. noon-9 P.M.

If you're in search of a romantic getaway, escape to the dim interior of Carmen's Cafe for an intimate meal, a perfect way to spend date night. Share a bottle of wine and some crusty bread before delving into Carmen's array of Italian specialties. You may want to pack a few pieces of gum—Carmen's chefs are heavy-handed with the garlic, resulting in a mellow yet powerful flavor that gives a signature tang to the entrées. Try the indulgent chicken spiedini, doused with a healthy portion of garlic butter, or any of the pasta dishes accompanied by a cream sauce.

LA CUCINA DI MAMMA $$

6229 Brookside Blvd., 816/444-5041,
www.kcbellanapoli.com
HOURS: Mon.-Thurs. 11 A.M.-8 P.M., Fri.-Sat. 11 A.M.-9 P.M.

It's only natural that a sumptuously stocked

Italian grocery like Bella Napoli includes an on-site Italian restaurant that offers filling fare in a casual, no-fuss atmosphere. Plop down your grocery bags and enjoy an array of antipasti, or opt for one of La Cucina di Mamma's pasta dishes like tagliatella bolognese or penne siciliana. Several *contorni,* or side dishes, are a great option as a quick snack if you're in search of a lighter meal. Try the sautéed spinach with butter and Parmesan or grilled peppers with olives and capers. Indoor seating is limited, but additional seating is available outside, weather permitting.

PIZZA

BLUE GROTTO $$

6324 Brookside Plaza, 816/361-3473,
www.bluegrottobrookside.com

HOURS: Mon.-Sat. 11 A.M.-10:30 P.M., Sun. 4-10 P.M.

Blue Grotto's sleek surroundings are a great place in which to unwind while you wait for your freshly baked artisan pizza to arrive, either on the main floor or the second-level, loft-like space. Caputo flour and San Marzano tomatoes form the base for Blue Grotto's pizzas, available in traditional combinations like margherita or more adventurous flavors like Thai chicken. A generous wine list and mouthwatering first plates are an ideal accompaniment to your pizza.

WALDO PIZZA $$

7433 Broadway St., 816/363-5242,
www.waldopizza.net

HOURS: Sun.-Thurs. 11 A.M.-10 P.M., Fri.-Sat. 11 A.M.-11 P.M.

Whether you come for the lunch pizza buffet (11 A.M.–2 P.M.) or head to Waldo Pizza for dinner, be sure to make time for one of Kansas City's favorite pizzerias. Try the honey wheat crust, a chewy, barely sweet base for your preferred pizza toppings. Waldo Pizza also serves gluten-free and vegan pizza. And here's a tip: Write your own coupon, within reason, and present it when you order. You'll get a personalized discount and support one of the best marketing campaigns in the city.

Northland

Map 5

ARGENTINEAN

PIROPOS $$$

4141 N. Mulberry Dr., 816/741-3600, www.piroposkc.com

HOURS: Mon.-Thurs. 5-9 P.M., Fri.-Sat. 5-10 P.M., Sun. 4-8 P.M.

Once you sample Piropos' Argentinean cuisine, you'll realize it's similar to the flavors inspired by the American Midwest. Grilled meats like peppercorn-encrusted filet in a brandy cream sauce make for a truly indulgent meal, or opt for a filling entrée-sized salad like the *ensalada de calamares,* topped with a skewer of calamari. Don't eat so much that you overlook the dessert menu. It's a sugary temptress that beckons with the restaurant's signature banana cake, among others. Perched on the second level of Kansas City's Briarcliff shopping area, Piropos' formal dining room features high ceilings, large windows, and colorful Argentinean sculptures. Reservations are recommended, as is dressy attire.

BRAZILIAN

EM CHAMAS $$$

6101 NW 63rd Terr., 816/505-7100, www.kansascitymenus.com/emchamas

HOURS: Mon.-Sat. 5-9 P.M.

Dinner at Em Chamas makes for a pricey night out, but once you've tasted the Brazilian restaurant's signature *churrasco* meats, you'll realize it was well worth the splurge. Roaming waiters circle the restaurant armed with skewers of freshly grilled meats like ham accompanied by slices of grilled pineapple or *alcatra,* tender top sirloin cuts. Switch your dual-sided dining token to indicate if you'd like more to eat, or you've had enough. The extensive *rodizio* menu is accompanied by a salad and hot hors d'oeuvres bar—just be careful not to fill up before you've sampled the 14 *rodizio* meats.

BREAKFAST AND BRUNCH

C CORNER CAFE $

4541 NW Gateway Ave., Riverside, 816/741-2570, www.thecornercafe.com

HOURS: Daily 5 A.M.-10 P.M.

Corner Cafe's cheerful red exterior and inviting dining rooms are welcome sights for hungry travelers in search of one of the city's best breakfasts. Former president George W. Bush may have only opted for one of the café's fluffy signature biscuits, but I recommend going all out with an omelet, hash browns, and one of the café's oversized cinnamon rolls or pecan-studded sticky buns, topped, as Corner Cafe puts it, "with extra sticky!"

LATTÉLAND $

4115 N. Mulberry Dr., 816/746-3808, www.lattelandkc.com

HOURS: Mon.-Wed. 6:30 A.M.-6 P.M., Thurs. 6:30 A.M.-8 P.M., Fri. 6:30 A.M.-6 P.M., Sat. 7 A.M.-6 P.M., Sun. 7 A.M.-5 P.M.

If you prefer your breakfast to be of the coffee and muffin variety, Lattéland is a great place to start the day. Freshly brewed coffee and espresso provide a much-needed pick-me-up, and you'll love Lattéland's seasonal concoctions. Try the heavenly winter dream tea latte during the holidays, or the iced caramella in the summer. Homemade muffins, cookies, biscotti, and other pastries just beg to be picked from a glass case—take my word for it and opt for the wedding cake cookie or low-fat cranberry nut muffin. Lattéland also has two locations on the Country Club Plaza.

© KATY RYAN

For coffee, pastries, juice, and friendly service, visit one of several Lattéland locations throughout Kansas City.

LE MONDE BAKERY $

308 Armour Rd., North Kansas City, 816/474-0055

HOURS: Mon.-Fri. 6 A.M.-2 P.M., Sat. 6 A.M.-noon

Sample a taste of France just minutes north of downtown Kansas City at Le Monde Bakery, a small shop that specializes in indulgent baked goods like *pain au chocolat* and baguettes that are simultaneously crusty and chewy. Stop in for lunch, when Le Monde offers soups like the creamy potage, a curried chicken soup, and sandwiches piled high on fresh croissants. Seating within Le Monde is limited, but you can get your food to go and enjoy a picnic in downtown North Kansas City or drive the few blocks to nearby Macken Park.

Greater Kansas City

Overview Map

RESTAURANTS

CONTEMPORARY AND NEW AMERICAN

CAFÉ TEMPO $$

12345 College Blvd., Overland Park, 913/469-8500, www.jccc.edu/cafetempo

HOURS: Tues.-Fri. 7 A.M.-3 P.M., Sat. 10 A.M.-3 P.M.

After you're done exploring the Nerman Museum of Contemporary Art, head to Café Tempo for a relaxed, upscale meal in spacious, airy surroundings. Choose from an expansive menu that includes salads, soups, paninis, sandwiches, and quiche, or try the café's daily fish special. Café Tempo also serves pastries, espresso drinks, and fresh fruit if you'd prefer to eat quickly and get back to the Nerman's extensive collection. Step up to the counter to place your order, then grab a seat at a table.

JUSTUS DRUGSTORE, A RESTAURANT $$$

106 Main St., Smithville, 816/532-2300, www.drugstorerestaurant.com

HOURS: Tues.-Thurs. 5:30-10 P.M., Fri.-Sat. 5:30-11 P.M., Sun. 5:30-9 P.M.

Since Justus Drugstore opened its doors, critical acclaim has poured in from area foodies, critics, and those simply in search of a good meal. Named after chef Jonathan Justus's family's drugstore that previously occupied the building, the restaurant is single-handedly transforming Kansas City's culinary reputation, appearing in publications such as *Food and Wine* and *Travel + Leisure* magazines. The modern interior is a pleasing contrast to the restaurant's small-town surroundings and includes a small yet spacious dining area and a bar outfitted with swivel stools, a homage to the building's drugstore past. Be prepared to drive—Smithville is about 35 minutes from downtown Kansas City—but it's well worth the trek to launch a culinary adventure. The Drugstore's menu is peppered with local ingredients coaxed out of their comfort zone by inventive combinations. The focus is on the food, so a meal here isn't a race; instead, it's a leisurely event meant to inspire not just your taste buds, but your soul—the perfect prescription for whatever ails you.

NIGHTLIFE

Although Kansas City has long been celebrated for its vibrant jazz culture, the city's nightlife has evolved to offer an eclectic mixture of bars, clubs, and live-music venues featuring all kinds of music. Kansas City's thriving local music scene means that you can find performances on most nights of the week, and the city now has several upscale clubs and lounges where long lines are common and pricey bottle service is the way to drink. Yet laid-back bars still welcome regulars and visitors alike, offering nightly drink specials, trivia contests, and an easygoing atmosphere conducive to conversation, whether you're making new friends or connecting with old ones.

Just as the city's culinary empire is expanding to offer sophisticated flavors and cooking techniques, the city's nightlife scene has embraced speakeasy-type establishments that channel the art of mixology, where cocktails are meant to be sipped, savored, and enjoyed rather than chugged or tossed back in a shot glass. Fresh herbs, fruit, and even locally produced milk have found their way behind the bar and are popping up in unexpected combinations that leave you craving more.

Whether you're seeking the modern surroundings of a wine bar or prefer to experience Kansas City's gay and lesbian clubs, the city has a nightlife venue that will entice you

COURTESY OF THE KANSAS CITY CONVENTION AND VISITORS ASSOCIATION

HIGHLIGHTS

LOOK FOR [icon] TO FIND RECOMMENDED NIGHTLIFE.

Most Inventive Cocktails: Start your evening at **The Drop** with an edible cocktail – think of it as the Jell-O shot's older, more sophisticated cousin (page 71).

Best Historic Bar: Drink at **Kelly's Westport Inn,** and you're drinking in the oldest building in Kansas City. Don't forget to raise a toast to Kansas City history (page 74).

Best Irish Bar: Irish culture lives at **O'Dowd's Little Dublin,** where Guinness is on tap and several varieties of whiskey line the bar (page 74).

Best Lounge: Pulsing music and a sleek interior have made the **Mint Ultra Lounge** a favorite drinking-and-dancing destination in Union Hill's Martini Corner District (page 78).

Best-Dressed Crowd: Unassuming bistro by day and gay club by night, **Bistro 303** serves up delicious cocktails and some of Kansas City's most beautiful people (page 79).

Best Bar in a Museum: While you enjoy your cocktails, take a look at the in-table memorabilia displays and impressive indoor mural dedicated to local jazz culture at **The Blue Room,** located inside the American Jazz Museum (page 81).

Best Live-Music Venue: Built specifically for live-music performances, **Crosstown Station** improves on the typical small-venue concert experience (page 81).

Best Live Jazz: Relax with Kansas City's official music during any of **Jardine's** mesmerizing jazz performances (page 82).

Most Iconic Nightlife Venue: If you can stay up late on Saturday or Sunday, you'll be rewarded with impromptu – and sometimes infamous – jazz jam sessions at the **Mutual Musicians Foundation** (page 83).

Best Cocktails: Celebrated local mixologist Ryan Maybee and his team of experts serve up the unexpected at **Manifesto,** a tiny, hard-to-find bar that's worth the effort (page 84).

Best Wine List: If you can't decide on a selection from the extensive wine list at **JP Wine Bar & Coffee House,** opt instead for a regional sampler featuring some of the world's premier wines (page 85).

© KATY RYAN

Kelly's Westport Inn is housed within Kansas City's oldest building.

to stay out until the wee hours as you find your own rhythm on the city streets.

Casual dress is accepted at most establishments, although the majority of the city's nightclubs enforce various dress codes, typically of the "dress to impress" variety.

Bars

THE BROOKSIDER BAR & GRILL

6330 Brookside Plaza, 816/363-4070, www.brooksiderbarandgrill.com

HOURS: Daily 11 A.M.-3 A.M.

COST: $5 cover

Map 4

The Brooksider has a great menu complete with pizza, burgers, and soft pretzels made in-house, but it's the spacious two-level layout with a sizable outdoor patio and multiple bars that has made it one of the most popular watering holes in the Brookside area. Frequented by the area's college students, The Brooksider often hosts local rock bands that keep the place hopping. The environment isn't conducive to conversation. If you seek a quieter spot to enjoy your drink, head outside to a patio table. The Brooksider is also a favorite destination for televised sporting events, including UFC fights.

BUZZARD BEACH

4110 Pennsylvania Ave., 816/753-4455, www.buzzardbeachkc.com

HOURS: Mon.-Thurs. 3 P.M.-3 A.M., Fri.-Sat. 2 P.M.-3 A.M., Sun. 8 P.M.-3 A.M.

COST: No cover

Map 3

Buzzard Beach has perfected the art of the dive bar. Creaky wooden booths and dim lighting help create a low-key ambience at a bar where the focus is on drinks, conversation, and good times. You won't find any sand at this beach, but you will find a wraparound deck that's a favorite after-work gathering spot for the happy-hour crowd. At night, you'll find few places that offer better people-watching than the Buzzard's deck. Come as you are, and make sure you have a pen to leave your personal graffiti on one of the bar's heavily inked bathroom stalls.

DARK HORSE TAVERN

4112 Pennsylvania Ave., 816/931-3663, www.thedarkhorsetavern.com

HOURS: Daily 3 P.M.-3 A.M.

COST: Varies

Map 3

Dark Horse Tavern is a no-fuss bar, with exposed brick walls, slightly worse-for-wear seating, and a jukebox—and that's the way the locals like it. You could go on Wednesday nights for live acoustic music, or Thursdays for a DJ. But the best time to visit Dark Horse is Friday or Saturday night for the bar's infamous power hour, when a $10 cover gets you bottomless beer or well drinks for two glorious alcohol-filled hours. If late-night debauchery is more your style, Dark Horse offers night-owl specials Sunday through Thursday. Luckily, you'll have no problem finding a cab in Westport, and you'll definitely need one—especially post–power hour.

THE DROP

409 E. 31st St., 816/756-3767, www.thedropbar.com

HOURS: Mon.-Fri. 11 A.M.-1 A.M., Sat.-Sun. 5 P.M.-2 A.M.

COST: No cover

Map 2

More than a sophisticated restaurant and lounge, The Drop is a study in the art of the cocktail.

A MODERN SODOM

Today Kansas City hosts its fair share of bars and clubs, a number that quickly pales in comparison to the huge number of drinking establishments that existed in the city's early history. In 1878 the *Kansas City Times* (now the *Kansas City Star*) pronounced Kansas City "a modern Sodom." With a population hovering near 50,000, Kansas City hosted 80 saloons: "triple the number of churches; four times the number of schools, colleges, libraries, and hospitals combined," write Rick Montgomery and Shirl Kasper in *Kansas City: An American Story*.

The city's rough and rowdy nature wasn't only a by-product of its wealth of drinking establishments. Research indicates that Jackson County's population in the late 1800s was 55 percent male and a mostly transient bunch, men constantly on the move in search of jobs, money, and booze. By the 1880s, Kansas City boasted the "wettest block in the world," an area between Gennessee and State Line on 9th Street and 1700 to 1800 West 9th. According to research compiled by Kansas City Public Television, "of the 24 buildings on this block, 23 were either saloons or liquor stores."

Try an edible two-bite cocktail in flavors like mojito, lemon drop, and amaretto. Or sample one of The Drop's signature martinis, with a selection that changes regularly. If you prefer to eat while you drink, The Drop serves an appetizing array of small plates—the bruschetta sampler is a must. And don't forget to bring dollar bills for The Drop's video jukebox, broadcast on several screens throughout the interior.

THE FOUNDRY AT MCCOY'S

424 Westport Rd., 816/960-0866, www.foundrykc.com

HOURS: Daily 4 P.M.-3 A.M.

COST: No cover

Map 3

Part game room, part dive bar, and part DJ showcase, The Foundry is a bar for the hip masses. Spend a low-key night at the pool tables or retro video games. If you're in the mood for a high-energy evening, The Foundry hosts local DJs nightly. When you're done dancing, cool off with a Super Model Martini, Sock It to Me shooter, or a drink from the Swingers Party section of the menu, which has oversized concoctions meant to be shared by four or more. An extensive beer list is also available, complete with lagers, pilsners, and several brews created next door at McCoy's.

FUEGO

1323 Walnut St., 816/442-8124, www.tengosedcantina.com

HOURS: Daily 11 A.M.-3 A.M.

COST: No cover

Map 1

An outpost of Mexican restaurant and bar Tengo Sed Cantina, Fuego is a great starting place to grab a beer or a cocktail and hang out in the Power and Light District's large, open-air area with seating and heat lamps. Before you order, ask about Fuego's drink specials. They aren't posted, but the bartender will fill you in on some of the cheaper choices.

HARRY'S BAR AND TABLES

501 Westport Rd., 816/561-3950, www.westportkc.com/places/harrys.html

HOURS: Mon.-Fri. 3 P.M.-3 A.M., Sat.-Sun. 5 P.M.-3 A.M.

COST: No cover

Map 3

Scotch and cigar connoisseurs will find a haven at Harry's Bar and Tables, where more than 50

© KATY RYAN

The patio at Harry's Bar and Tables offers prime Westport people-watching.

brands of scotch and 30 types of cigars await. The laid-back yet classy bar has ample indoor and outdoor seating, and large windows make for prime Westport people-watching (especially entertaining during late-night hours.) Harry's is a preferred watering hole for foodies and restaurateurs, so you just may find yourself embroiled in conversation with a local culinary legend.

HARRY'S COUNTRY CLUB

112 Missouri Ave., 816/421-3505, www.kansascitymenus.com/harryscountryclub

HOURS: Mon.-Sat. 11 A.M.-1:30 A.M.

COST: Cover during performances; price varies

Map 1

Leave the khakis and polo shirt at home when visiting what its owners call "a hip but irreverent take on a 1940s honky-tonk roadhouse." Come for lunch or dinner and stay for a tasty cocktail menu (try the bombpop martini) and a staggering array of specialty beers and liquors. On a budget? Opt for one of Harry's "yard beers": Schlitz, Pabst, Falstaff, or Hamm's, $2.25 a can. A jukebox usually supplies the bar's soundtrack, but Harry's is also host to frequent live musicians on its spacious patio. Be prepared to pay a cover during performances.

THE INDIE ON MAIN

1228 Main St., 816/283-9900, www.midlandkc.com

HOURS: Thurs.-Fri. 4 P.M.-3 A.M., Sat.-Sun. 8 P.M.-3 A.M.

COST: No cover

Map 1

An extensive renovation to Kansas City's Midland Theater introduced The Indie on Main, an adjacent music-themed bar that makes a great pre-show party spot. With a full bar and lounge-style seating, The Indie is a low-key place to grab a few drinks and people-watch on one of downtown's busier corners. If there's no show, The Indie's open Thursday–Sunday, so you still have an excuse to check out The Midland Theater's upgraded digs.

JOHN'S UPPER DECK

928 Wyandotte St., 816/474-5668

HOURS: Daily 11 A.M.-3 A.M.

COST: No cover

Map 1

As the name implies, John's boasts a deck—a really big deck—on the building's rooftop, offering one of the best views of Kansas City (and plenty of photo ops!). Indoor seating is available on the ground floor, and a DJ usually reigns on the second, but as long as the weather cooperates the deck is the place to be. Deck features include numerous tables, a full-service bar, and a small stage area that frequently hosts live musicians or karaoke. A popular spot for post-work cocktails, John's is also jumping through the late night, so arrive early to snag a deck table.

KELLY'S WESTPORT INN

500 Westport Rd., 816/561-5800,
www.kellyswestportinn.com

HOURS: Mon.-Sat. 11 A.M.-3 A.M., Sun. 10 A.M.-3 A.M.

COST: No cover

Map 3

Forget the expansive interior, the oversized beers, and the lack of cover charge. Kelly's Westport Inn is the oldest building in Kansas City, making it a true icon that continues to see a packed house nearly every night of the week. Weekends are especially busy as a diverse and fun-loving crowd arrives to start, or finish, the night. For the true Kelly's experience, order a round of homemade $1 Jell-O shots—and yes, you definitely want whipped cream. If you get the late-night munchies while you're there, make a beeline to the back and order a slice from the Joe's Pizza Buy the Slice window. Pizza and beer in a historical icon? It's an equation for a great night out.

KENNEDY'S

501 W. 75th St., 816/361-9788

HOURS: Mon.-Sat. 11 A.M.-1:30 A.M.

COST: No cover

Map 4

After a devastating fire gutted the building, Kennedy's reopened in early 2009 with a new multilevel space designed to accommodate eaters, drinkers, and special events. The self-proclaimed Irish bar stocks a healthy supply of whiskey and other spirits, in addition to a large beer selection that includes local favorites Boulevard Wheat and Pale Ale, as well as Guinness and Sam Adams Lager. A weekday happy hour, 4–7 P.M., features domestic and import draw specials, as well as $5 domestic pitchers. Kennedy's occasionally hosts live music, although for the most part you'll find a laid-back, welcoming bar where the beer flows and regulars dot the spacious interior.

LEW'S GRILL AND BAR

7539 Wornall Rd., 816/444-8080,
www.lewsgrillandbar.com

HOURS: Mon.-Sat. 11 A.M.-1:30 A.M., Sun. 11 A.M.-midnight

COST: No cover

Map 4

Feeling extra thirsty? Then try your hand at Lew's infamous "Das Boot," filled with 100 ounces of beer. Those who prefer their drinks in more manageable glasses have an extensive liquor and beer menu from which to choose. Stop by for Wednesday trivia night, a local favorite. Or head to Lew's to watch your favorite sporting event on any of the 18 large-screen TVs. And with Waldo's only outdoor heated patio, it's the place to go to drink outside even in the colder months. Lew's offers daily drink specials from 6 P.M. to 3 A.M., making the casual bar a great spot for budget-minded drinkers.

O'DOWD'S LITTLE DUBLIN

4742 Pennsylvania Ave., 816/561-2700,
www.odowdslittledublin.com

HOURS: Daily 11 A.M.-3 A.M.

COST: No cover

Map 3

In a city with as rich an Irish heritage as Kansas City, you're bound to find numerous Irish bars sprinkled throughout the metro area. O'Dowd's Little Dublin captures an ethnic authenticity that's made it a favorite bar since the ornately carved double doors swung open in 1996. Favorite Irish beers and whiskeys are in plentiful supply, and for those who prefer sweeter libations O'Dowd's offers a quarterly cocktail menu that captures the tastes of the season. O'Dowd's often hosts live music, and on New Year's Eve bar patrons ring in the Irish New Year at 6 P.M. with free champagne. When you're there, don't forget an Irish toast: Slainte!

VELVET DOG

400 E. 31st St., 816/753-9991, www.velvetdog.com

HOURS: Mon.-Fri. 3 P.M.-3 A.M., Sat. 6 P.M.-3 A.M.

COST: No cover

Map 2

One of several bars in Union Hill's "Martini Corner," The Velvet Dog exudes a low-key ambience with a plush, dimly lit interior and sprawling patio out back. To match its aura of casual sophistication, The Velvet Dog offers a martini menu that ranges from classics like cosmopolitans and dirty martinis to more inventive combinations like dreamsicle, schnozberry, and the martini navratalova. Head to the Dog's back room for billiards and plush seating, or come early to grab a prime table in front of the bar's floor-to-ceiling windows.

THE WELL

7421 Broadway St., 816/361-1700, www.waldowell.com

HOURS: Mon.-Sat. 11 A.M.-1:30 A.M., Sun. 11 A.M.-midnight

COST: No cover

Map 4

The eye-catching interior of The Well is a stylish place in which to enjoy cocktails, whether

© KATY RYAN

Quench your thirst at The Well, and enjoy the rooftop patio that overlooks Waldo.

you snag a high-top table or grab a seat at the lengthy bar. Yet the true attraction at The Well is the spacious rooftop patio set against the backdrop of Waldo's bustling business district. In the summer, you'll want to make a beeline for this bar: The Well's owners boast that they serve the coldest beer in town, thanks to aluminum bottles that are chilled to a frigid 22 degrees before serving.

Casinos

AMERISTAR CASINO HOTEL KANSAS CITY

3200 Ameristar Dr., 816/414-7000,
www.ameristar.com
HOURS: Daily 24 hours
Map 5

Try your luck at the 3,000 slot and video poker machines and 60 table games at Ameristar, one of the biggest casinos in the Kansas City area. A live poker room deals out hands of Texas Hold 'em, Omaha, and Stud Poker (Sun.–Thurs. 8 A.M.–4:30 A.M., Fri.–Sat. 24 hours). When you're ready for a meal, Ameristar hosts numerous restaurants including Arthur Bryant's barbecue, Horizons Buffet, and Pearl's Oyster Bar. On Friday and Saturday nights live musicians perform in Depot No. 9, a historic Pullman railroad car located at the casino's entrance. Bar service in the Depot begins at 4 P.M., and bands start at 8:30 P.M.

COURTESY OF THE KANSAS CITY CONVENTION AND VISITORS ASSOCIATION

Ameristar Casino Hotel Kansas City is open 24 hours a day and boasts one of Missouri's largest gaming floors.

ARGOSY CASINO HOTEL & SPA

777 Argosy Pkwy., 816/746-3100,
www.stayargosy.com
HOURS: Daily 24 hours
Map 5

Argosy's Mediterranean-inspired aesthetic adorns the casino with an impressive domed stained-glass ceiling, in-laid terrazzo floors, and handmade Moroccan tile. The expansive gaming floor features slot machines and table games and a VIP lounge area. Restaurants ring the perimeter of the casino. For speedy service and affordable entrées, try Crazy Olives, a spacious restaurant complete with multiple jumbo-screen TVs and a menu that includes sandwiches, pizza, appetizers, and entrées. Book a session at Argosy's on-site spa for the ultimate in relaxation. Because the spa fills quickly, consider reserving your session before your trip to ensure availability.

HARRAH'S NORTH KANSAS CITY

1 Riverboat Dr., North Kansas City, 816/472-7777,
www.harrahsnkc.com
HOURS: Daily 24 hours
Map 5

Modeled after Harrah's properties in Las Vegas and Atlantic City, Harrah's North Kansas City combines gaming, dining, shopping, and entertainment into one inclusive property complete with an on-site hotel. After a thrilling table game or fast-paced session of video keno, head to one of Harrah's casino bars or try Toby Keith's I Love This Bar & Grill, where down-home cooking is served in an exciting atmosphere filled with Toby Keith and country music memorabilia. After dark, escape to the VooDoo Lounge for dancing, live DJs, and an expansive cocktail menu.

7TH STREET CASINO

803 N. 7th St., Kansas City, Kansas, 913/371-3500, www.7th-streetcasino.com

HOURS: Daily 24 hours

Overview Map

Modeled after a 1920s casino, 7th Street Casino is a tribal-owned slots-only gaming venue and the only Kansas City casino located in a downtown district. More than 400 slots await for a night of fast-paced fun. The casino is also home to Lucky's Steak and Chophouse, a fine-dining restaurant that specializes in thick-cut perfectly cooked steaks. Or head to Zaper's for nostalgic cocktails amid historic surroundings. Parking is available in surrounding city lots.

Dance Clubs

ANGEL'S ROCK BAR

1323 Walnut St., 816/896-3943, www.angelsrockbarkc.com

HOURS: Wed. 9 P.M.-2 A.M., Thurs.-Sat. 9 P.M.-3 A.M.

COST: No cover

Map 1

If you like your angels as scantily clad waitresses and occasional go-go dancers, then you'll find heaven within Angels Rock Bar, a nightclub-lounge hybrid devoted to all things rock-and-roll. A 130-foot bar is the centerpiece, around which tables and low-slung seating areas offer plenty of room to sit back and enjoy the show. DJ-mixed rock music, ranging from classic to current, keeps the party going at high volume until the wee hours. For big spenders Angels offers premium bottle service, complete with mixers, priced from $125 for several varieties of champagne, vodka, whiskey, and other spirits.

BLONDE

100 Ward Pkwy., 816/931-2525, www.blondekc.com

HOURS: Mon.-Tues. 11 A.M.-2 P.M. and 4 P.M.-1 A.M., Wed.-Sat. 11 A.M.-2 P.M. and 4 P.M.-2:30 A.M., Sun. 8 P.M.-2:30 A.M.

COST: Cover varies

Map 3

In 2005, Blonde exploded onto the scene as one of the Plaza's first ultra-lounges. By day, the sleek, contemporary interior and soaring bar are reminiscent of an upscale eatery. At night, pulsing dance beats and a tireless crowd transform Blonde into one of the city's must-see nightspots. But be advised: A dress code is strictly enforced, and it's best to arrive early to ensure entry. Late arrivals are often stuck in a line that snakes halfway around the block. Keep your camera ready, as Blonde is a favorite spot for visiting celebrities, musicians, and athletes, making the people-watching well worth the price of a few cocktails.

DENIM & DIAMONDS

1725 Swift Ave., 816/221-5741, www.denimanddiamondskc.com

HOURS: Wed.-Sat. 7 P.M.-3 A.M.

COST: $5 cover

Map 5

Dust off your boots and cowboy hat and head to Denim & Diamonds for country music and dancing. An oversized dance floor allows plenty of room to whirl, twirl, and stomp. If your moves are a little rusty, Denim & Diamonds offers dance lessons most evenings. Different dances are featured in each lesson, including the cha cha, bomshel stomp, West Coast swing, and wave on wave. Drinking on a budget? Wednesday is ladies night and features a reduced cover and lower drink prices, and on Friday and Saturday the $5 cover, plus an additional charge, gets you a wristband good for bottomless drafts.

MINT ULTRA LOUNGE

334 E. 31st St., 816/561-2640, www.mintkc.com

HOURS: Thurs.-Sat. 9 P.M.-3 A.M.

COST: No cover

Map 2

Known as "the place to dance," Mint serves an intoxicating combination of cool cocktails and bumping beats designed to keep you moving. On Friday and Saturday nights, So Sick DJs spin dance and top 40, while the gay and lesbian crowd flocks to Mint on Thursday nights. While you're there, try the club's signature drink, the Mintini, and head downstairs for a peek at the Mile High Lounge, modeled after early 1970s TWA style. Take a break from the dancing and enjoy a slightly quieter atmosphere while perky flight attendants take your order for drinks—mixed, of course, by the Captain.

MOSAIC LOUNGE

1331 Walnut St., 816/442-8134, www.mosaicmo.com

HOURS: Wed.-Sat. 9 P.M.-3 A.M.

COST: Cover varies

Map 1

For a sleek, sophisticated lounge atmosphere, Mosaic delivers with a luxe interior, adjacent outdoor patio, and an expansive cocktail menu that includes champagne by the glass. DJ Spinstyles is the featured performer on Bounce Thursdays, and throughout the rest of the week Mosaic hosts local, regional, and even celebrity DJs like Samantha Ronson who keep the dance floor packed and the atmosphere electric. Dress to impress, and arrive on the early side to avoid waiting in lengthy lines, especially on Friday and Saturday nights.

VOODOO LOUNGE

1 Riverboat Dr., 816/889-7320, www.voodookc.com

HOURS: Fri.-Sat. 6 P.M.-1:30 A.M.

COST: $5 cover

Map 5

Adjacent to the gaming floor at Harrah's casino, the VooDoo Lounge is a nightlife experience complete with dancing, flair bartenders, and the VooDoo Doll Dancers. DJs from around the country are flown in weekly, giving clubgoers the very best in hip-hop and dance music. If you're feeling especially indulgent or want to celebrate a special occasion, reserve space in VooDoo's VIP area, complete with bottle service and a velvet rope. Dress code is strictly enforced, so if you're spending the day at the casino consider bringing a change of clothing or returning to your hotel to freshen up before entering VooDoo.

Gay and Lesbian

BALANCA'S PYRO ROOM

1809 Grand Blvd., 816/474-6369, www.balancaskc.com

HOURS: Mon.-Fri. 6 P.M.-3 A.M., Sat. 2 P.M.-3 A.M.

COST: No cover

Map 2

Come as you are to Balanca's, a two-story inclusive bar that welcomes everyone "regardless of lifestyles, ethnicity, or sexual preference." If you love to dance, head to Balanca's on Friday and Saturday nights for DJs and live music. For a quieter, more laid-back atmosphere, head upstairs where a jukebox provides the soundtrack for pool, darts, and socializing. On Wednesday, game night starts at 7 P.M. with Atari, Twister, and assorted board games, followed by a rousing karaoke session. The parking lots surrounding Balanca's are private, so be sure to park on the surrounding streets instead.

BISTRO 303

303 Westport Rd., 816/753-2303, www.bistro303kc.com

HOURS: Mon.-Thurs. 3 P.M.-1:30 A.M., Fri.-Sat. 11 A.M.-1:30 A.M.

COST: No cover

Map 3

For a casual lunch in sophisticated surroundings, Bistro 303 is an ideal choice. Around happy hour, the after-work crowds flock to 303 for cocktails and conversation and during the late-night hours a mixed, fashionable crowd swaps stories after partying at nearby dance clubs. The sizable interior leads to a diminutive brick-lined patio that's simultaneously cozy and cosmopolitan in its seclusion. Out-of-towners are encouraged to stop by 303 and take advantage of the knowledgeable, hospitable bartenders. They'll give you insider tips about the city while mixing one of the bistro's signature cocktails, or inventing a concoction based on your flavor preferences.

FLEX KC

1522 McGee St., 816/471-1522, www.flexkc.com

HOURS: Fri. 9 P.M.-1:30 A.M.

COST: $3 cover

Map 2

Head to the second floor of live-music venue Crosstown Station to find Flex KC, a Friday-only dance club that welcomes the hottest DJs and live performers. The state-of-the-art atmosphere features live video mixology by DVJ Synematix, an eye-catching montage that races to the pulsing beats of Flex KC's dance soundtrack. Loud, energetic surroundings make for an upbeat night out, but don't expect to hold much conversation with your fellow clubgoers. Dress to impress and wear your best dancing shoes; you've only got one night to take advantage of Flex KC so make it count.

FLO'S CABARET

1911 Main St., 816/283-3567, www.floscabaret.com

HOURS: Mon.-Sat. 4 P.M.-1:30 A.M.

COST: $5 cover starting at 7 P.M. Sat. only

Map 2

Flo is, simply put, a Kansas City icon. Garish makeup and a brash demeanor disguise John Koop, who as Flo is one of the most recognizable drag queens in the city. After performing "The Flo Show" for several years at area gay clubs, Flo opened her own cabaret reminiscent of a dinner theater, albeit one with leopard-print carpeting. She takes the stage Wednesday, Friday, and Saturday nights. Desiree Love headlines Monday nights, Bryce Lane hosts Tuesday Lesbian Night, and Wednesdays are Latin Night. Come early for weekend dinner and avoid the cover charge. Menu service starts at 3 P.M. and the kitchen closes at midnight.

MISSIE B'S

805 W. 39th St., 816/561-0625, www.missiebs.com

HOURS: Daily 4 P.M.-3 A.M.

COST: $3 cover

Map 3

What started as a piano lounge in 1994 has grown into one of the city's most popular gay and lesbian venues that also features regular (and well-attended) drag shows. The two-story establishment is part live-performance stage and part dance club complete with firemen's poles and elevated dancing platforms. Bars are placed throughout Missie B's, ensuring you'll never wait long for a cocktail. Although the club is cash-only, an ATM is located by the front door in case you run out of funds. And if you're in the market for leather apparel, head upstairs to Bootleggers, a leather shop open Thursday through Sunday nights.

OUTABOUNDS

3611 Broadway St., 816/931-0501

HOURS: Tues.-Sat. 11 A.M.-2 A.M.

COST: No cover

Map 3

In contrast to the gay and lesbian clubs and lounges found mostly in Midtown and Westport, Outabounds offers a laid-back sports bar environment complete with numerous televisions, darts, and pool tables. Outabounds hosts a variety of special events, including poker and trivia nights, '70s-music Sundays, and more. The sports bar also offers a grill menu if you're in need of a pre- or post-drinking snack.

SIDE KICKS SALOON

3707 Main St., 816/931-1430

HOURS: Mon. 8 P.M.-3 A.M., Tues.-Sat. 3 P.M.-3 A.M., Sun. 4 P.M.-3 A.M.

COST: No cover

Map 3

Described as a country-and-western bar for "cowboys who love cowboys," Side Kicks is a divey, unassuming nightspot for Kansas City's alternative community. Stop at the ATM before bellying up to this cash-only bar. The early-evening country soundtrack later gives way to a mix of hip-hop and top 40 dance favorites. There are plenty of tables encircling the often-packed dance floor, so you'll have a prime view of the action.

TOOTSIE'S

1818 Main St., 816/471-7704, www.tootsieskc.com

HOURS: Tues.-Sun. 11 A.M.-1 A.M.

COST: $5 cover Fri. and Sat.

Map 2

Known as Kansas City's oldest lesbian bar, Tootsie's bar and lounge is complete with DJs, live entertainment, and ample seating. An oversized hardwood dance floor complete with a stage and mirrored columns is the place to see and be seen, and surrounding tables are prime spots from which to survey the crowd or see one of Tootsie's live shows. High-definition screens broadcast music videos and other televised entertainment, and multiple bars ease drink lines and wait times.

Live Music

THE BEAUMONT CLUB

4050 Pennsylvania Ave., 816/561-2560,
www.beaumontkc.com

HOURS: Daily 7 P.M.-3 A.M.

COST: Cover varies

Map 3

Whether you love discovering local music or enjoy larger touring acts, The Beaumont Club is a must for live music in Kansas City. The sprawling interior hosts musicians and DJs in varying styles of music, including country, rock, and hip-hop. Next door, Sidecar offers a more intimate setting where musicians and DJs perform nightly. Outside, The Back Yard hosts concerts in a festival-like atmosphere. Dress to impress on Saturday night when ladies dance night is in full effect at The Beaumont Club, with the city's biggest dance floor.

KANSAS CITY'S JAZZ SCENE

Listen closely as you wander Kansas City's streets and you may catch the faint sounds of jazz, the city's unofficial soundtrack. In the 1920s and '30s 18th and Vine shot to popularity as jazz bars and clubs popped up in the predominantly African-American area. Musicians from around the United States flocked to Kansas City to study, jam, and perfect the art of their instruments. George E. Lee, Lester Young, Count Basie, Ben Webster, Walter Page, Julia Lee, and Charlie Parker were all products of the Kansas City jazz scene. During the mid-1930s and '40s, jazz clubs and bars were so prevalent that Kansas City earned the moniker "Paris of the Plains," a nickname that evoked images of smoke-filled rooms ringing with the sounds of brass instruments, sometimes accompanied by a haunting, mellow voice.

THE BLUE ROOM

1616 E. 18th St., 816/474-8463,
www.americanjazzmuseum.com

HOURS: Mon. and Thurs. 5-11 P.M., Fri. 5 P.M.-1 A.M., Sat. 7 P.M.-1 A.M.

COST: Free Mon. and Thurs., $10 cover Fri. and Sat.

Map 2

Not many museums feature an adjacent live-music club, but it seems only natural that the American Jazz Museum include a jazz venue to entice musicians from throughout the region. Modeled after a 1930s nightclub, The Blue Room is an exhibit designed to showcase the city's connection to jazz and its evolution. Nine tables grouped near the stage double as display cases for rare artifacts collected from Kansas City's musical prime. The Blue Room also features memorabilia-filled shadowboxes and The Massenburg Mural, which according to American Jazz Museum literature "celebrates the history of jazz and the African-American experience through compelling interpretations of jazz legends and inspiring words."

CROSSTOWN STATION

1522 McGee St., 816/471-1522,
www.crosstownstation.com

HOURS: Mon.-Fri. 4 P.M.-1 A.M., Sat. 5 P.M.-1 A.M.

COST: Free-$25

Map 2

Other bars and clubs may host live music, but Crosstown Station was built from the ground up specifically to host concerts and performances by mainly rock, alternative, and blues bands. An elevated stage and a gently inclined standing area allow for prime views no matter your location. Expert sound and lighting production and a carefully calibrated acoustic modeling program ensure clear sound and sight for performers that range from local favorites to nationally known acts. Acoustic performers shine during happy hour if you'd prefer a more mellow crowd and atmosphere. Whether you prefer to sit, dance, or stand your way through shows, Crosstown Station has the space to accommodate.

DAVEY'S UPTOWN RAMBLERS CLUB

3402 Main St., 816/753-1909, www.daveysuptown.com

HOURS: Daily 1 P.M.-3 A.M.

COST: No cover

Map 3

Since 1925, Davey's Uptown has perfected a formula of equal parts dive bar and live-music institution. Step through the doors on any evening and you're nearly guaranteed to a performance from a local or regional musician. Daily drink specials on wells, pints, and pitchers ensure you'll never go thirsty. Although the music varies from country and rock to metal and DJ-produced electronica, a prevalence of country and folk performers have left their rockabilly mark on the charmingly grimy venue.

ERNIE BIGGS CHICAGO-STYLE DUELING PIANO BAR

4115 Mill St., 816/561-2444, http://kansascity.erniebiggs.com

HOURS: Wed.-Thurs. 8 P.M.-1:30 A.M., Fri. 7 P.M.-1:30 A.M., Sat. 8 P.M.-1:30 A.M.

COST: Cover varies

Map 3

Good times are guaranteed at this venue thanks to Ernie Biggs' rollicking atmosphere. Dueling piano players keep the crowd screaming for more while they play a mix of favorite sing-along numbers and slighty naughty renditions dedicated to birthday celebrants and bachelorettes. Come early to grab a table; the standing room is cramped and it's hard to stay clear of waitresses and thirsty patrons moving back and forth from the bar. Ernie Biggs is great for a group outing; if you feel up to sharing, order one of the bar's signature cocktails served in a large plastic fishbowl. Bring small bills to tip the piano players to ensure they'll play your favorite song.

JARDINE'S

4536 Main St., 816/561-6480, www.jardines4jazz.com

HOURS: Tues.-Thurs. 4:30 P.M.-midnight, Fri. 4:30 P.M.-3 A.M., Sat. 6 P.M.-3 A.M., Sun. 5:30 P.M.-midnight

COST: No cover

Map 3

If Kansas City's unofficial cuisine is barbecue, then its soundtrack comes courtesy of jazz's mellow, sensual tones. And for some of the best jazz performances in the city, Jardine's is the place. In 2009, *Down Beat* magazine named Jardine's one of the 100 great jazz clubs of the year. Come for dinner, and when you're finished stick around for an incredible performance from some of the best names in the jazz industry. Reservations are recommended for meals and performances.

KC BLUES & JAZZ JUKE HOUSE

1700 E. 18th St., 816/472-0013, www.kcjukehouse.com

HOURS: Mon. and Thurs. 8 P.M.-midnight, Fri.-Sat. 8 P.M.-1 A.M.

COST: No cover

Map 2

In April of 2009, Benny and Calvin Shelby opened the KC Blues & Jazz Juke House as "a place where people can start quenching their appetite for some down-home blues and good food in the same venue." The 215-seat bar and restaurant features live blues on Monday, Thursday, Friday, and Saturday nights; on Monday and Thursday nights jam sessions draw musicians from throughout the region. Located in downtown's 18th and Vine District, the city's jazz music stronghold, the juke house adds to the soundtrack by showcasing the best in local blues music. Tables grouped around the stage make for an intimate environment, a throwback to the cozily crowded clubs that put 18th and Vine on the map.

MUTUAL MUSICIANS FOUNDATION

1823 Highland Ave., 816/471-5212,
www.thefoundationjamson.org

HOURS: Sat.-Sun. midnight-6 A.M.

COST: Suggested donation to the Historic Jazz Foundation

Map 2

Once the home of the Black Musicians' Protective Union Local 627 AF of M., the Mutual Musicians Foundation remains an integral part of Kansas City's jazz history and the site of late-night jam sessions that attract local, regional, and national performers into the foundation's intimate setting. Photos and other jazz memorabilia line the walls of the historic club, designated a National Historic Landmark and the site of special events like the Bird Lives Festival in honor of Kansas City jazz legend Charlie "Yardbird" Parker.

THE PHOENIX

302 W. 8th St., 816/221-5299, www.phoenixjazzkc.com

HOURS: Mon.-Sat. 11 A.M.-1:30 A.M.

COST: No cover

Map 1

After more than a century in business, The Phoenix is still one of the top spots in Kansas City to hear live jazz. Known for an uplifting environment and lively performances, The Phoenix also dishes up smoked meats, sandwiches, soups, and appetizers. Past performers include Tim Whitmer, Dan Doran, Pat Morrissey, and The Scamps. If you arrive early enough, you just might score a seat at the piano bar, although patrons agree that any seat in the house allows for a prime stage view. Thanks to the club's laid-back atmosphere, you can stay as long as you like, so grab a few cocktails, get comfortable, and spend the evening in a sultry embrace of mellow melodies.

THE RECORD BAR

1020 Westport Rd., 816/753-5207,
www.therecordbar.com

HOURS: Mon.-Fri. noon-1:30 A.M., Sat. 4 P.M.-1:30 A.M., Sun. noon-midnight

COST: Varies by performance

Map 3

Tucked in a strip mall next to one of the city's best bets for breakfast, The Record Bar's appealing mix of live shows, special events, and gourmet food has made the venue a Kansas City nightlife VIP. National acts like Howie Day and Ting Tings share the stage with local favorites Be/Non, The Elders, and other rock and alternative bands. And on Monday nights, test your rock-and-roll prowess with Bob's Yer Uncle music trivia. Cost? A cover charge. A reputation as a trivia genius? Priceless. Before you leave, don't forget to swing by The Record Bar's store and pick up a logo tee, tank, or pair of hot pants.

Lounges

CZAR BAR

1531 Grand Blvd., 816/221-2244, www.czarbar.com

HOURS: Mon.-Thurs. 4 P.M.-1:30 A.M., Fri. 4 P.M.-3 A.M., Sat. 5 P.M.-3 A.M.

COST: No cover

Map 2

Czar Bar's smallish interior retains an intimate feeling, whether you've come to enjoy the bar's happy-hour food and drink specials or to see live music or a DJ showcase. You'll find boutique and small-batch liquors on the cocktail menu, and knowledgeable waitstaff and bartenders are happy to make recommendations if you'd like to step outside your cocktail comfort zone. Before you leave, make sure to stop in Czar Bar's photo booth for a strip of souvenir snapshots.

© KATY RYAN

Drink and food specials make Czar Bar a popular spot for afternoon happy hours.

FIREFLY

4118 Pennsylvania Ave., 816/931-3663

HOURS: Thurs. 6 P.M.-3 A.M., Fri-Sat. 4 P.M.-3 A.M., Sun. 10 P.M.-3 A.M.

COST: No cover until 10 P.M., late-night cover varies

Map 3

Billed as a modern-day speakeasy, Firefly opened as a tribute to the city's colorful nightlife history. Firefly has minimal signage and awaits at the rear of a narrow 50-foot hallway—you might even be tempted to whisper a password as you breeze by the doorman. One step into the sleek lounge makes the effort worthwhile, and you'll be rewarded with some of the city's most inventive and delicious cocktails. Managers Matt Jones and Todd Gambal are no strangers to the area; they're the managerial brains behind Dark Horse Tavern and Torre's Pizza. After one visit to Firefly you'll agree it's a stylish step up for the duo.

MANIFESTO

1924 Main St., 816/536-1325

HOURS: Daily 5 P.M.-1:30 A.M.

COST: No cover

Map 2

Manifesto is difficult to enter, but it's the challenge that gives the nightspot a true speakeasy ambience. Located below 1924 Main, Manifesto's interior seats only 40 people. Look for the keypad, hit "call," and, if space allows, you'll be buzzed into a dimly lit, intimate room filled with mostly white decor. Head to the bar where Manifesto co-owner Ryan Maybee might be mixing up some of the most inventive cocktails in existence. Manifesto's other mixologists are equally talented, combining spirits with unusual ingredients like dried juniper berries and even Shatto root beer milk to create flavorful cocktails that are an experience, rather than a mere drink. If you're planning to visit Manifesto Thursday through Saturday, call for a reservation to ensure one of the hottest tables in the city.

SKIES

2345 McGee St., 816/398-4845, www.skieskc.com

HOURS: Sun.-Thurs. 5-10 P.M., Fri.-Sat. 5 P.M.-midnight

COST: No cover

Map 2

Here you can sip a cocktail while enjoying what is, hands down, the best view in Kansas City. Skies is a posh revolving restaurant perched atop the towering Hyatt Regency Crown Center. Settle in one of Skies' plush lounge chairs and enjoy the sweeping, panoramic view of downtown and Midtown as the restaurant makes a full revolution each hour. It's a beautiful vista whether you're at Skies for happy hour or a late nightcap. Dressy attire is encouraged, and although the restaurant fills quickly you'll be able to secure a lounge seat with a minimal wait.

Wine Bars

BOOZEFISH WINE BAR

1511 Westport Rd., 816/561-5995, www.boozefish.com

HOURS: Tues.-Thurs. 4 P.M.-12:30 A.M., Fri. 4 P.M.-1:30 A.M., Sat. 10 A.M.-1:30 A.M.

COST: No cover

Map 3

Affectionately known as The Fish, Boozefish is a wine lover's dream. Owner Maija Diethelm channeled a European-bistro vibe when she opened the bar, whose claim to fame is an extensive wine menu that doesn't only appeal to sophisticated palates; it's also meant to educate about wine's flavorful nuances. In a cheeky nod to male-dominated sports nights, Boozefish hosts First Wednesdays, a girls-night-out extravaganza complete with cosmopolitans, manicures, and uncensored episodes of iconic HBO drama *Sex and the City.* The Fish also boasts weekly and happy-hour specials and expertly prepared food that makes a fitting accompaniment to a favorite vino.

CAFE TRIO AND STARLET LOUNGE

4558 Main St., 816/756-3227, www.cafetriokc.com

HOURS: Mon.-Sat. 11 A.M.-11 P.M.

COST: No cover

Map 3

Along with an ample menu and signature martinis, Cafe Trio serves up an alluring atmosphere of pure urban sophistication. Locally painted canvases lend an additional vibrancy to the dining area, and are rotated regularly as part of Trio's art program. Five nights a week, local performers take center stage in the adjoining Starlet Lounge. Small plates such as Prince Edward Island black mussels and blue cheese bistro *satay* are an ideal accompaniment to any of Trio's signature cocktails or wine selections, a combined collection so extensive that Trio has been locally recognized for both best bar and best martini. Now, it's your turn to judge.

JP WINE BAR & COFFEE HOUSE

1526 Walnut St., 816/842-2660, www.jpwinebar.com

HOURS: Mon.-Sat. 4 P.M.-1:30 A.M.

COST: No cover

Map 2

The bar's stylish interior reflects an understated yet upscale ambience that blends seamlessly with the almost daunting cocktail list and accompanying food menu that includes a savory blend of entrées and appetizers. Wine flights blended by region are a popular choice for those eager to sample a variety of wines, and if you're feeling especially celebratory, try the "little bubbles" flight. JP's seating accommodates both small and large groups. Snuggle with a date in one of the more intimate booths, or hold court with a large group in a plush lounge-type area or a cluster of booth-backed high-top tables.

SAVVY COFFEE AND WINE BAR

1201 Main St., 816/471-7044, www.savvykc.com

HOURS: Mon.-Wed. 7 A.M.-4 P.M., Thurs.-Fri. 7 A.M.-midnight, Sat. 9 A.M.-midnight

COST: No cover

Map 1

Savvy's prime location in the Power and Light District makes it a popular stop for passersby in need of caffeine, alcohol, or an appetizer. A pastry case oozes goodness with treats from Prairie Village bakery Dolce. A three half-glass sampler is available for those who want to mix and match their wines, and Savvy also serves up several varieties of beer. Thanks to extensive hours, you could swing by for coffee and pastry in the morning, and head back to the bar for an evening aperitif. Now that's some savvy thinking.

ARTS AND LEISURE

Nationally renowned museums, concentrated gallery districts, annual festivals, and a state-of-the-art performing-arts venue have helped make Kansas City a regional arts and culture leader filled with options for those who want to explore the creative side of the city. In the midst of downtown redevelopment, public art installations add vibrancy and life to city streets. Eclectic gallery districts are the nucleus of Kansas City's creative community, and the monthly First Fridays gallery crawl is one of the most consistently attended events in the city.

On stage, Kansas City's dancers, musicians, and performers exude a passion and talent that reflects a devotion to local arts. And whether you attend the Kansas City Literary Festival or the must-see American Royal, Kansas City hosts festivals throughout the year that are great ways to truly feel the pulse of the city.

A large number of lush green spaces, both in urban areas and in the suburbs, encourage walking, jogging, or simply spending time outside. Many parks also reflect local history, like Swope Park, named for one of the leaders in Kansas City's parks and boulevard movement that transformed the city in the early 1900s.

If you're eager for a new way to explore the city, numerous walking tours showcase architecture, history, hauntings, and even gangsters in entertaining, interactive environments.

COURTESY OF THE KANSAS CITY CONVENTION AND VISITORS ASSOCIATION

HIGHLIGHTS

LOOK FOR [icon] TO FIND RECOMMENDED ARTS AND ACTIVITIES.

Best Local Art: The art energy is electric at **Arts Incubator,** a multifaceted space that hosts galleries, studios, and arts-related programming (page 89).

Best Architectural Icon: The **Kauffman Center for the Performing Arts'** 2011 opening is highly anticipated as the architectural marvel welcomes the ballet, opera, and symphony, in addition to traveling performances (page 95).

Best City Celebrations: Kansas City is recognized nationwide for its Irish celebrations, and **Irish Fest** and the **St. Patrick's Day Parade** are two ways to celebrate all things green (pages 99 and 104).

Best Festival: Barbecue, live music, and rodeos – the **American Royal** truly knows how to throw a party. Bring your appetite, comfy shoes, and extra napkins (page 100).

Best Art Splurge: Artists from around the United States exhibit during the annual **Plaza Art Fair,** a great place to start – or add to – your art collection (page 102).

Best Way to Explore Downtown: **First Fridays** are hopping with gallery openings, boutiques, street performances, and a lively crowd that breathes life into an evolving downtown (page 104).

Best Place to Picnic: With sprawling acreage and an exquisite rose garden, **Loose Park** is a lush respite perfect for picnics or an outdoor nap (page 105).

Best Places for Family Fun: Whether you crave high-speed roller coasters, water slides, or bumper cars **Oceans of Fun** and **Worlds of Fun** are great for a high-octane, family-friendly day (pages 106 and 107).

Best Tours: Explore the history and architecture of Kansas City with expertly guided tours sponsored by the **Historic Kansas City Foundation,** a great way to truly see the city (page 112).

COURTESY OF THE KANSAS CITY CONVENTION AND VISITORS ASSOCIATION

The Kauffman Center for the Performing Arts is scheduled to be completed in 2011.

The Arts

GALLERIES

ART BIDZ

1830 Locust St., 816/471-3737, www.artbidz.net

HOURS: First Fridays 5-9 P.M.

COST: Free

Map 2

Each month, Art Bidz hosts a gallery show and art-buying event that's 90 percent silent bidding and 10 percent live auction. Art in a variety of mediums from both local and national artists is displayed within Art Bidz, a sort of clearinghouse that offers an array of price points from $50 to $20,000. The mostly silent auction is a great way to peruse and bid on art in a low-pressure setting, and entertainment is often offered for those who simply want to browse the art and watch the ensuing proceedings. Check the website for a preview of upcoming art displays.

ARTS INCUBATOR

115 W. 18th St., 816/421-2292, www.artsincubatorkc.org

HOURS: Thurs.-Fri. 11 A.M.-5 P.M.

COST: Free

Map 2

A multifaceted arts education and expansion space, Arts Incubator includes 47 active studios, a gallery, and a third-floor event space designed to promote local artists and their work and help them build a solid foundation on which to continue their art careers. The on-site Cocoon Gallery hosts several exhibits throughout the year in a variety of mediums. Artist receptions are typically held on First Fridays,

FIRST, SECOND, AND THIRD FRIDAYS

In 2005, inspired by an increasingly active arts community and a growing number of galleries in a relatively confined area, organizers unveiled First Fridays, a free monthly gallery crawl held throughout the Crossroads Arts District. The event has since grown to encompass galleries, local retailers, street performers, and more, and sometimes coincides with larger events like June's Gay Pride Festival.

Bars and restaurants throughout the Crossroads get into the spirit, offering drink and appetizer specials throughout the evening. Yet the main attraction is the art, with dozens of galleries flinging open their doors (admission is free) to display the latest and greatest of the local arts community. Select galleries host performances and even live-action art, during which visitors can watch a group of artists create canvases during a fixed period of time using spray paint and other materials.

Not to be outdone, other parts of the city began their own arts campaigns planned around later Fridays in the month. The second Friday brings an eclectic mix of arts-related activities, whether it's the Nelson-Atkins Museum of Art's Young Friends of Art networking happy hour, movies at the Kansas City Public Library, or the Follow the Dotte Artwalk, an art crawl similar to First Fridays that takes place within the galleries of downtown Kansas City, Kansas.

The Charlotte Street Foundation, a local arts support organization, commandeers third Fridays with artist receptions and shows at its public spaces. Part of the Urban Culture Project, the spaces transform unused buildings and storefronts into temporary galleries that host a variety of shows, from video and performance art to mixed media and other stationary displays. Shows are accessible from both inside the gallery as well as from the street through large windows, a dualistic approach designed to make art accessible to everyone, regardless of whether they feel comfortable entering a gallery space.

and exhibits are shown through the end of the month. The variety of local art exhibited, combined with Arts Incubator's enduring commitment to promoting and assisting local artists, has made the gallery a favorite with residents and visitors alike, earning "best independent gallery" accolades from *KC Magazine.*

ARTSPACE–KANSAS CITY ARTS INSTITUTE

16 E. 43rd St., 816/561-5563,
www.kcai.edu/hr-block-artspace
HOURS: Tues.-Fri. noon-5 P.M., Sat. 11 A.M.-5 P.M.
COST: Free
Map 3

Compelling work in a variety of mediums is regularly rotated throughout Artspace, the H&R Block–funded gallery space for the Kansas City Arts Institute. Exhibits from both students and other arts organizations are displayed for several weeks, and each kicks off with an artist reception. In addition, Artspace hosts educational programs, professional development opportunities, and partnerships, all in the name of furthering the creation, presentation, and appreciation of art and visual education.

BLUE GALLERY

118 Southwest Blvd., 816/527-0823,
www.bluegalleryonline.com
HOURS: Tues.-Sat. 10 A.M.-5:30 P.M.,
First Fridays 10 A.M.-9 P.M.
COST: Free
Map 2

A stunningly simple space, highlighted by glossy concrete floors and ample white wall space, is a contemporary yet unintrusive backdrop for some of the best that Kansas City artists have to offer. The gallery's ability to create a refined yet welcoming setting has made it a local favorite. The Blue Gallery is described as a sanctuary for the art experience, a space that hosts contemporary fine art that makes you think, yearn, and wonder. Exhibits are rotated monthly and include works in mixed media, paint, sculpture, and more.

BYRON C. COHEN GALLERY FOR CONTEMPORARY ART

2020 Baltimore Ave., Ste. 1N, 816/421-5665,
www.byroncohengallery.com
HOURS: Thurs.-Sat. 11 A.M.-5 P.M.
COST: Free
Map 2

This fine-arts gallery founded by Byron Cohen features significant collections of contemporary art and has recently expanded to include works from master and emerging artists from mainland China. Cohen, who graduated from Columbia University with an art history degree, has collected contemporary art for more than 40 years and has channeled his love of the style into one of the city's premier galleries and an anchor in Kansas City's arts-centric Crossroads District.

KANSAS CITY ARTISTS COALITION

201 Wyandotte St., 816/421-5222,
www.kansascityartistscoalition.org
HOURS: Wed.-Sat. 11 A.M.-5 P.M.
COST: Free
Map 1

Self-described as "an artist-centered, artist-run alternative space," the Kansas City Artists Coalition simultaneously hosts three contemporary art exhibits in three spaces: Mallin Gallery, Jacqueline B. Charno Gallery, and the Underground. In addition to monthly shows, the coalition also hosts the annual River Market Regional Exhibition in July, a collective showing that highlights creations of neighborhood artists. Although the coalition also offers various programming to assist artists with creative growth, its primary function is hosting exhibits that attract public viewings and increase exposure not just to individual artists, but to the local arts community in general.

KEMPER AT THE CROSSROADS

33 W. 19th St., 816/753-5784, www.kemperart.org

HOURS: Fri. noon-8 P.M., Sat. noon-6 P.M.

COST: Free

Map 2

Part museum, part gallery space, Kemper at the Crossroads is an outpost of the Kemper Museum of Contemporary Art. The newest addition to the museum, Kemper at the Crossroads showcases contemporary works from a variety of local and national artists and is certainly a must-see during the monthly First Fridays gallery crawl. Design firm Kem Studio said the goal was to design a gallery that is "flexible, transparent, and communal," an ideal backdrop for the often dramatic contemporary artwork that graces the gallery walls. A large movable interior wall allows for easy reconfiguration of the space in order to accommodate a variety of exhibits both large and small.

LA ESQUINA

1000 W. 25th St., 816/221-5115, www.charlottestreet.org/urban-culture-project

HOURS: Vary according to performance schedule

COST: Free

Map 2

Part of the Urban Culture Project, La Esquina is a 2,500-square-foot white box/black box that hosts staged performances and large-scale exhibits and installations. Two 14-foot moveable walls allow for easy reconfiguration of the space, which also hosts video screenings, public programs, and other special events. Check the Charlotte Street Foundation's website for a complete performance schedule.

LEEDY-VOULKOS ART CENTER

2012 Baltimore Ave., 816/474-1919, www.leedy-voulkos.com

HOURS: Wed.-Sat. 11 A.M.-5 P.M.

COST: Free

Map 2

Founded in the mid-1980s by Jim Leedy, the Leedy-Voulkos Art Center showcases local art work while offering resources to professional artists in an effort to expand and promote Kansas City's arts community. Rotating exhibits display a variety ranging from painting and sculpture to jewelry and mixed-media collage. The art center also hosts one-day workshops designed to introduce various artistic techniques. Workshop admission includes light refreshments and materials; check the website for a complete schedule.

LIGHTWORKS

215 W. 19th Terr., 913/262-1763, www.vankeppelartglass.com

HOURS: Vary

COST: Free

Map 2

Stop into Lightworks and you may find yourself leaving with a piece of custom lighting or glass sculpture. Exquisite art glass in vibrant colors and gently curved shapes is displayed alongside dome lamps, wall sconces, and pendants that add a distinct touch of style to any room. Created by Merriam, Kansas–based Dierk Van Keppel, Lightworks serves as a downtown showroom and gallery space that exhibits the latest in cutting-edge glass techniques. If you can't make it for First Fridays, call the gallery to schedule an appointment.

PARAGRAPH + PROJECT SPACE

21 and 23 E. 12th St., 816/221-5115, www.charlottestreet.org

HOURS: Thurs. and Sat. noon-5 P.M.

COST: Free

Map 1

These spaces are part of the Urban Culture Project, a movement started by the Charlotte Street Foundation. A rolling wall separates the Paragraph and Project spaces, and can be moved to accommodate large-scale shows and other special events. When divided, Project is ideal for installations and smaller exhibits; Paragraph's larger interior works for both individual and group exhibitions.

PI

419 E. 18th St., 816/210-6534, www.piartgallery.com

HOURS: Wed.-Sat. 11 A.M.-4 P.M.

COST: Free

Map 2

When you open a gallery in a district filled with art spaces, you've got to find a way to set yourself apart. And at Pi, art meets food in a gallery-cum–coffee shop that serves espresso-based drinks, breakfast, lunch, and, yes, there's pie. If you're eager to start an art collection but find yourself on a budget, no worries—the Pi gallery hosts one of the state's few Art*O*Mat vending machines (actually a repurposed cigarette dispenser), into which you insert a $5 token and are rewarded with an original piece of artwork.

SLAP-N-TICKLE GALLERY

504 E. 18th St., 816/716-5940, www.letyourfreakflagfly.com

HOURS: First Fridays 6-11 P.M. and by appointment

COST: Free

Map 2

Defined as "an exceptional gallery for very silly people," the provocatively named Slap-n-Tickle Gallery hosts thought-provoking exhibits from local and national fringe artists often accompanied by live music, burlesque dancers, and other entertainment. Because exhibits often contain mature content, gallery visitors should be over 18. Slap-n-Tickle is owned by April McAnerney, an artist whose work focuses on women by reinventing them in a commentary on the gender's proclivity to make sacrifices and assume various forms in order to evoke happiness and please others.

THIRD EYE

2024 Main St., 816/931-7160, www.thirdeyekc.com

HOURS: Mon.-Fri. 9 A.M.-5 P.M. and by appointment

COST: Free

Map 2

A commercial production studio, Third Eye also houses a 5,000-square-foot loft-style event space and an accompanying art gallery that regularly rotates exhibits from area artists. The 1,000-square-foot gallery can accommodate a variety of exhibits, and on warmer nights a huge garage door is flung open to allow guests access to a landscaped courtyard. Although the gallery's address is listed on Main Street, enter on Baltimore Street for the most convenient access to the gallery.

PERFORMING ARTS

COTERIE THEATER

2450 Grand Blvd., 816/474-6552, www.coterietheater.org

COST: Varies

Map 2

Named "one of the five best theaters for young audiences in the U.S." by *Time* magazine, the Coterie Theater is a nonprofit organization that displays both classic and contemporary theater performances, as well as providing dramatic outreach programs to the surrounding community. *Travel + Leisure* magazine praised the Coterie not only as one of its top 10 children's theaters, but also for refusing to talk down to its audience regardless of the type of performance. Plays are designed for a variety of age levels, and the Coterie also hosts the annual Young Playwrights' Festival, which includes the thought-provoking Young Playwrights' Roundtable.

H&R BLOCK CITY STAGE

30 W. Pershing Rd., Ste. 850, 816/460-2020, www.unionstation.org

HOURS: Vary

COST: $8

Map 2

Funded by Kansas City–based H&R Block, the City Stage is a kid-friendly performance venue that features dramas, comedies, and musicals during the day and evening. Located in the lower level of Union Station, the City Stage is a great alternative to a movie—and for parents, an excuse to sit still after hours spent exploring Union Station's attractions. Tickets are available online, by phone, and at the City Stage box office.

KANSAS CITY BALLET

1616 Broadway Blvd., 816/931-2232, www.kcballet.org

COST: $80-160

Map 2

Under the direction of artistic director William Whitener and executive director Jeffrey Bentley, the 25-member Kansas City Ballet performs three mixed repertory seasons annually, in addition to the always-anticipated performance of *The Nutcracker*. The local company specializes in a mix of shows, both classical and

COURTESY OF THE KANSAS CITY CONVENTION AND VISITORS ASSOCIATION

The exquisite dancers of the Kansas City Ballet have earned a reputation as one of the best mid-sized ballet organizations in the country.

contemporary, to offer gracious and high-energy performances that have made the ballet a much-loved event in Kansas City. If your visit in 2010 coincides with a ballet performance, seize the opportunity to witness the Kansas City Ballet's last season at the Lyric Theater before moving to the state-of-the-art Kauffman Center for the Performing Arts and the Bolender Center for Dance and Creativity in 2011.

KANSAS CITY REPERTORY THEATRE

4949 Cherry St., 816/235-2707, www.kcrep.org

COST: Varies

Map 3

Under the artistic direction of Eric Rosen, the Kansas City Repertory Theatre, founded in 1964, continues to produce lively, thought-provoking, and elaborate stage productions. The region's only member of the prestigious League of Resident Theatres, the Rep is the professional theater-in-residence for the University of Missouri–Kansas City. Plays and musicals are performed on two stages: Spencer Theatre (main stage) and Copaken Stage, adjacent to H&R Block world headquarters at 13th and Walnut Streets.

KANSAS CITY SYMPHONY

1020 Central St., 816/471-0400, www.kcsymphony.org

Map 1

Michael Stern's 2005 designation as music director and conductor was an appointment met with excitement and acclaim by area and national symphony fans alike. With an extensive resume, Stern brings a youthful, energetic approach and has received praise for fueling a noticeable artistic growth within the symphony. Kansas City Symphony's season kicks

COURTESY OF THE KANSAS CITY CONVENTION AND VISITORS ASSOCIATION

The Kansas City Repertory Theatre is the professional theater-in-residence at the University of Missouri–Kansas City.

off in mid-September with a sophisticated Symphony Ball, followed by various performances until the season's conclusion in early June. The symphony will permanently relocate to the Kauffman Center for the Performing Arts upon its scheduled completion in 2011.

KAUFFMAN CENTER FOR THE PERFORMING ARTS

Broadway and Wyandotte Sts. btwn. 16th and 17th Sts., www.kauffmancenter.org

COST: Varies

Map 2

One of Kansas City's newest architectural marvels, the Moshe Safdie–designed Kauffman Center for the Performing Arts is a state-of-the-art performance venue that will become the home of the Kansas City Ballet, Kansas City Symphony, and Lyric Opera in late 2011. Curved steel and thick glass combine to create a statuesque lobby that moves gently in the wind and offers panoramic views of downtown. Surrounding acoustic joints allow for simultaneous performances, and individual screens on each chair back allow for operatic and other translations to several languages.

LYRIC OPERA

1029 Central St., 816/471-4933, www.kcopera.org

COST: Varies

Map 1

Originally known as the Capri Theatre, the space now known as the Lyric Theatre changed names in 1974 after housing the Lyric Opera for several years. What began as a struggling venture in the mid-1950s has grown to one of Kansas City's performing-arts staples, operating with a budget of just over $5 million. New

COURTESY OF THE KANSAS CITY CONVENTION AND VISITORS ASSOCIATION

The historic Lyric Theatre will host the Kansas City Symphony, Lyric Opera, and the Kansas City Ballet until 2011.

production, office, and rehearsal spaces are being constructed in Kansas City's Crossroads Arts District, and in 2011 the Lyric Opera will make the move to the Kauffman Center for the Performing Arts. The Lyric Opera performs four productions, each with four performances, throughout its season, which begins in mid-September and concludes in early May.

THE MIDLAND THEATER

1228 Main St., 816/471-8600, www.midlandkc.com

COST: Varies

Map 1

The Midland Theater first opened its doors in 1927 and, after an extensive renovation in 2007, the historic theater reopened with a kick-off performance by Leavenworth, Kansas, native Melissa Etheridge. The Midland Theater hosts regional and national touring acts in a concert season that spans the year. Performers like Journey, Widespread Panic, and Rick Springfield perform on a stage once graced by Bob Dylan, The Moody Blues, Jethro Tull, and Willie Nelson. The ornate, historic surroundings of the Midland make any concert an unforgettable experience, made even more enjoyable by the adjacent Indie on Main, a fully stocked bar that's a perfect before-show meeting place.

QUALITY HILL PLAYHOUSE

303 W. 10th St., 816/421-1700, www.qualityhillplayhouse.com

COST: Varies

Map 1

Within the intimate surroundings of Quality Hill Playhouse you'll find professional musical theater performances in a season that includes six musical and cabaret revues annually. One of the playhouse's most beloved productions, *Christmas in Song*, is held mid-November through late December and celebrates the holiday season with a traditional cabaret revue dedicated to classic and contemporary songs. Throughout each show, pianist and emcee J. Kent Barnhart peppers the performance with little-known facts about the music, as well as anecdotes drawn from his personal experiences. For a lively, relaxed theater experience, make Quality Hill Playhouse a stop on your Kansas City agenda.

QUIXOTIC PERFORMANCE FUSION

Various locations, www.quixoticfusion.com

COST: Varies

Take flight with Quixotic Performance Fusion, a majestic ensemble of musicians, dancers, aerialists, composers, designers, and choreographers. Far from limiting themselves to one art form, the members of Quixotic instead embrace many art forms to bring audience members a multisensory experience that in 2009 included a breathtaking performance along the towering walls of the Nelson-Atkins Museum of Art. Check Quixotic's performance schedule prior to your visit, as they perform at various venues in Kansas City and also travel throughout the region for select shows.

STARLIGHT THEATER

4600 Starlight Rd., 816/363-7827, www.kcstarlight.com

COST: Varies

Overview Map

Kansas City's majestic outdoor theater flung open its doors in 1950, and for more than five decades has welcomed concerts, musicals, and performing acts to its sizable stage flanked by impressive brick turrets. The second-largest theater of its kind in the United States, Starlight also hosts special events like corporate parties and weddings. While you're there, be sure to find the Walk of Stars, to which 24 famous performers have already been inducted. Today only three self-producing outdoor theaters remain in the United States, making Starlight Theater a must-see while you're in Kansas City.

MOVIE THEATERS

SCREENLAND

1656 Washington St., 816/421-2900, www.screenland.com

HOURS: Vary according to show times

Map 2

Once you decide to see a movie at Screenland (and you definitely should), arrive early and score one of the theater's premium seats in a row of plush red leather recliners that add luxury and glamour to any movie-going experience. Modeled after older movie houses, Screenland boasts a full-service bar and retro decor that's a pleasing antithesis to the corporate-owned movie theaters so popular today. Although the smallish theater only shows a handful of movies at a time, you'll find local, independent, and Hollywood blockbuster films, creating a mix that's sure to please even the most selective of movie watchers. On your way out, visit the Screenland gift shop for some theater souvenirs.

TIVOLI CINEMAS

4050 Pennsylvania Ave., 913/383-7756, www.tivolikc.com

HOURS: Vary according to show times

Map 3

For independent, foreign, and documentary films, Tivoli Cinemas is your best choice in Kansas City. Voted best movie theater in Kansas City by both *Pitch Weekly* and *KC Magazine,* the Tivoli also hosts a yearly film festival that shows classic movies. Pick an afternoon or early-evening movie, and afterwards walk to dinner at any of Westport's several restaurants. Or take your ticket stub to nearby Broadway Cafe, a favorite coffee and gathering spot, for half off one drink.

Festivals and Events

Visit Kansas City at the right time and your itinerary will be enhanced by a number of festivals and outdoor events. St. Patrick's Day and Irish Fest bring out teeming masses of green-clad celebrants, while Rhythm and Ribs honors two of the city's greatest pastimes: barbecue and jazz. Other must-see festivals include a tribute to the Bard, a sophisticated art fair (and another founded as a satire of the first), and a tribute to 16th-century England. And for a weekend-long barbecue feast complete with other activities like concerts and rodeos, the annual American Royal event is not to be missed—just don't forget your appetite!

SPRING

FESTA ITALIANA

8640 Dixson St., www.zonarosa.com

Map 5

Eat, drink, and be Italian at this lively annual celebration of Italian culture held during the first weekend in June. The smell of garlicky chicken spiedini and other Italian delicacies fills the streets of Zona Rosa during the weekend-long festival. Browse arts and crafts booths and cultural exhibits and enjoy live performances, cooking demonstrations, and evening fireworks displays. After more than three decades in Kansas City, Festa Italiana unofficially kicks off the city's summer festival season and is worth a trip to the Northland—your taste buds will thank you!

JAZZOO

6800 Zoo Dr., 816/585-1545, www.jazzookc.org

COST: $200

Overview Map

A pricey but well-attended fundraiser, Jazzoo is an annual benefit for the Kansas City Zoo held on the first Friday in June. Guests are encouraged to wear animal-themed attire as part of the creative black-tie dress code. More than 80 restaurants set up booths throughout the zoo offering a taste of their signature entrées, appetizers, and cocktails. Jazzoo culminates with a concert featuring a national headliner and opening act. Proceeds benefit the zoo's children's educational programs and are also used to purchase feed for more than 1,000 animals.

KANSAS CITY LITERARY FESTIVAL

Country Club Plaza, 48th and Jefferson Sts., www.kansascitylitfest.org

Map 3

If your trip coincides with the annual Kansas City Literary Festival in early May, you just may find yourself listening to a lecture or reading presented by a nationally renowned author. The celebration of all things books features local, regional, and national authors, as well as book sales, children's activities, and other literary-minded exhibits set amid the blooming landscape of the Plaza. Admission is free, but bring cash if you want to buy books.

RHYTHM AND RIBS

18th and Vine Sts., 816/474-8463, www.kcrhythmandribs.com

COST: $18-35 adult, $20 senior, $10 child

Map 2

On Father's Day weekend follow the smoky smell of barbecue to the annual Rhythm and Ribs festival, which unites two of Kansas City's favorite things: jazz music and barbecue. The historic 18th and Vine District hosts a nonstop lineup of local, regional, and national musicians on two stages while pit masters prepare mouthwatering feasts of barbecue classics. Other festival highlights include a barbecue contest, children's activities, and educational jazz programming that covers local jazz history, musical techniques, and more.

SUMMER

ETHNIC ENRICHMENT FESTIVAL

Swope Park, 816/513-7553, www.eeckc.org

COST: $3 adult, free child under 12

Overview Map

From an idea that sparked during Kansas City's 1976 bicentennial came the Ethnic Enrichment Commission, a mayoral commission that includes membership from 66 countries and ethnic groups. In addition to outreach programming and related functions, the commission's most anticipated event in late August is the annual Ethnic Enrichment Festival, a sensory explosion of sights, sounds, and tastes from dozens of ethnic groups that give Kansas City such a widespread cultural diversity. Watch a tae-kwon-do demonstration from the Republic of Korea or a performance from Israeli Tikvah dancers, or make your way through a mouthwatering array of multicultural foods.

FRINGE FESTIVAL

Fringe 411 ticket booth, 2450 Grand Blvd., 816/516-4750, www.kcfringe.org

COST: Fringe Festival buttons $5, ticket prices vary

Map 2

The week-long festival during the third week of July celebrates the best in local theater, dance, performance art, visual art, spoken word, puppetry, and more. What started as a spontaneous 1947 festival in Edinburgh, Scotland, has grown to an annual arts showcase in cities worldwide. Fringe Festival performances are held in venues from downtown to the Plaza and are offered throughout the day, including several late-night shows and exhibitions. Stop at the Fringe 411 ticket booth in Crown Center's first-floor atrium for tickets, Fringe Festival memorabilia, maps, and more. Although individual tickets are available at each venue, it's more economical to purchase a Fringe Festival button for discounted admittance throughout the festival.

HEART OF AMERICA SHAKESPEARE FESTIVAL

47th and Oak Sts., 816/531-7728, www.kcshakes.org

Map 3

The annual Shakespeare festival in July salutes the enduring contributions of the Bard as envisioned by festival founder Marilyn Strauss. Despite inclement weather, the first festival opened in 1993 and has since nearly quadrupled in size. The festival's highlight, a performance of a Shakespearian drama, is intertwined with classes, a poster and sonnet contest, and related lectures that make for a truly comprehensive event. Shakespeare under the stars—it really is a mid-summer night's dream.

IRISH FEST

2450 Grand Blvd., 816/997-0837, www.kcirishfest.com

COST: $10 adult, free child under 12

Map 2

If you absolutely can't wait until St. Patrick's Day, head to Kansas City over Labor Day weekend for the next best thing. Held on the grounds of Crown Center, Irish Fest unites the best in cuisine, culture, and live performances in a tribute to Kansas City's Irish population.

COURTESY OF THE KANSAS CITY CONVENTION AND VISITORS ASSOCIATION

Irish dancers at the annual Irish Fest

Trace your Irish ancestry at a genealogy booth, or head to the stage for the city's beloved O'Riada Academy of Irish Dance. Consistently voted best festival in the Convention and Visitors Association's annual survey, the Irish Fest is a lively, family-friendly way to spend the weekend.

RIVERFEST

Berkley Riverfront Park, East Front St. and Lydia Ave., www.kcriverfest.com

Map 1

Since its founding in 2004, Kansas City's Riverfest (July 3–4) is becoming one of downtown's biggest festivals complete with entertainment, food, and fireworks. Vendors and entertainers gather in downtown's Berkley Park along the banks of the Missouri River for two days of fun in the sun that culminates on the Fourth of July with an explosive fireworks show over the water. Come hungry for festival staples like curly fries, funnel cakes, gyros, and corn dogs. Or tempt a more adventurous palate with falafel or alligator on a stick. The kids will be occupied for hours in a fully equipped children's area complete with games and inflatable bounce houses, and the shops of the Riverfest Marketplace offer one-of-a-kind souvenirs. Parking is available throughout the River Market neighborhood, and several free shuttles regularly cruise Grand Boulevard.

FALL

AMERICAN ROYAL

1701 American Royal Ct., 816/221-9800, www.americanroyal.com

Map 2

What began in 1899 as the National Hereford Show has evolved into the American Royal, otherwise known as "the world's largest barbecue." Typically held in early October, the Royal is equal parts barbecue competition, rodeo, and live-music event. More than 70,000 flock to the Royal to eat, drink, and celebrate. Come hungry, wear comfortable shoes, and savor the unofficial cuisine of Cowtown. Parking is available at the American Royal complex, and shuttles also run to and from Union Station.

COURTESY OF THE KANSAS CITY CONVENTION AND VISITORS ASSOCIATION

Each October, the American Royal festival draws more than 70,000 people.

ART WESTPORT

Broadway and Pennsylvania Sts., 913/533-2656, www.artwestport.net

Map 3

For more than three decades, Art Westport has united local artists—and yes, they're definitely local. Participating artists must live no more than 40 miles from the Westport post office, ensuring a display of local art that ranges in subject matter and media. Browse the various displays that march along the streets of

Westport, duck into one of several bars or restaurants for an energizing meal or cocktail, then head back out to continue exploring the art. Local bloggers have called this one of the best art fairs of the year—visit while you're in Kansas City and judge for yourself!

CROSSROADS MUSIC FEST

Various venues, www.cmfkc.com

COST: $10-15

Although the monthly First Fridays gallery crawl has propelled the Crossroads Arts District into the go-to arts destination in Kansas City, the annual Crossroads Music Fest is shining an increasingly bright spotlight on the city's local music scene. Musicians such as the Barclay Martin Ensemble and Bacon Shoe meet dance and visual arts groups like Quixotic in an all-day performance spectacular that begins with several Friday-night preparties. Purchase festival passes prior to the event or the day of the show to avoid venue-specific cover charges. Several Crossroads-area bars host performances, including The Brick, Crosstown Station, and Czar Bar.

GREASERAMA

Boulevard Drive-In, Kansas City, Kansas, 913/831-2694, www.greaserama.com

Overview Map

Channel your inner hot-rod enthusiast or pin-up girl during the annual Greaserama car show over Labor Day weekend. Carefully restored custom hot rods and motorcycles are displayed by their proud owners as car fans from around the nation flock to Kansas City, Kansas, for car conversation and prime photo opportunities. Greaserama also hosts several rockabilly and other bands, as well as Lily's Greasy Gallery, a mobile art show that features "kustom kulture art" from artists nationwide. At night, the Boulevard Drive-In's massive screen lights up with cult movie classics, the perfect backdrop for the high-octane car festival.

HOLIDAY MART

Overland Park Convention Center, 6000 College Blvd., Overland Park, Kansas, 816/444-2112, www.jlkc.org

COST: Ticket prices vary

Overview Map

Shop for a cause during the annual Holiday Mart, a retail benefit organized by the Junior League of Kansas City. More than 200 specialty retailers convene on the show floor of the Overland Park Convention Center in late October to display clothing, home accessories, baked goods, and other gifts in a shopping spectacle so huge it's said to unofficially kick off the holiday shopping season. Proceeds raised at Holiday Mart benefit the Junior League of Kansas City and its longstanding volunteer and financial commitments to children's literacy. Tickets are available at a variety of price ranges, including an all-access VIP pass that includes buffet, cocktails, schwag bag, and more.

JAPAN FESTIVAL OF GREATER KANSAS CITY

The Carlsen Center, Johnson County Community College, 12345 College Blvd., Overland Park, Kansas, www.kcjapanfestival.com

Overview Map

Kansas City's Japanese population may be small, but the annual mid-September celebration of all things Japanese is anything but. Enjoy performances including Ottawa suzuki strings, Okinawa dance and drum, and Yosakoi dance, among others. Exhibits such as a miniature Japanese tearoom, wedding kimono display, and bonsai display provide a visual homage to important elements of Japanese culture, and traditional Japanese food service is available all day in the nearby Regnier–Cap Fed Room for an authentic taste of Japanese cuisine. Other events include a Japanese beer and sake tasting, lecture series, and a shopping and cultural village in which festival visitors can experience authentic Japanese surroundings including a bank, craft shop, and face and nail painting.

KANSAS CITY IMPROV FESTIVAL

Off Center Theater, Crown Center, 2450 Grand Blvd., 816/842-9999, www.kcimprov.com/festival

COST: $15-25

Map 2

Get ready to laugh—a lot—during the annual Kansas City Improv Festival. Local improvisational performers unite with national acts during a four-day comedic showcase. In 2009 *Saturday Night Live* cast member and Kansas City native Jason Sudeikis made an appearance. "We've done TV commercials and public pranks and shows for hundreds of people, but this is the most exciting thing we do all year," said Tim Marks, KCiF director. "We get to bring superstars in from L.A., New York, and Chicago and set them up in Crown Center to do one-time-only shows."

KANSAS CITY URBAN FILM FESTIVAL

Screenland Theater, 1656 Washington St., 816/421-9700, www.screenland.com

Map 2

The urban film festival debuted in 2009 to an appreciative local response. The two-day event in early September includes a short-film showcase, in addition to screenings of documentaries and webisode-based mini marathons. Feature-length films are followed by a locally produced film both days. Fox 4 News movie critic Shawn Edwards called the debut festival "a celebration of seat-of-the-pants moviemaking," recognizing that many of the films cover subjects that fall outside the mainstream. The festival is also designed to bring a wider audience to the Screenland Theater, a locally owned movie house that displays local and independent movies as often as it does major Hollywood blockbusters.

PLAZA ART FAIR

Country Club Plaza, www.countryclubplaza.com

Map 3

More than 300,000 visitors flock to the Plaza during the third weekend in September to view (and purchase) works from nearly 250 local, regional, and national artists. Born out of despair, the Plaza Art Fair began after the Great Depression as a way to entice local businesses to relocate to the shopping district. Since then, the festival has evolved into a three-day spectacle that lines nine blocks. Art booths are interspersed with local restaurants offering cuisine and cocktails that transcend the culinary experience typical of festivals.

RENAISSANCE FESTIVAL

628 N. 126th St., Bonner Springs, Kansas, 913/721-2110, www.kcrenfest.com

COST: $17.95 adult, $15.50 student/senior, $8.95 child

Overview Map

Wander the streets of a 16th-century village during the Renaissance Festival (Labor Day weekend through mid-October), one of Kansas City's largest festivals. Witness the heart-pounding action of live jousting, or become hypnotized by a troupe of exotic belly dancers. More than 500 costumed characters wander the tree-lined streets of the village. Hundreds of artisans display their work, and a mouthwatering array of food vendors serve the best in traditional Renaissance fare. Don't leave the festival without trying its signature snack, the

COURTESY OF THE KANSAS CITY CONVENTION AND VISITORS ASSOCIATION

Raise a glass at the Kansas City Renaissance Festival, a nearly month-long celebration of all things 16th century.

turkey leg. For a complete and educational view of the festival and life during the Renaissance, take the living-history tour.

UN-PLAZA ART FAIR

4501 Walnut St., 816/561-1181,
www.peaceworkskc.org/unplaza.html

Map 3

In a playful jab to its pricey counterpart, the Un-Plaza Art Fair in mid-September represents more than 85 artists in a laid-back environment. Although the fair is a juried art show, a lack of entry fee makes the fair more accessible to up-and-coming artists. Proceeds from the event benefit Peaceworks KC, an entirely volunteer-run organization that, simply, works for peace. Programs that benefit from Peaceworks' funding include Adopt-A-Minefield, Unitown, and peace studies scholarships available through Park University and Avila University.

WATERFIRE KANSAS CITY

Brush Creek, Country Club Plaza, Ward Pkwy. and Main St., www.visitkc.com/waterfire

Map 3

Created by artist Barnaby Evans, WaterFire is an annual spectacle of water and fire in late October that's not to be missed. At dusk, more than 55 floating bonfires will be illuminated along Kansas City's Brush Creek, one at a time, until all are ablaze in a fiery demonstration of public art installation glory. Evans' WaterFire originated on the three rivers of Providence, Rhode Island, and remains one of the city's signature events. In its few years in Kansas City, WaterFire has quickly become a favorite local occurrence, a way to celebrate the fall season and yet another piece to add to a long list of public art installations. During the show, food and refreshments are available from Plaza restaurants.

WINTER

PLAZA LIGHTING CEREMONY

Country Club Plaza, 47th St. btwn. Jefferson and Broadway Sts., www.countryclubplaza.com

Map 3

With the flip of a switch, more than 80 miles of Christmas lights illuminate building exteriors along the Country Club Plaza on Thanksgiving night. What started with a string of 16 lights over a doorway in 1925 has blossomed into an eagerly anticipated annual tradition. If you plan to attend the ceremony, be advised that hotel reservations on the Plaza fill up months, even years, in advance. For a sneak peek of the lights without the crowds, grab an extra-strong espresso and head to the plaza from 2 to 6 A.M. the day before Thanksgiving, when they test the lights.

ST. PATRICK'S DAY PARADE

Broadway St., Linwood to 43rd St., www.kcirishparade.com

Map 3

See the city through green-tinted glasses during the annual St. Patrick's Day Parade, a miles-long display that remains one of Kansas City's favorite traditions. The March 17 parade dates back to the late 1800s, when processions of "great pomp and circumstance" marched through city streets, according to the parade committee. After a hiatus in the mid-1900s, the parade made a triumphant return in 1974, and since then the St. Patrick's Day Parade has grown to include nearly 4,000 participants and, most recently, huge character balloons similar to those in the Macy's Thanksgiving Day Parade.

COURTESY OF THE KANSAS CITY CONVENTION AND VISITORS ASSOCIATION

the Plaza Lighting Ceremony

YEAR-ROUND

FIRST FRIDAYS

18th and Wyandotte Sts., 816/994-9325, www.crossroadskc.com

Map 2

What began as a small gallery crawl has evolved into one of the city's favorite Friday-night events. On the first Friday of the month, galleries, shops, and restaurants throughout the Crossroads Arts District stay open late for exhibits, artist receptions, and special events. Sporadic street performers provide outdoor entertainment throughout the area. Most galleries open between 5 and 6 P.M.; arrive early for the best parking. First Fridays are especially crowded during the warmer months, and the artwalk sometimes coincides with other events like Kansas City's Pride Festival, increasing area congestion. If you choose to dine out in the Crossroads during First Fridays, eat early or be prepared to wait for a table.

Sports and Recreation

Boaters, fishers, hikers, bicyclists, and sports enthusiasts will find no shortage of activities and destinations in Kansas City. Pack a picnic and enjoy a number of local parks, or take advantage of several extensive trail systems for a decidedly different view. Numerous organizations host various walking tours that cater to a range of interests from local history to the supernatural. Golfers have a number of courses from which to choose, and for those who prefer sports of the spectator variety, Kansas City is home to several professional and minor-league teams, as well as the first professional sports stadiums to be built side-by-side.

PARKS

BERKLEY RIVERFRONT PARK

East Front St. and Lydia Ave.,
www.berkleyriverfrontpark.org

Map 1

With 70,200 square feet of uninterrupted green space, Berkley Park is a lush oasis within the city's urban core. Celebrate the River Market's roots as a trading post as you stroll along the banks of the Missouri River. A two-thirds-mile lighted walkway is perfect for walking, jogging, and cycling, and the path now connects to the Riverfront Heritage Trail System. The park's size and picturesque surroundings make it ideal for downtown events, including the city's annual Riverfest celebration. Berkley Park also offers prime photo opportunities of the Missouri River and the Kansas City skyline, as well as the eye-catching uphill Broadway Bridge.

LOOSE PARK

5200 Pennsylvania Ave., 816/784-5300,
www.kcmo.org

Map 3

The sprawling grounds of Loose Park have made it a local favorite for picnics, walks, and relaxation.

© KATY RYAN

The tranquil settings in Loose Park are ideal for walks and picnics.

Loose Park is home to a lake, shelter house, tennis courts, a wading pool, and several historic Civil War markers. The park's most popular attraction, the Laura Conyers Smith Municipal Rose Garden, is a fragrant oasis of more than 4,000 flowers that represent 150 varieties of roses. A popular venue for local weddings, the rose garden is carefully maintained thanks to the dedicated volunteers of the Kansas City Rose Society.

MACKEN PARK

1000 E. 27th Ave., North Kansas City

Map 5

A renovation funded by North Kansas City's Parks and Recreation Department and the city council added a playground and tennis facility to this large park that often hosts sporting events and practices for the nearby North Kansas City High School, as well as recreational leagues. A paved one-mile track surrounds the park and is ideal for walking and jogging. The park also features sporadically placed life-fitness stations that include demonstrations for various strength training and flexibility exercises.

MILL CREEK PARK

47th St. and J. C. Nichols Pkwy., www.kcmo.org

Map 3

Anchored by the picturesque J. C. Nichols Fountain, Mill Creek Park is a sizable landscaped retreat nestled in the heart of Kansas City's Country Club Plaza. In addition to ample seating around the fountain, Mill Creek Park features a jogging track and eco pond. Thanks to an irresistible combination of stunning views and lush landscaping, Mill Creek Park is often the site of wedding photo shoots throughout the year. Keep your eyes peeled while you're there and you may catch a glimpse of a blushing bride and groom having pictures taken before or after the ceremony.

SWOPE PARK

6900 Elmwood Ave., 816/471-3472, www.kcmo.org

Overview Map

Much more than a park, Swope Park hosts the Kansas City Zoo, Starlight Theater, Swope Memorial Golf Course, Blue River Golf Course, and Lakeside Nature Center. Ten shelters and numerous picnic spots are ideal places for an outdoor meal. A volunteer-built 1.35-mile urban hiking and mountain bike trail is a challenging route that offers unmatched views of the surrounding parkland. Created on land donated by Colonel Thomas Swope in 1896, Swope Park is one of the city's first and largest parks.

THEIS PARK

Oak and 47th Sts., www.kcmo.org

Map 3

Adjacent to the Plaza and the Nelson-Atkins Museum of Art, Theis Park is a popular spot for walking, jogging, and picnics. A large open field is a prime area for outdoor games like Frisbee, croquet, and catch, and a jogging path along Brush Creek is a scenic way to see parts of the city. An on-site amphitheater often hosts live performances. When you visit Theis Park, don't forget your camera—the park's ideal location offers a great shot of the Nelson-Atkins, a hard building to capture because of its sheer size.

AMUSEMENT PARKS

OCEANS OF FUN

4545 Worlds of Fun Dr., 816/454-4545, www.worldsoffun.com

HOURS: Vary

COST: $28.99 adult, $15.99 child/senior

Map 5

With 60 acres of rides, slides, and pools, Oceans of Fun is the Midwest's largest tropically themed water park. A variety of family and thrill rides make for an exciting water-soaked day, whether you brave the 72-foot-tall Hurricane Falls slide or go careening down Typhoon, the park's dual racing slides. Kids will love Paradise Falls, a watery funhouse complete with water cannons, sprays, and more. Several dining options are available, including Calypso Cafe for burgers, chicken sandwiches, fries, and dessert, or head to Captain Cook's Nook for sandwiches, chips, and drinks. If you're planning a full day at the park, consider purchasing a Ride and Slide pass that gets you discounted combination admission into Oceans of Fun and Worlds of Fun.

WORLDS OF FUN

4545 Worlds of Fun Dr., 816/454-4545, www.worldsoffun.com

HOURS: Vary

COST: $40.99 adult, $18.99 child/senior

Map 5

Since 1973, Worlds of Fun has delivered high-octane entertainment with an array of state-of-the-art roller coasters, thrill rides, and the family-friendly Camp Snoopy play area complete with miniaturized versions of some of the park's most popular rides. In 2009, Worlds of Fun debuted the Prowler, a 3,074-foot wooden roller coaster that's valued at $8 million and reaches top speeds of 51 mph. For one of the best views of the greater Kansas City area, brave the Mamba, one of the highest roller coasters in the world. Some of the park's older, more classic rides include Autobahn, a bumper car arena, and Le TaxiTour, guest-operated antique taxi replicas. A variety of walk-up or dine-in restaurants satisfy any craving, from hamburgers and buffalo wings to funnel cakes and Dippin' Dots. And if you find yourself in Kansas City during weekends in September and October, head to Worlds of Fun's Halloween Haunt. Family-friendly ghouls and goblins roam the park during the day, while at night more gruesome creatures prowl the grounds as visitors enjoy late-season rides.

FEAR FACTORY

Let's play a game of word association. I say haunted house, and you probably think of a ramshackle contraption most likely held at a local community center with a fog machine, some creepy stuffed zombies, and maybe a fake spider web or two. Yet in Kansas City, several permanent haunted houses rise to terrifying, pulse-pounding heights.

Aptly situated among the dilapidated warehouses of Kansas City's West Bottoms, a once-thriving industrial district, haunted houses like **The Beast** (1401 W. 13th St., 816/842-4280, www.kcbeast.com) and **The Edge of Hell** (1300 W. 12th St., 816/842-4279, www.edgeofhell.com) truly immerse visitors in room after room of frights. Carefully costumed and made-up actors and actresses silently patrol the hallways or lurk in dim corners, waiting to jump out and scare on-edge visitors simply searching for a way out. These haunted houses are so elaborate, in fact, that animatronics and live animals are used to add even more authenticity to gruesome sets that include a werewolf forest, Jack the Ripper's London, the Macabre Cinema, and the Chambers of Edgar Allan Poe.

Should you survive the horrors within, you'll find yourself high atop the multi-story buildings with no escape but via a steep slide, down which you'll hurtle until you arrive on the ground floor. Although not for the faint of heart, the haunted houses have become nationally known and are a must-see if you're in town from Labor Day until early November. As you plan your trip check The Beast or The Edge of Hell's websites; hotels like the Sheraton and Hyatt Regency Crown Center offer haunted house and hotel travel packages that include admission to the hair-raising fear factories.

HIKING AND BIKING

BLUE RIVER PARKWAY AND MINOR PARK

E. 118th St. and Lydia Ave., www.kcwildlands.org

Overview Map

The more than 2,300 acres of the Blue River Parkway run alongside the Blue River and include a 10-mile trail ideal for cycling, mountain biking, hiking, and cross-country skiing. Other features of Blue River Parkway include a radio-controlled airplane field, hiking trails, horseback riding area, soccer fields, shelter houses, and picnic areas. Because much of Blue River Parkway is heavily treed, opportunities for bird-watching are numerous, and the land also hosts a wide array of native plants and wildflowers.

INDIAN CREEK TRAIL

105th St. and Roe Ave., Overland Park, Kansas, www.opfd.com

Overview Map

This 17-mile multi-use trail is a scenic way to see much of Johnson County before the trail crosses the state line to connect with Kansas City. Comprised of mostly level terrain, the Indian Creek Trail is ideal for biking and hiking. Mileage markers are placed every half-mile to assist with trail navigation. As you make your way along the trail, stop to enjoy amenities along the way, including several parks, playgrounds, and tennis courts. Leashed dogs are permitted on the trail.

GOLF

HEART OF AMERICA GOLF COURSE

7501 Blue River Rd., 816/513-8940, www.hellokansascity.com

COST: Nine holes $14 adult ($15 Sat.-Sun.), $12 senior, $10 child, additional $4 for second nine

Overview Map

Choose from two nine-hole layouts that wind throughout Kansas City's Swope Park at Heart of America. The "old" course, a par 35, features tight target areas. The newer course, designed by Richard Allen, is a par 27 and includes a water feature and a tee box atop a cliff face. On-site facilities include a snack bar, pro shop, locker facilities, putting and chipping greens, and a large driving range. Cart rental is available for $7/person for 9 holes, or $14/person for 18 holes.

OVERLAND PARK GOLF CLUB

12501 Quivira Rd., Overland Park, Kansas, 913/897-3809, www.opkansas.org

COST: Greens fees $27 (18-hole) Mon.-Fri., $33 (18-hole) Sat.-Sun. and holidays, $20 (9-hole); cart $15/person (18-hole), $7.50/person (9-hole)

Overview Map

At Overland Park Golf Club 27 regulation golf holes are spread out over three 18-hole courses. Lush fairways, scenic views, and bentgrass greens make for picturesque surroundings, and the courses are designed for players of all skill levels. Food is available at the course grill with a large patio area, and a driving range, putting and chipping greens, and a full-service golf shop are also available. The club uses a wave method of tee times, meaning groups are started off each course simultaneously. Thirteen tee times are available per course in a one hour, 44-minute period, after which the course is closed until groups begin their second nine.

TENNIS

PLAZA TENNIS CENTER

4747 J. C. Nichols Pkwy., 816/784-5100, www.plazatenniscenter.com

HOURS: Mon.-Fri. 9 A.M.-10 P.M., Sat. 9 A.M.-6 P.M., Sun. 11 A.M.-7 P.M.

COST: $4-9/hour tennis court, $10-15/hour ball machine rental

Map 3

Practice your serve or your backswing at Plaza Tennis Center, a public facility located in the heart of the Country Club Plaza. Guests of any Plaza hotel are invited to use the center, and lessons, clinics, and use of the ball machine can be arranged with a phone call prior to your visit. The Plaza Tennis Center frequently hosts league and tournament play, as well as group clinics that focus on specific skill sets. If you arrive in Kansas City without your tennis gear, visit the center's fully equipped on-site pro shop that also offers next-day racquet stringing and grip service, in addition to shoes, clothing, and other tennis accessories for purchase.

BOWLING

LUCKY STRIKE LANES

1370 Grand Blvd., Ste. 2, 816/471-2316, www.bowlluckystrike.com

HOURS: Tues.-Thurs. 3 P.M.-midnight, Fri.-Sat. noon-3 A.M., Sun. noon-1 A.M.

COST: Varies

Map 1

Part bowling alley, part cocktail lounge, Lucky Strike Lanes stands in homage to the iconic Hollywood Star Lanes, famous for its appearance in *The Big Lebowski*. This is one of more than 20 locations across the country, specializing in bowling served with a side of alcohol. The plush interior is as conducive to ten-pin victory as it is to relaxing and enjoying time with friends. The posh bowling alley also offers a menu of small plates, perfect for refueling between games. On Friday, Saturday, and Sunday evenings Lucky Strike keeps the pins flying with sounds from local and regional DJs. After 8 P.M. daily, patrons must be 21 to enter. A dress code requires "smart casual" attire and is strictly enforced.

PIN-UP BOWL

1859 Village West Pkwy., Kansas City, Kansas, 913/788-5555, www.pinupbowl.com

COST: Varies; $3 shoe rental

Overview Map

Test your ten-pin skills at Pin-Up Bowl, a bowling alley meets martini lounge outfitted with plush seating and a full bar. Pin-Up Bowl's food menu features appetizers, pizzas, sandwiches, and bowls of Campbell's soup, an inexpensive but filling way to fuel up for a night of bowling. Twelve lanes accommodate up to six players each. Reservations are recommended, especially on weekend nights. After 9 P.M., guests must be over 21. Before you leave Pin-Up Bowl, commemorate your bowling experience with one of the alley's signature T-shirts emblazoned with an oh-so-appropriate slogan: "Get your mind out of the gutter!"

ICE-SKATING

CROWN CENTER ICE TERRACE

2450 Grand Blvd., www.crowncenter.com

HOURS: Vary

COST: $6 admission, $3 skate rental

Map 2

Kansas City's favorite public outdoor ice rink is a popular spot for both residents and visitors during the colder months, beginning the first week of November. From Thanksgiving until Christmas, enjoy the colorful view of the Mayor's Christmas Tree, a towering evergreen perched in front of Crown Center and draped with thousands of lights. Skaters are welcome to bring their own skates. On Tuesdays, receive two-for-one admission after 5 P.M. (skate rental not included).

ICE SPORTS KANSAS CITY

19900 Johnson Dr., Shawnee, Kansas, 913/441-3033, www.icesportskc.com

HOURS: Daily noon-2 P.M.

COST: $6 admission, $3 skate rental

Overview Map

Skate year-round on Ice Sports Kansas City's

indoor rink, which also hosts area adult and youth ice hockey leagues and programs. In addition to general skating sessions, Ice Sports Kansas City offers adult and youth pickup hockey and broomball, a competitive sport similar to ice hockey. If you need to thaw yourself after a skating session, head outside to the adjoining nine-hole miniature golf course. Other on-site amenities include a concession stand, pro shop, and Wi-Fi.

SPECTATOR SPORTS

KANSAS CITY CHIEFS

1 Arrowhead Dr., 816/920-9400, www.kcchiefs.com

COST: Single tickets from $35

Overview Map

Even if you're not completely sold on NFL football, a visit to a Chiefs game is worth the experience to visit Arrowhead Stadium, the loudest outdoor stadium in the NFL. Wear red and prepare to join the throngs of screaming masses as they cheer the city's beloved team to victory. Single-game tickets can be difficult to find, but if you head to Kansas City later in the season, it can be easier to get seats (depending on the team's performance that year). Dress warmly for late fall and winter games—Arrowhead's wide-open layout provides little to no protection against frigid winds. Arrive early to meander through crowds of faithful tailgaters camped out across the parking lot, some of whom spare no expense when preparing for a game.

KANSAS CITY ROLLER WARRIORS

Municipal Auditorium, 301 W. 13th St., 913/636-7894, www.kcrollerwarriors.com

COST: $16 adult, $8 child

Map 1

For fast-paced rough-and-tumble action, head to a Kansas City Roller Warriors roller derby, called "a true blend of sport and spectacle." Kansas City's all-female league joins amateur leagues in more than 80 U.S. cities, all of whom deliver high-speed neo-derby bouts throughout the team's season, April–August. Eighty players are divided into four teams—Black-Eye Susans, Dreadnought Dorothys, The Knockouts, and Victory Vixens—that skate against each other and teams outside of Kansas City. A portion of derby ticket sales benefit local charities.

KANSAS CITY ROYALS

1 Royal Way, 800/676-9257, http://kansascity.royals.mlb.com

COST: Tickets from $7

Overview Map

Kansas City often has a love-hate relationship with the Royals, yet a favorite summer pastime is an afternoon or evening game at Kauffman Stadium, affectionately known as "The K." Lush landscaping, fountains, and a crown-topped jumbotron have helped The K consistently rank as one of the country's most beautiful ballparks. A $250 million renovation, completed in 2009, added a new scoreboard, suites, more concessions, two additional dining and lounge options, and more. For an inexpensive night out, head to a Royals game on "buck night" and enjoy peanuts, hot dogs, and small sodas for $1 each.

KANSAS CITY T-BONES

CommunityAmerica Ballpark, 1800 Village West Pkwy., Kansas City, Kansas, 913/328-5618, www.tbonesbaseball.com

COST: Tickets from $6

Overview Map

Lively, promotion-heavy games have made the T-Bones a popular choice for those eager to spend an evening at the ballpark. Kansas City's independent baseball team arrived in

2003, and in 2008 became Northern League Champions. Western Wyandotte County's CommunityAmerica Ballpark is home to the T-Bones, putting gamegoers within walking distance of the shops, bars, and restaurants of Legends at Village West. Parking is free; while you're at the stadium stop by the Meat Locker team store for the latest and greatest in T-Bones apparel and memorabilia.

KANSAS CITY WIZARDS

1800 Village West Pkwy., Kansas City, Kansas, 913/387-3400, http://kc.wizards.mlsnet.com

COST: Tickets from $15

Overview Map

Fiery, fast-paced action is a signature of Kansas City Wizards' games. The local Major League Soccer team delivers tireless performances at CommunityAmerica Ballpark against teams from around the country, encouraged by lively fans including those in the Cauldron, a vocal group of the Wizards' most die-hard supporters. If you plan on attending a game, purchase your tickets before traveling to Kansas City, as they often sell out prior to game day. A new stadium is scheduled to be built in the coming years; check the Wizards' blog, Hillcrest Road (www.hillcrestroadblog.com), for the latest information.

WATER SPORTS AND ACTIVITIES

BLUE SPRINGS LAKE

22807 Woods Chapel Rd., Blue Springs, www.jacksongov.org

HOURS: Beach Fri.-Sun. 11 A.M.-7 P.M.; marina daily 7 A.M.-sunset

COST: Beach admission $5 adult, $3 child/senior

Overview Map

Power boating, water skiing, tubing, and riding personal watercraft are the preferred methods of transportation at Blue Springs Lake, a 720-acre body of water located within Blue Springs' Fleming Park. A sand beach provides a waterfront oasis perfect for lounging, walking, and building sand castles. If you'd prefer to be on the water, stop at Blue Springs Lake's marina for one-day boating licenses, boat rental, fishing tackle, and state fishing licenses. Boat rental fees range $10–45/hour depending on the type of craft.

LAKE JACOMO

7401 West Park Rd., Blue Springs, 816/795-8888, www.jacksongov.org

HOURS: Marina daily 7 A.M.-sunset

Overview Map

Located next to Blue Springs Lake in Fleming Park, Lake Jacomo offers 970 acres of sparkling waters ideal for boating, sailing, windsurfing, and fishing. Visit Lake Jacomo's on-site marina to rent one of 80 available watercraft, including pontoon boats, paddle boats, canoes, and fishing boats. Boat rental fees range $10–45/hour depending on the type of craft. If you'd prefer to sit back and relax, book a spot on the Lake Jacomo cruise tours, which depart at 2 P.M. and 4 P.M. Saturday and Sunday through the summer. Tickets go on sale at noon and are $10 for adults, $5 for children 12 and under. The tour lasts approximately an hour; no pets are allowed.

WALKING TOURS

CROSSROADS DISTRICT WALKING TOUR

1705 Baltimore Ave., www.kccrossroads.org

HOURS: Second Sat. of month, times vary

COST: Varies

Map 2

Past meets present on the Crossroads District walking tour, part of the Second Saturday education and enrichment program. You'll explore the area while learning about the district's history and stop by up-and-coming galleries, studio spaces, and restaurants. Tours are four hours but include artist meet-and-greets, food demonstrations and samplings, and an introductory coffee. Wear comfortable shoes and bring a camera and a bottle of water, although refreshments will be available during the lunch stop. To enroll, email 2ndsaturdays@kccrossroads.org.

GHOST TOURS OF KANSAS

411 N. 6th St., Kansas City, Kansas, 785/383-2925, www.paranormaladventuresusa.com

HOURS: 8 P.M., dates vary

COST: $17.50

Overview Map

Discover the haunted—and historical—side of Kansas City, Kansas, declared by ghost hunters to be the most haunted city in the state. You'll travel by bus to several locations throughout the downtown area, including a cursed cemetery and high school, while knowledgeable tour guides deliver anecdotes detailing the gruesome history found in this mecca for the supernatural. Tours depart from the Ghost Tours' unofficial headquarters, Fat Matt's Vortex, a divey watering hole haunted by a man who committed suicide in one of the booths. Participants must be over 12, and tours are held rain or shine.

HISTORIC KANSAS CITY FOUNDATION

201 Westport Rd., 816/931-8448, www.historickansascity.org

COST: Varies depending on type of tour

Map 3

Led by knowledgeable volunteers of the Historic Kansas City Foundation, numerous walking tours provide an up-close look at the architecture and buildings that shaped the city's history. Choose from Art Deco downtown, 18th and Vine, the Garment District, or Quality Hill, among others, and enjoy informative lectures paired with prime photo opportunities. Founded in 1974, HKCF is the only Greater Kansas City nonprofit corporation dedicated to the preservation of the city's architectural heritage. Additional programming, including slide shows, heritage hikes, and other special events, increase awareness of the city while showcasing the benefits of—and need for—historic preservation.

SHOPS

With an enticing array of locally owned boutiques, specialty shops, and large shopping centers that offer recognizable national names, it's easy to shop your way through Kansas City. You'll find the greatest concentrations of local boutiques and shops in pockets throughout downtown, Westport, and the Plaza; although some may be hard to find, the inviting interiors filled with carefully arranged displays make the journey worthwhile.

To coincide with the city's flourishing arts community, local fashion is becoming more prominent thanks to boutiques like Tomboy that offer custom-made clothing and accessories. If you're in Kansas City in mid-June, check to see if your trip coincides with the brilliantly energetic 18th Street Fashion Show, an annual display of locally created fashion that, in just a few years, has attracted a sizable crowd eager to see the evolution of the city's favorite designers. Smaller fashion shows are held throughout the year to accommodate an increasing number of designers and a greater demand for locally created garments and accessories.

Head outward to the suburban areas and you'll be greeted by a sea of shopping centers and strip malls. Outdoor districts built as walkable mixed-use environments are the current trend; just two indoor shopping malls remain in Kansas City. Most of the shopping

COURTESY OF THE KANSAS CITY CONVENTION AND VISITORS ASSOCIATION

HIGHLIGHTS

LOOK FOR ☾ TO FIND RECOMMENDED SHOPS.

☾ **Best Local Bookstore:** A cozy shop, knowledgeable employees, and some of the city's biggest author events have made **Rainy Day Books** an independent bookselling authority in Kansas City (page 117).

☾ **Best Kids' Store:** From Legos to alligator skulls, **Brookside Toy and Science** has it all – when you manage to tear yourself away, you just might be taking most of the playful inventory with you (page 117).

☾ **Best Lingerie Haven: Birdie's** stocks an impressive array of practical and sexy lingerie and swimwear (page 118).

☾ **Best Picnic Supplies:** Choose from fruits, veggies, bread, local cheese, and wine at the **City Market** and plop down in the adjacent park for a relaxing, sumptuous picnic (page 124).

☾ **Best Home Decor:** Asian antiques and home decor create a luxe, stylish environment within **Black Bamboo** that provides plenty of ideas for redecorating your entire home (page 125).

☾ **Best Local Boutique: Bon Bon Atelier** is the boutique of dreams, artfully stocked with art books, sewing supplies, home accessories, and locally made jewelry, as well as a fabric department that will make you want to spend hours at a sewing machine (page 125).

☾ **Best Candles:** One whiff of **5B & Co. Candle Makers**' happy camper candle and you'll wonder how a scent so realistic can be re-created in a burning pillar of wax (page 126).

☾ **Best Paper Products:** The work of an enterprising Kansas City Art Institute graduate, **Hammerpress** is a paper lover's dream, stocked with cards, concert posters, and prints created on letterpress plates (page 127).

☾ **Best Edible Artwork:** It's hard to eat the exquisite works of art available at **Christopher Elbow Artisanal Chocolates,** but with ingredients like fleur de sel caramel and champagne, resistance is futile (page 132).

☾ **Best Pet Treats:** Stop in at **Three Dog Bakery** for delicious homemade dog and cat treats (page 134).

☾ **Best Local Shops:** Pint-sized fashion boutiques that pack a punch create a cosmopolitan shopping aura along **18th and Wyandotte** that's not to be missed (page 135).

18th and Wyandotte shops

centers average a 20-minute drive from downtown Kansas City and feature a plethora of dining and entertaining options on the premises. Several of the newer developments, billed as destination shopping districts, combine movie theaters, concept restaurants, and other interactive attractions that offer much more than a mere shopping trip.

Antiques

ANTIQUES AND ODDITIES ARCHITECTURAL SALVAGE

2045 Broadway Blvd., 816/283-3740,

www.aoarchitecturalsalvage.com

HOURS: Thurs.-Sat. 10 A.M.-5 P.M.

Map 2

Remnants of Kansas City's rich art deco history live within the nooks and crannies of Antiques and Oddities, an almost overwhelmingly large shop dedicated to found objects and antiques. Pedestal bath tubs, vintage store displays, and art deco wall sconces represent merely a fraction of what you might find while combing through the extensive inventory. Wear comfortable shoes and be prepared to devote an afternoon to exploring—your inner treasure hunter will thank you.

ARTS AND ANTIQUES DISTRICT

45th St. and State Line Rd.

HOURS: Vary

Map 3

Tucked in a mostly residential area, the arts and antiques district is a small yet mighty collection of shops that boasts an impressive array of antiques, home accessories, art, and other luxurious necessities. Businesses include **Christopher Filley** (antique furnishings, accessories, Asian-inspired pieces), **Parrin & Co.** (antiques and collectibles), **Kincaids** (Chinese antiques specialists), **Earl's Court** (antiques and collectibles), **Show-Me Antiques** (antiques and consignment), **Portabello Road** (antiques), and **Morning Glory** (fine European antiques).

RIVER MARKET ANTIQUE MALL

115 W. 5th St., 816/221-0220,

www.rivermarketantiquemall.com

HOURS: Daily 10 A.M.-6 P.M.

Map 1

Pause before you go into the River Market Antique Mall for a photo in front of the 6,000-square-foot Lewis and Clark mural, a visual homage to the area's historic beginning as a Missouri River trading post and a stopping point on the duo's legendary trip west. Once inside, browse antiques and collectible wares from more than 100 dealers spread throughout the mall's four-story 30,000-square-foot interior. With a product range described as "fine to funky," the River Market Antique Mall knows no limits when it comes to satisfying an antiquing urge. The wares may be vintage, but the methods of payment are not—all major credit cards are accepted.

URBAN MINING HOMEWARES

3923 Main St., 816/529-2829,

www.urbanmininghomewares.com

HOURS: First Fri.-Sat. 9 A.M.-6 P.M., Sun. noon-5 P.M.

Map 3

Since it's only open on the weekend of the month's first Friday, a small window of opportunity exists to visit Urban Mining and scour affordable vintage furniture, textiles, accessories, and more offered by more than a dozen hunter-gatherer-artists who comb the city throughout the month, searching for discarded treasure begging for a home. Whether you collect china, doilies, or architecturally salvaged goods, Urban Mining Homewares has the next addition to your collection. If you're worried about forgetting the next sale, email reminders are available through Urban Mining's website. Happy hunting!

WEBSTER HOUSE

1644 Wyandotte St., 816/221-4713,
www.websterhousekc.com

HOURS: Mon.-Tues. 10 A.M.-5 P.M., Wed.-Sat. 10 A.M.-8 P.M.

Map 2

A carefully restored former schoolhouse, Webster House is now a multi-room shop filled with gifts, collectibles, and the Midwest's largest selection of fine antiques. Knowledgeable staff members can help guide your search for the perfect piece, whether a stately example of Georgian walnut or mahogany furniture or pieces constructed from French oaks. Take a break from shopping in Webster House's English country–inspired dining room that serves lunch, happy hour, and dinner complemented by an extensive wine list.

Bath and Beauty

BEAUTY BRANDS

438 Ward Pkwy., 816/753-8822,
www.beautybrands.com

HOURS: Mon.-Sat. 8 A.M.-9 P.M., Sun. 10 A.M.-6 P.M.

Map 3

Owned by prominent local advertising company Bernstein-Rein, Beauty Brands is a hair and beauty mecca that's equal parts salon, spa, and beauty store. Walk-ins are easily accommodated if you find yourself in need of salon or spa services while you're in town. Otherwise, browse the sizable collection of shampoo, conditioner, styling products, and a recently expanded makeup line that includes brands like Too Faced, Philosophy, Smashbox, and more. Beauty Brands frequently hosts popular in-store events like the $6.98 hairspray sale and $12.98 liter sale; check the website for a look at current specials.

DERMADOCTOR

1901 McGee St., 816/472-5700,
www.dermadoctor.com

HOURS: Mon.-Fri. 10 A.M.-5 P.M.

Map 2

You can't miss the impressively large sign that graces the exterior of DERMAdoctor's first flagship store to open in the United States. For skin-care addicts, the cartoon doctor has become a symbol of exemplary skin care, illustrating DERMAdoctor's products that channel the latest in skin-care technology and research to deliver proven results without surgery. Knowledgeable staff members help you pinpoint the products you need, whether you prefer to shop by brand or skin condition. And with an easy-to-navigate online ordering system, you'll be able to quickly replenish your products from outside the Kansas City area.

Books and Music

PROSPERO'S BOOKS

1800 W. 39th St., 816/531-9673,
www.prosperosbookstore.com
HOURS: Call for hours
Map 3

The store's motto is simple: Step away from the box (your television) and opt for a book. With more than 45,000 titles filling two floors, Prospero's is a retreat for bibliophiles. If you're unable to decide on a book (or four), consider purchasing a volume from Prospero's Desert Island Picks, a short list of significant works guaranteed to move readers. Prospero's also sells works from local artists in a variety of media, making the store not just a book lover's dream, but an undeniable contributor to the betterment of local arts and culture.

RAINY DAY BOOKS

2706 W. 53rd St., Fairway, Kansas, 913/384-9209,
www.rainydaybooks.com
HOURS: Mon.-Wed. and Fri. 10 A.M.-6 P.M., Thurs. 10 A.M.-7 P.M., Sat. 10 A.M.-5 P.M.
Map 3

Roger Doeren and Vivian Jennings aren't merely owners of one of Kansas City's favorite independent bookstores. They're veritable literary powerhouses, attracting nationally acclaimed authors and espousing their industry opinions in publications including the *New York Times.* Once inside the store's cozy interior, you'll find shelves packed with fiction, non-fiction, children's, and other genres. Friendly yet non-intrusive staff are eager to help and share their favorites, which also appear on the store's website.

SPIVEY'S BOOKS

825 Westport Rd., 816/753-0520,
www.spiveysbooks.com
HOURS: Mon.-Sat. 10 A.M.-4 P.M., Sun. noon-4 P.M.
Map 3

Spivey's reeks of history, thanks to a celebrated assortment of rare books, maps, and fine art. Inhale the scent of old books as you gaze at a selection of true literary treasures, including a six-volume original bound set of *Don Juan* or a first American edition leather-bound copy of Mark Twain's *Life on the Mississippi.* Spivey's selection of historic maps dates back to the late 1700s, offering evocative illustrations of cities, states, and countries.

Children's Stores

BROOKSIDE TOY AND SCIENCE

330 W. 63rd St., 816/523-4501,
www.brooksidetoyandscience.com
HOURS: Mon.-Fri. 10 A.M.-6 P.M., Sat. 10 A.M.-5 P.M., Sun. noon-4 P.M.
Map 4

Teeming with curiosities and toys designed to spark any child's imagination, Brookside Toy and Science is consistently rated best Kansas City toy store by its visitors. Browse Lego and Erector sets, Lincoln Logs, curiosity kits, and railroad toys from Thomas & Friends. Brookside Toy and Science also stocks an impressive collection of science fair supplies and materials with which to start bug and butterfly collections, the perfect gifts for your little Einstein. Beware creepy stuff like skeletons, alligator heads, and toad purses!

READING REPTILE

328 W. 63rd St., 816/753-0441, www.readingreptile.com

HOURS: Mon.-Fri. 10 A.M.-6 P.M., Sat. 10 A.M.-5 P.M., Sun. noon-5 P.M.

Map 4

The Reading Reptile could easily become a second home for any young bookworm. This quirky children's bookstore stocks an impressive array of picture, fiction, and educational books, even in foreign languages. The shop hosts weekly story hours, and while your kids explore you can browse the small treasure troves of adult books located around the store (be sure to check near the register), including past volumes of *McSweeney's Quarterly Concern.*

Clothing, Shoes, and Accessories

BIRDIE'S

116 W. 18th St., 816/842-2473, www.birdiespanties.com

HOURS: Tues.-Sat. noon-7 P.M.

Map 2

Dedicated to the fine art of lingerie, Birdie's is a tiny yet well-stocked store that features an array of silky, sophisticated undergarments and swimwear created by local and national designers. Owner Peregrine Honig is an expert at on-the-spot recommendations if you're not sure what to choose. If you'd like a less expensive alternative to some of the boutique's pricier pieces, try a pair of Birdie's signature panties with various designs hand-screened onto American Apparel briefs and bikinis.

BUNKER

4056 Broadway St., 816/561-7407, www.thebunkeronline.com

HOURS: Mon.-Sat. 11 A.M.-7:30 P.M., Sun. noon-6 P.M.

Map 3

Although it stocks several stylish apparel brands, Bunker is particularly known for its impressive inventory of eyewear and accessories. Browse watches from Paul Frank and Harajuku Lovers, or shield your eyes with a chic pair of sunglasses from Original Penguin.

KATE SPADE'S HANDBAG LEGACY

Her chicly streamlined bags have become instantly recognizable in the fashion world, but what you may not know is that Kate Spade grew up in Kansas City. Her father owned a construction company that created many of the city's roads and bridges, and after she graduated high school, Kate moved out of Kansas City to pursue a career in fashion. She started as accessories editor at *Mademoiselle* magazine, and after being decidedly unsatisfied with a season's handbags, she decided to take matters into her own hands – literally.

She founded Kate Spade in 1993 with her husband, Andy, and created six prototypes from pieces of white drawing paper and Scotch tape. Her eye for detail and proportion shone through, and now Kate sees tens of millions of dollars in annual sales from a company that's expanded to shoes, accessories, stationery, home decor, and men's accessories under the label Jack Spade.

Although there's not yet an exclusive Kate Spade boutique in Kansas City, **Halls Plaza** carries an extensive collection of Kate's bags and wallets. Surely her hometown isn't far from her mind – go to www.katespade.info and you'll find clocks that display three times: Paris, New York City, and Kansas City.

Or try on jackets from BB Dakota or Nixon bags, belts, beanies, and sleek headphones available in several styles and models. Goggles, shoes, and prescription eyewear round out the store's inventory, much of which is also available online.

DONNA'S DRESS SHOP

1415 W. 39th St., 816/931-0022,
www.donnasdressshop.com

HOURS: Mon.-Sat. 11 A.M.-7 P.M., Sun. noon-5 P.M.

Map 3

Led by an owner who was trained in the art of vintage and flea market shopping at an early age, Donna's Dress Shop is a local favorite for vintage clothing and accessories. Thanks to a much-needed expansion in 2009, Donna's Dress Shop continues its commitment to stocking classic vintage pieces with a focus on timeless style as opposed to too-trendy clothing that's quickly discarded. Clothing and accessories are added weekly, so stop by often to browse the latest finds. Although limited sizes are available in each piece of clothing, it's Donna's philosophy that you also won't find yourself wearing the same thing as dozens of other people—and individuality is about as timeless as well-made vintage attire.

HABITAT SHOE BOUTIQUE

4569 W. 119th St., Leawood, Kansas, 913/451-6360,
www.habitatshoes.com

HOURS: Mon.-Sat. 10 A.M.-9 P.M., Sun. noon-6 P.M.

Overview Map

If you're shopping for shoes in Kansas City, look no further than Habitat. Within the boutique's streamlined, contemporary interior you'll find instantly recognizable brands like Puma and Timberland, but you also may discover a lesser-known but just as stylish brand such as Rachel Comey, Chie Mihara, or Coclico. Habitat stocks footwear for men, women, and kids, as well as a small yet stylish array of accessories and jewelry to complete your ensemble. Be prepared to plan an exciting evening out once you've purchased a pair of Habitat shoes; footwear this fabulous deserves a night on the town as soon as possible.

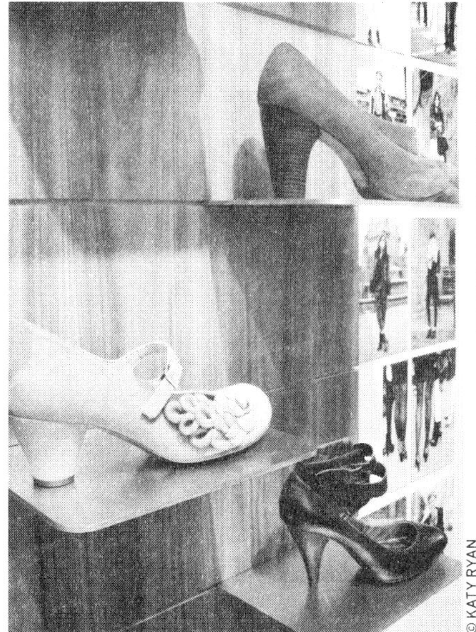

© KATY RYAN

Browse a trendy selection of shoes, boots, apparel, and accessories at Habitat Shoe Boutique.

HEMLINE

610 W. 48th St., 816/753-0150,
www.shophemline.com

HOURS: Mon.-Sat. 10 A.M.-7 P.M., Sun. noon-5 P.M.

Map 3

With more than 200 lines of clothing, shoes, and accessories, Hemline is a shopaholic's dream. Women flock to Hemline for the latest apparel trends, including both casual and formal styles. Owned by three sisters eager to help shoppers select the perfect outfit, Hemline raises the bar for personable, memorable shopping experiences. Designers include Free People, Theme, Seychelles, and Report, and the inventory changes regularly to reflect upcoming trends and newly released styles.

MICHAEL'S FINE CLOTHING FOR MEN

1830 Main St., 816/221-0000

HOURS: Mon.-Sat. 9:30 A.M.-5:30 P.M.

Map 2

For more than a century, Michael's has outfitted Kansas City men with stylish, tailored clothes. Stocked with a range of suits, business wear, and casual clothing as well as accessories, Michael's specializes in individualized service. Sizes 36–60 are available, as are a variety of fits in regular, tall, extra tall, short, extra short, and athlete. Out-of-town visitors can take advantage of Michael's immediate alteration services, ensuring you'll leave Kansas City with new clothes that fit perfectly. Brands include Burberry, Cole Haan, Tommy Bahama, Stetson, Ike Behar, and more. And if you're in the area for First Fridays, Michael's stays open until 8 P.M.

MITZY LONDON'S

4541 W. 119th St., Leawood, Kansas, 913/661-1775, www.mitzylondons.com

HOURS: Mon.-Fri. 10 A.M.-8 P.M., Sat. 10 A.M.-7 P.M., Sun. 11 A.M.-6 P.M.

Overview Map

Forget the adorable apparel and accessories within Mitzy London's—the pink and black interior serves as an eye-catching backdrop for this lifestyle boutique that carries a mix of vintage and modern fashions. Think ballet flats, party dresses, handbags, and jewelry that add a bit of stylish flair to any outfit. You'll also find a small yet chic selection of home accessories within Mitzy London's, the perfect way to inject a bit of British glamour into your residence. Visit the first Saturday of the month and join fellow shoppers for the Fashionista High Tea, a full British tea service complete with sandwiches, scones, and sweets.

PEGGY NOLAND

124 W. 18th St., 816/221-7652, www.peggynoland.com

HOURS: Tues.-Sat. noon-7 P.M.

Map 2

Step inside Peggy Noland's pint-sized boutique and enter a world of whimsical, sometimes crazy, fashion and accessories created by Noland, a nationally renowned fashion designer. Recent hits include low-crotch leggings and bodysuits—in other words, fashion for those not faint at heart! Noland regularly switches up her store's decor to better showcase her latest pieces, such as floor-to-ceiling cotton clouds that make you feel like you're inside a giant cone of cotton candy. Noland's off-beat style has attracted several musical followers including Lovefoxxx, VIP Party Boys, and Tilly and the Wall.

PERUVIAN CONNECTION

1803 Wyandotte St., 816/221-2163, www.peruvianconnection.com

HOURS: Mon.-Sat. 10 A.M.-6 P.M.

Map 2

Peruvian Connection began as a mail-order business in Tonganoxie, Kansas, a small town about 35 minutes from Kansas City. Thanks to continued popularity of Peruvian Connection's signature woven sweaters, tops, and other brightly colored clothing inspired by Peruvian textiles, several stores have opened throughout the United States, including one in Kansas City's Crossroads District. Look for jackets in exquisitely soft yet sturdy materials like alpaca, or scarves woven from delicate pima cotton.

Peruvian Connection also stocks jewelry and home decor, and the brightly lit well-arranged store is a pleasure to browse even if you can manage to bypass shelf after shelf of tempting wares.

SEDUZIONE LEGGS

1911 McGee St., 816/221-0153, www.seduzioneleggs.com

HOURS: Wed.-Sat. 10:30 A.M.-5:30 P.M.

Map 2

Co-owner Lisa Goshon describes Seduzione Leggs, a designer hosiery and leggings boutique, as the first of its kind in the United States. Designers include Sisi, Girardi, Just My Size, and Pretty Polly, among others, creating an inventory that spans from funky to downright saucy in materials like silk, cotton, and soft wool. Goshon also stocks a range of fashion-forward jewelry hand-selected from New York City's Fashion District, making Seduzione an essential accessories stop as you shop Kansas City.

SOHO 119

4419 W. 119th St., Leawood, Kansas, 913/338-5800, www.soho-119.com

HOURS: Mon.-Sat. 11 A.M.-8 P.M., Sun. noon-5 P.M.

Overview Map

Contemporary music, designer brands, and attentive service make a trip to SoHo 119 a shopping experience complete with a look at the latest fashion trends as found in New York and L.A. From men's and women's apparel to sleek, structured handbags and accessories, SoHo 119 stocks a complete range of high-fashion apparel. To complete the experience, a restaurant and vinotherapy medspa await in the back of the boutique, ready to serve deliciously prepared meals or a menu of pampering services to ease away the fatigue of the day.

SPAGHETTI WESTERN

112 Main St., Parkville, 816/442-7749

HOURS: Tues.-Sat. 10 A.M.-6 P.M.

Map 5

Outfit your inner cowgirl with a full stock of vintage ranchwear including boots, hats, and jewelry against a warm backdrop of bright red walls. Worn-in leathers are buttery soft, the perfect complement to a pair of frayed jeans. Spaghetti Western also stocks music, art, kid's stuff, and collectibles, making this a one-stop shop while you're touring scenic downtown Parkville. While you're at Spaghetti Western, pick up one of their signature ringer tees emblazoned with the shop's logo.

SPOOL

122 W. 18th St., 816/842-0028

HOURS: Tues.-Fri. noon-7 P.M.

Map 2

Don't be fooled by Spool's tiny interior. The boutique, voted by *Pitch Weekly* readers in 2008 as the "Best Alternative to Urban Outfitters," stocks a surprisingly large array of locally designed T-shirts, as well as apparel, accessories, handbags, wallets, and more by designers from throughout the United States, as well as right here in Kansas City. Spool also stocks a select variety of body products and candles.

STANDARD STYLE BOUTIQUE

451 W. 47th St., 913/312-1097, www.standardstyle.com

HOURS: Mon.-Sat. 10 A.M.-7 P.M., Thurs. 10 A.M.-9 P.M., Sun. noon-6 P.M.

Map 3

The brainchild of married couple Matt and Emily Baldwin, Standard Style has quickly earned a reputation as the city's go-to boutique for men's and women's fashion, including an extensive denim bar. Marc by Marc Jacobs, 3.1 Phillip Lim, Ever, and Citizens of

Humanity comprise a partial roll call of the boutique's featured designers. After moving to Kansas City from the West Coast, Matt and Emily fulfilled their dream to open a one-stop destination that's a true shopping experience. For help navigating Standard Style's extensive inventory, personal shoppers are ready and willing to consult on the season's must-have apparel and accessories, available at a variety of price points.

TIVOL

220 Nichols Rd., 816/531-5800, www.tivol.com

HOURS: Mon.-Wed. and Fri.-Sat. 10 A.M.-5:30 P.M., Thurs. 10 A.M.-8 P.M.

Map 3

What started as a small downtown jewelry shop opened in 1910 by immigrant Charles Tivol has grown into one of Kansas City's favorite jewelry and watch boutiques. The name Tivol has become synonymous with quality, thanks to the dedication and attention paid to each piece and the exquisite work of designers who continue to produce elegant timepieces and jewelry. Brands like Cartier, David Yurman, Patek Philippe, and Tag Heuer have made Tivol's timepiece collection unmatched throughout the city, while jewelry designers like David Yurman, Judith Ripka, Mikimoto, and Scott Kay signify the jeweled elegance found within Tivol's subtly illuminated display cases.

TOMBOY

1817 McGee St., 816/472-6200, www.tomboydesign.net

HOURS: Tues.-Sat. 10 A.M.-6 P.M.

Map 2

Inventory tends to be on the more selective side at Tomboy because owner Laura McGrew and her employees focus on custom-made women's clothes. Whether you're searching for a pair of perfectly fitted jeans or something more elaborate like a business suit or gown, Tomboy's expert seamstresses use the finest fabrics and supplies to create one-of-a-kind garments. Tomboy does offer seasonal apparel in-store, but be aware that pieces may only be available in a handful of sizes. Take home a silky Tomboy logo T-shirt as a memento, or browse accessories for the latest in scarves, pins, and more.

Crafts and Collectibles

MISKNITS YARN SHOP

3904 Terrace St., 816/531-5809, www.misknits.com

HOURS: Tues. 11 A.M.-7 P.M., Wed. 11 A.M.-9 P.M., Thurs.-Sat. 11 A.M.-7 P.M.

Map 3

Described as "a curious little yarn shop," hip and well-stocked MisKnits has the supplies for you, whether you knit or crochet, all neatly stocked against the store's soothing purple walls. MisKnits also offers several cozy sitting spots, perfect if you'd like to plop down and start work on your latest project in the company of other yarnaholics. MisKnits stocks a small inventory of apparel and accessories graced with the store's inventive logo, from T-shirts and slip-ons to roomy totes perfect for carting projects around town.

POPTOPIA

4126 Pennsylvania Ave., 816/931-9800, www.poptopia-online.com

HOURS: Tues.-Sat. 11 A.M.-7 P.M., Sun. noon-5 P.M.

Map 3

After browsing Poptopia's bright, cheerful

© KATY RYAN

Handmade jewelry is among many of the DIY goods stocked at Urban Arts + Crafts.

interior, you may find yourself reverting to your childhood and buying every collectible toy in sight. Described as "urban vinyl paradise," Poptopia stocks a wide range of collectible toys including Munny, Domo, Kaiju Kidz, and more. In addition you'll find a small but eclectic mix of art magazines and graphic novels, as well as a selection of Poptopia logo T-shirts that definitely put the "chic" in "geek chic." If your toy tastes run a little more old-school, try one of Poptopia's 3-D wooden models in designs like black widow spider, bulldozer, and carousel.

URBAN ARTS + CRAFTS

4157 N. Mulberry Dr., 816/234-1004, www.urbanartsandcrafts.com

HOURS: Mon.-Wed. 10 A.M.-6 P.M., Thurs. 10 A.M.-8 P.M., Fri.-Sat. 10 A.M.-6 P.M., Sun. noon-5 P.M.

Map 5

If you fancy yourself an artist, a crafter, or simply like to spend time around pretty things, a visit to UA+C is a must while you're in Kansas City. The carefully stocked crafts store isn't your grandmother's; instead you'll find delicate papers and embellishments for book-making, an extensive jewelry and beading section, vibrantly hued cardstock that screams to be transformed into stationery, and a yarn section filled with plush, colorful yarns eager to be made into scarves or socks. An ever-expanding fabric line stocks Amy Butler's easily recognizable graphic prints, as well as fabrics from other designers. Patterns, notions, and how-to books round out the store, which also hosts seasonal crafting classes for beginners and advanced creators alike.

Farmers Markets

CITY MARKET

20 E. 5th St., 816/842-1271, www.thecitymarket.org

HOURS: Vary throughout the year

Map 1

Whether you crave the crisp flavor of fresh produce or simply want to immerse yourself in local culture, a weekend visit to City Market is a must. Celebrated as one of the region's largest (and most enduring) farmers markets, City Market offers shoppers a vibrant mix of produce, baked goods, and crafts from local farmers and artisans, as well as an alluring array of more than 30 full-time, year-round merchants that hock specialty foods, spices, gifts, and more. During spring and summer months, the historic market (which dates back to 1857) offers numerous events, including kid-friendly petting zoos, cooking demonstrations, and in-depth seminars that educate attendees about in-season produce, as well as concerts from local, regional, and national acts. Arrive early, bring cash and plastic or reusable bags, and pick up ingredients for a picnic lunch—a picturesque park just behind City Market provides a lush respite amid the heart of downtown's scenic River Market neighborhood.

DOWNTOWN OVERLAND PARK FARMERS MARKET

Marty Ave. btwn. 79th and 80th Sts., Overland Park, Kansas, 913/642-2222, www.downtownop.org/farmers_market

HOURS: Mid-Apr.-Oct. Wed. 7:30 A.M.-sell-out, Sat. 6:30 A.M.-sell-out

Overview Map

If you plan to spend time exploring Johnson County, start your day at the Downtown Overland Park Farmers Market, an open-air market located on the streets of Overland Park's historic downtown area. Local growers offer a tempting selection of pies, pasta, bread, and other specialty food items, in addition to freshly grown produce and herbs. After you've shopped, take a seat for the Clock Tower Series (Sat. 10:30 A.M.–12:30 P.M.), a weekly concert session that's ideal for the entire family.

FARMERS COMMUNITY MARKET AT BROOKSIDE

63rd St. and Wornall Rd., www.farmerscommunitymarket.com

HOURS: Apr.-Oct. Sat. 8 A.M.-1 P.M.

Map 4

Local and certified organic farmers gather on Saturdays to present a tantalizing array of fresh produce and herbs. You'll also find organic freshly prepared food, fair-trade coffee, baked goods, and organic hand-crafted soap. Several tables are scattered around the market, perfect for an impromptu breakfast or early lunch. The Farmers Community Market hosts several events throughout the season, including herb, flower, tomato, and fall festivals. You'll also find live music, children's activities, and cooking demonstrations, making the Farmers Community Market a perfect way to start your Saturday.

Gift and Home

ACME BICYCLE COMPANY

412 E. 18th St., 816/221-2045,
www.acmebicyclecompany.com
HOURS: Tues.-Wed. and Fri. 11 A.M.-6 P.M.,
Thurs. noon-7 P.M., Sat. 10 A.M.-3 P.M.
Map 2

Bicycle enthusiasts, meet your nirvana. Acme Bicycle Company specializes in custom frames, as well as a complete range of cycling accessories to ensure you're road-ready. Acme is also a great spot for bicycle repairs, and stocks one of the largest selections of used bikes and parts in the city. The shop specializes in urban bikes, perfect for tooling around the streets of downtown and outfitted with baskets if you'd prefer to do your grocery—or other shopping—on two wheels.

ART FLEA KC

1522 Holmes St., 816/461-0201,
www.artflea.blogspot.com
HOURS: Sat. 10 A.M.-5 P.M.
Map 2

Throughout the week, ArtsTech is a spacious gallery that displays the latest and greatest in local art. On Saturdays, however, the space transforms into one of Kansas City's best weekly flea markets bursting with local art, handmade items, and vintage collectibles priced from $1 to $50. Wares are neatly stacked along tables and in bins, and you may have to dig to find what you're after. The low prices and eclectic items make it a worthwhile experience, however, and inventory changes weekly. Look for hand-knitted goods, fragrant cakes of handmade soaps, glassware, clothing, journals—you name it, Art Flea's probably got it.

BLACK BAMBOO

1815 Wyandotte St., 816/283-3000,
www.black-bamboo.com
HOURS: Tues.-Fri. 10 A.M.-6 P.M., Sat. 10 A.M.-5 P.M.
Map 2

Owner Timothy Butt travels to China annually and returns with Asian antiques and home accessories that have made his boutique a true home decor retreat within the Crossroads District. Clean, modern lines complemented by ornate trim and details make Black Bamboo pieces one-of-a-kind finds, whether you're shopping for a piece of furniture or are in need of some colorful vases to accent an end table. If you find yourself headed to Asia in the near future, visit Black Bamboo's website for Tim's travel tips.

BON BON ATELIER

314 Westport Rd., 816/756-0855,
www.bonbonatelier.com
HOURS: Mon.-Sat. 10 A.M.-6 P.M.
Map 3

Bon Bon Atelier isn't so much an arts and crafts store as it is a boutique for those who simply covet style. A carefully selected assortment of photography, craft, and other books mingles with decorative paper, cards, and sewing notions. Colorfully patterned fabrics beg to be transformed into a bag, skirt or apron, and if you're in a guessing mood, pick up one of Bon Bon's grab bags. A brown paper bag conceals a mix of fabric, yarn, and other remnants that add a whimsical finishing touch to your own project. Sisters and co-owners Sheila Blodgett and Emily Blodgett-Panos have a knack for creating store displays that are simultaneously homey and stylish. Both are also crafters, and sell their handmade goods in-store.

© KATY RYAN

Bon Bon Atelier is filled with crafting supplies, handmade goods, and other must-have curiosities.

ECLECTIC LEOPARD

400 Grand Blvd., Ste. 412, 816/739-8547, www.eclecticleopard.com

HOURS: Wed.-Fri. 10 A.M.-4 P.M., Sat. 9 A.M.-4 P.M., Sun. 10 A.M.-4 P.M.

Map 1

Think of Eclectic Leopard as a garage sale—a hip, funky garage sale in which you find treasures like old furniture, collectible glassware, and decorative bowling balls adorned with costume jewelry and bottle caps. Owner M. J. George opened the shop in 2009 when, after the death of her husband, she decided to begin selling a lifetime's accumulation of furniture and collectibles. And although you may not find much leopard-themed merchandise within the store, you will find plenty of leopard-inspired decor that fits perfectly with the store's name.

FENG

5029 W. 119th St., Overland Park, Kansas, 913/498-0530, www.fenglookeast.com

HOURS: Mon.-Sat. 10 A.M.-6 P.M.

Overview Map

East meets West within the calming interior of Feng, an Asian lifestyle boutique that offers a pleasing mix of Asian-inspired home decor and accessories alongside cutting-edge Asian fashions from designers like Chan Luu, Anna Sui, Richard Chai, and Alice Roi. Silky scarves, delicately made dresses, and exquisitely embroidered handbags imbibe a touch of Asian flair into any wardrobe. Feng also features a jewelry collection and a wide range of Asian teas, perfect for bringing a bit of Asian flavor into your home.

THE FIDDLY FIG FLORIST

22 W. 63rd St., 816/363-4313, www.fiddlyfig.com

HOURS: Mon. and Sat. 9 A.M.-5:30 P.M., Tues.-Fri. 9 A.M.-7 P.M.

Map 4

For more than three decades, The Fiddly Fig Florist has been a local go-to destination for exquisite floral arrangements, gift baskets, and assorted gifts that range from fragrant Voluspa candles to Missouri-made Hot Fresco Pottery. If you find the perfect bouquet for a friend or family member back home, don't fret—The Fiddly Fig ships worldwide and even includes suggestions for prolonged plant care on its website.

5B & CO. CANDLE MAKERS

6231 Brookside Plaza, 816/361-6393, www.5bandco.com

HOURS: Mon.-Fri. 10 A.M.-6 P.M., Sat. 10 A.M.-5 P.M., Sun. noon-5 P.M.

Map 4

The intoxicating scent of 5B & Co.'s hand-poured candles hits as soon as you walk through the shop door. A soy/paraffin base ensures ultimate scent distribution and a clean burn, two important qualities in candle quality. You'll be amazed at the array of scents available and how realistic they are, like happy camper, which smells like a campfire. To satisfy an olfactory craving, try the burnt sugar, a tantalizing blend of oatmeal and maple. Various sizes, including tealights and votives, are available, as are candle accessories and decorative accents.

GALLUP MAP COMPANY

1733 Main St., 816/842-1994,
www.gallupmaps.com
HOURS: Mon.-Fri. 9 A.M.-5 P.M.
Map 2

Forget MapQuest and Google Maps and head to Gallup Map Company to browse print maps in their original artistic glory. The 120-year-old company specializes in a variety of regional and national maps, atlases, globes, and software to meet all of your mapping needs. If you're in the mood to splurge on a true cartographic statement, purchase a $295 84-inch-by-84-inch map of Kansas City, complete with an accompanying atlas, for a one-of-a-kind trip memento.

GEORGE

315 E. 55th St., 816/361-2128,
www.georgelifestyle.com
HOURS: Mon.-Sat. 10 A.M.-5 P.M.
Map 4

Simply described as "a lifestyle shop," George is so much more. Expertly arranged home decor items mingle with timeless handmade leather bags, art books, and cashmere throws in vignettes so stylish they seem as if every item has its exact place within the boutique's calm, chic interior. At George you'll also find a select supply of bath products, exquisite place settings, and all of the luxe touches you need to make your home a palace.

GOOD JUJU

1412 W. 12th St., 816/421-1930,
www.goodjujukc.com
HOURS: Fri. 9 A.M.-9 P.M., Sat. 9 A.M.-5 P.M., Sun. noon-4 P.M.
Map 1

You won't need a healthy dollop of "good juju" as much as really good timing to browse the second-hand treasures of this salvage boutique. Open only the first weekend of the month, Good JuJu is home to artisans, second-hand dealers, and collectors who gather together to present a month's worth of finds, creations, and other repurposed items. Owner Trish Moore created Good JuJu to reflect her own expansive decorating style. Each month, Good JuJu spotlights a local artist, heaping emphasis not only on the value of repurposed finds, but the merits of those who create them.

HAMMERPRESS

110 Southwest Blvd., 816/421-1929,
www.hammerpress.net
HOURS: Tues.-Fri. 10 A.M.-5:30 P.M., Sat. noon-5 P.M.
Map 2

Worship the intricate art of letterpress printing at Hammerpress, created by Kansas City Art Institute graduate Brady Vest. Take home stationery, art prints, and posters all graced with letterpress-created type and designs that reflect a truly distinctive design aesthetic that's appeared in a variety of press outlets, including the book *1,000 Music Graphics: A Compilation of Packaging, Posters, and Other Sound Solutions.* If you'd prefer to wear your love for Hammerpress on your sleeve, pick up one of the shop's screen-printed unisex T-shirts.

HUDSON HOME

1500 Grand Blvd., Ste. 2, 816/421-3629,
www.hudsonhomeonline.com

HOURS: Wed.-Sat. 11 A.M.-5:30 P.M.

Map 2

Modern home furnishings and accessories comprise the inventory within Hudson Home's sprawling 4,000-square-foot showroom. BluDot, Knoll Space, and Urban Farm are a small sampling of contemporary brands available at Hudson Home, which relocated to a second-floor space above Retro Inferno in 2007 in order to take advantage of increased foot traffic in the surrounding the Power and Light District. If your trip doesn't coincide with Hudson Home's business hours, call and schedule an appointment to view the in-store collection and wealth of trade binders.

J DESIGN

1803 Baltimore Ave., 913/269-0470,
www.360kc.com/Shopping/Furniture/JDesign

HOURS: Tues.-Sat. 11 A.M.-6 P.M.

Map 2

The tranquil surroundings of J Design envelop you as soon as you walk in. It's a multisensory experience made possible by the gentle tinkling of indoor waterfalls, the soft lighting from several of J Design's light fixtures, and the fresh, addictive scent of La Cucina kitchen and body products. Look past the accessories, and it's easy to see that J Design stocks an impressively stylish array of furniture suitable for a modern loft, condominium, or traditionally built home. Nestled among the furniture are carefully arranged vignettes of gifts, eco-friendly products, and pieces of local art that J Design's owner personally selects to display in-store.

THE KNOTTY RUG CO.

4510 State Line Rd., Kansas City, Kansas, 913/677-1877,
www.knottyrug.com

HOURS: Tues.-Sat. 10 A.M.-5 P.M.

Map 3

The Knotty Rug Co. is best known in Kansas City for two things: an unmatched selection of rugs, and cheeky advertisements that run slogans like "Does your rug match your drapes?" and "I love it when you walk all over me." If you're searching for a new floor covering or simply want to browse their impressive selection, wander through the sizable showroom stacked with rugs in various patterns, colors, and textures, all of which are Persian hand-knotted rugs. The Knotty Rug Co. also stocks a selection of furnishings, accessories, art, and pillows, the perfect complement to your new rug.

NELL HILL'S

4101 N. Mulberry Dr., 816/746-4320,
www.nellhills.com

HOURS: Mon.-Sat. 10 A.M.-6 P.M., Sun. noon-5 P.M.

Map 5

Owner Mary Carol Garrity opened Nell Hill's home interiors store in Atchison, a boutique that became so popular she has since expanded to Kansas City's Briarcliff Village. Inside the sprawling interior you'll find home furnishings and accessories, each chosen with Garrity's impeccable eye to style and detail. She changes the decor seasonally in order to provide tablescape and other decorative ideas to shoppers eager to bring a touch of luxury and beauty into their own homes. Check the store's online calendar before you go; Nell Hill's often hosts special events including sales, open houses, and philanthropic gatherings throughout the year.

THE ORCHIDLOFT

1803 Wyandotte St., Ste. 105, 816/225-7900,
www.orchidloft.com

HOURS: Fri.-Sat. 1-7 P.M.

Map 2

Exquisite orchids are the focus of the aptly named Orchidloft, a floral sanctuary that specializes in orchids and urban gardening products. Choose from a spellbinding selection of blooms available in a delicate wash of colors, from milky white to petal pink and a mix of hues in between. If you live nearby, enroll in Orchidloft's Exchange Program in which you take home a plant and later exchange it as many times as you like. Monthly charges are dependent on the number of plants and range from $15–40.

THE PLANTERS SEED AND SPICE COMPANY

513 Walnut St., Ste. A, 816/842-3651,
www.plantersseed.com

HOURS: Mon.-Fri. 7 A.M.-6 P.M., Sat. 7 A.M.-5 P.M.

Map 1

Walk through the doors of The Planters Seed and Spice Company and you're met with an oversized high-ceilinged room filled with gardening paraphernalia and a mouthwatering bulk spice section. Turn to your right or left, however, and the realization hits that The Planters stretches through two additional rooms on each side, creating a creaky-floored mecca of gardening, planting, and lawn supplies. The Planters also stocks totes, decorative accessories, and a full range of Mrs. Meyer's cleaning supplies. Your nose will guide you through the store's spice section, which offers a wide range of bulk spices as well as rubs, powdered dressing mixes, and popcorn seasoning. Because most spices are priced around $2 for a hefty bag, you may just find yourself with a sack full of aromatic souvenirs that will add a dash of Kansas City flavor to your home-cooked meals.

RETRO INFERNO

1500 Grand Blvd., 816/842-4004,
www.retroinferno.com

HOURS: Mon.-Sat. 11 A.M.-6 P.M.

Map 2

As the name implies, Retro Inferno is a collection of retro-inspired furniture, accessories, and collectibles that channel some of the most recognizable and colorful periods in interior design history. Vibrant pieces of art glass are clustered atop tables like a coveted Charles and Ray Eames design. Seating, lighting, storage, and objects round out the store's eclectic mix, creating an inventory that's time-consuming, yet worthwhile, to explore.

SILK ROAD TRAVELERS

500 Delaware St., 816/241-2211,
www.silkroadtravelers.com

HOURS: Tues.-Fri. 9 A.M.-5:30 P.M., Sat. 9 A.M.-3:30 P.M., Sun. 9 A.M.-3 P.M.; winter Wed.-Fri. 10:30 A.M.-6 P.M., Sat.-Sun. 10 A.M.-3:30 P.M.

Map 1

Several times each year, Pamela Johnson and Robert Eppes travel to China to explore and shop. They return with antiques, jewelry, and accessories that find a home within the tranquil environment of Silk Road until a lucky customer seizes the opportunity to own a piece steeped in Asian history and culture. From ornately carved chests to vibrantly colored freshwater pearls, Silk Road specializes in the stylish, the rare, and the truly remarkable. And even if you leave Silk Road without a purchase, you'll know you have friends in Kansas City, eagerly awaiting your return.

STUDIO DAN MEINERS

1700 Wyandotte St., 816/842-7244,
www.danmeiners.com

HOURS: Mon.-Fri. 10 A.M.-5 P.M.

Map 2

Shopping for floral arrangements while on vacation may not be the most practical decision, but the incredibly stylish designs at Studio Dan Meiners are worth at least a peek. Meiners has quickly earned a reputation as Kansas City's go-to florist, whether for special events, weddings, or simply a beautiful pick-me-up. Studio Dan Meiners offers local and national delivery, and can create a customized floral arrangement depending on your specifications and budget. If you could truly speak through the language of flowers, those who use Studio Dan Meiners would never be at a loss for words.

STUFF

316 W. 63rd St., 816/361-8222,
www.pursuegoodstuff.com

HOURS: Mon.-Sat. 10 A.M.-6 P.M., Sun. noon-5 P.M.

Map 4

This eclectic boutique is packed full of, well, stuff, but a carefully chosen conglomeration of local artisan goods, body products, stationery, jewelry, and quirky art like painted switchplates, found art sculptures, and vibrant wall hangings. Sisters (and co-owners) Casey and Sloane Simmons carefully research each in-store item so that they know how and when it was created. Stuff also hosts classes, trunk shows, and other special events designed to highlight the surrounding creative community and uncover the beauty of the stuff that's all around us.

URBAN DWELLINGS DESIGN

412 Delaware St., Ste. 101, 816/569-4313,
www.urbandwellingsdesign.com

HOURS: Mon. 11 A.M.-5 P.M., Tues.-Fri. 10 A.M.-6 P.M., Sat. 10 A.M.-5 P.M.

Map 1

Within the relaxed, welcoming interior of Urban Dwellings Design are all the ingredients for a chic, stylish home, complete with furniture from Mitchell Gold + Bob Williams and Oly Studio, among others, as well as accessories and decorative touches. Take home a tube of decorative scented drawer liners, or one of the pungent soy candles that shop owners say fill the room with fragrance even when unlit. Urban Dwellings Design also hosts special events and participates in the Wine Walk on Delaware, held the third Saturday of the month from May to October. Before you go, check the shop's website and blog for an up-to-date event schedule.

Local Flavor

Take home the tastes of Kansas City, from cheese and savories to handmade chocolates and other confections. Many local barbecue restaurants sell sauces, rubs, and other gifts, and at brewpubs like McCoy's Public House you can take home a growler of beer or root beer.

ANDRE'S CONFISERIE SUISSE

5018 Main St., 816/561-6484, www.andreschocolates.com

HOURS: Tues.-Fri. 8:30 A.M.-5:30 P.M., Sat. 8 A.M.-5 P.M.

Map 3

After Andre and Elsbeth Bollier emigrated to Kansas City from Switzerland in 1955, they opened Andre's Confiserie Suisse, which has since been a local go-to for rich, handmade chocolates, cookies, tortes, wedding cakes, and sinfully delicious seasonal favorites. Stop in for a gourmet lunch at Andre's Tearoom, 11 A.M.–2:30 P.M., but be sure to save room for dessert. Online ordering is available if you find you can't live without Andre's once you leave Kansas City. And you won't be alone—Andre's ships chocolates worldwide.

BADSEED

1909 McGee St., 816/472-0027, www.badseedfarm.com

HOURS: May 1-Nov. 20 Fri. 4:30-9 P.M.

Map 2

At what may be Kansas City's only night-time farmer's market, BADSEED offers colorful produce and other locally and sustainably grown

MUST-HAVE SOUVENIRS

You'll find no shortage of shopping in Kansas City, but while you're exploring the best the city's retailers have to offer, you may want to pick up a few of these must-have souvenirs. Keep them for yourself as a lasting memory of your trip. Or bestow them on lucky friends and family and it'll be apparent you have a heart of gold! (Just don't forget to get an extra for yourself.)

Stroll the streets of the Plaza, and you may notice the large banners suspended from streetside light poles. The banners change depending on the season or upcoming event, and if you stop into **Plaza Customer Service** you, too, can own one of these sizable pieces of vinyl artwork. Select designs are marked down throughout the year, but otherwise you can expect to spend between $20 and $40 per banner.

Even if you choose to forego the **Boulevard Brewing Co.** tour, stop in to peruse the brewery's well-stocked gift shop. Pick up a Boulevard hoodie, a set of pint glasses, or a jar of the brewery's famous pale ale mustard, a tangy blend that goes with everything from pretzels to burgers. And speaking of edible gifts, Kansas City offers some of the best food in the country. Stop into **Christopher Elbow Artisanal Chocolates** for a box of the exquisite hand-painted truffles, filled with uncommon ingredients like champagne, key lime, and fleur de sel caramel. Sizable bars of pure chocolate are also a must-have, as are the cheery white tins of the chocolatier's signature drinking chocolate mix – think of it like hot chocolate on steroids. Really, really delicious steroids.

If you enjoy Kansas City's barbecue culture as much as the natives, don't even think about leaving the city without a bottle (or three) of barbecue sauce. Most barbecue restaurants including **Gates Bar-B-Q** sell sauces and rubs, fragrant ways to imbibe a bit of Kansas City flavor into your next barbecue. And if you prefer your sauces south of the border, check out **Original Juan** for an astounding selection of freshly made salsas, dips, wing sauces, and more from mild to off-the-chart spicy.

foods like goat cheese, eggs, and free-range meat, most of which is produced at BADSEED's organic farm. Browse heirloom tomatoes, several varieties of beets, red velvet okra, and culinary and medicinal herbs, among other produce. BADSEED also hosts events throughout the year, and is a stop on the annual Kansas City Urban Farms Tour (early June).

THE BETTER CHEDDAR

604 W. 48th St., 816/561-8204,
www.thebettercheddar.com

HOURS: Mon.-Sat. 9 A.M.-9 P.M., Sun. 10 A.M.-6 P.M.

Map 3

Cheese lovers, rejoice. Tucked on a side street of the Plaza, The Better Cheddar awaits hungry shoppers with a staggering array of cheese. Owner Ron Shalinsky boasts that the store carries the largest selection of cheese in a four-state area. Once you've exhausted the store's cheese supply, turn to a gourmet array of oils, vinegars, pastas, sweets, mixes, and other specialties guaranteed to leave a tantalizing taste in your mouth.

CHRISTOPHER ELBOW ARTISANAL CHOCOLATES

1819 McGee St., 816/842-1300,
www.elbowchocolates.com

HOURS: Tues.-Sat. 10 A.M.-6 P.M.

Map 2

Sure, the sleekly modern interior of Christopher Elbow's boutique is worth a second look. But just try and peel your eyes away from a tantalizing glass case filled with exquisite hand-painted chocolates graced with unexpected flavors like champagne, lime, and cinnamon. During the winter, a sinfully rich cup of Christopher Elbow's drinking chocolate is a must, with a handmade marshmallow garnish instead of whipped cream. The city's celebrated chocolatier also makes delicately sugared pate de fruits and lightly dusted truffles, perfect for satisfying any sweet tooth.

GREEN ACRES MARKET

4175 N. Mulberry Dr., 816/746-0010,
www.greenacres.com

HOURS: Mon.-Sat. 8 A.M.-9 P.M., Sun. 10 A.M.-7 P.M.

Map 5

For organic foods and produce, Green Acres Market is a must-see in Briarcliff Village, a quick five-minute drive from downtown. Although you might not do much grocery shopping while on vacation, Green Acres has an extensive deli and carry-out section filled with freshly made sandwiches, sides, and an organic salad bar. Try the Give Thanks sandwich, a holiday-inspired blend made with turkey, cream cheese, cranberry sauce, and whole-grain bread. Soups, drinks, and energy bars are also ideal purchases when you're in need of a quick pick-me-up.

ORIGINAL JUAN

111 Southwest Blvd., Kansas City, Kansas,
913/432-5228, www.originaljuan.com

HOURS: Mon.-Fri. 9 A.M.-4:30 P.M., Sat. 10 A.M.-3 P.M.

Map 2

Sure, you thought Kansas City was the Midwest's barbecue capital. And it is—but after a visit to Original Juan, Purveyors of Specialty Foods, you'll realize a completely different side of the city's cuisine. Flavor-soaked salsas made in micro-batches—and at a variety of heat levels—are Original Juan's specialty. For the faint of heart, try Original Juan's mild salsa. If you're feeling especially adventurous (or maybe a little crazy) try anything from the Off the Chart category, including Da' Bomb The Final Answer Hot Sauce. Just do your traveling companions a favor and have some milk standing by.

PRYDE'S OLD WESTPORT

115 Westport Rd., 816/531-5588,
www.prydeskitchen.com

HOURS: Mon.-Sat. 10 A.M.-6 P.M.

Map 3

If you're an aspiring chef or you know someone who is, Pryde's is a must-visit while in Kansas City. It's easy to be overwhelmed by the two-story space literally crammed with pots, pans, recipe books, spices, dishes, and assorted kitchen gadgetry. But despite the store's massive inventory, employees keep the shelves and display areas organized and neat. After a thorough walk-through, restore your energy with a homemade treat from The Upper Crust bakery, located in the lower level. Fruit, cream, and seasonal pies are the perfect pick-me-up, as are the several varieties of cookies. Try the burnt sugar frosted banana or coconut macaroons—they make ideal gifts, if you can ignore temptation long enough to get them home!

© KATY RYAN

Pryde's Old Westport is stocked floor-to-ceiling with every food gadget imaginable.

Pet Supplies

LAND OF PAWS

4155 N. Mulberry Dr., Ste. A, 816/587-2275, www.landofpaws.com

HOURS: Mon.-Sat. 10 A.M.-6 P.M., Sun. noon-5 P.M.

Map 5

Founded in 1993 by two veterinarians and their wives, Land of Paws specializes in accessories, treats, collars, and more for dogs and cats. Upscale products like shampoos, conditioners, and aromatherapy spritzers ensure your beloved pooch has a clean, shiny coat. For a pet constantly on the go, Land of Paws stocks several kinds of carriers and car seats, ensuring your pet's safety and comfort while you're on the road. Visit Land of Paws in the early fall and you'll be able to choose from an adorable array of pet costumes to allow your pet to masquerade as a tasty taco or a Snow White princess.

THREE DOG BAKERY

612 W. 48th St., 816/753-3647, www.threedog.com

HOURS: Mon.-Fri. 10 A.M.-7 P.M., Sat. 11 A.M.-5 P.M.

Map 3

Call it a meeting of the minds, or a good old-fashioned case of serendipity. When Dan Dye met Mark Beckloff, the two realized they shared a love of dogs, and Three Dog Bakery was born. The company specializes in all-natural, oven-baked doggie treats made with ingredients like peanut butter, carob, molasses, and cranberries. The results are tasty tidbits that show your dog how much you care. For those feline fans, don't fret. Three Dog Bakery also makes We Pity the Kitties treats in cat-friendly flavors like chicken, salmon, and lobster and Alaskan pollock. And if your hometown is lacking a Three Dog Bakery or affiliated retailer, you can replenish your supplies through the company's online dogalog.

Shopping Districts and Centers

The majority of Kansas City's shopping is found in outdoor districts, so bring comfortable shoes and be prepared for rain or other inclement weather. Most of the shopping areas include a mix of boutiques, restaurants, and other attractions, including movie theaters, making them prime places to spend a large part of the day.

BRIARCLIFF

4151 N. Mulberry Dr., 816/584-2655, www.briarcliffvillagekc.com

HOURS: Vary

Map 5

A smaller walkable outdoor shopping center, the shops at Briarcliff are all locally owned and offer a variety of goods, from urban-inspired craft supplies to upscale dresses, home goods, and kitchen necessities. Briarcliff also hosts a surprising number of restaurants and coffee shops, making this a picturesque spot for breakfast, lunch, or dinner, a mere five minutes north of downtown Kansas City. Try the patio at **Lattéland** for a great view of the surrounding Briarcliff area and, on a clear day, the Kansas City skyline.

COUNTRY CLUB PLAZA

47th St. from Roanoke Rd. to Main St., www.countryclubplaza.com

HOURS: Vary

Map 3

The Spanish-style district isn't just a premier

example of new urbanism, a design principle that touts walkable, dense developments designed for retail, residential, and commercial use. The Plaza is one of the city's most prized shopping meccas, a place where upscale vendors such as **Tiffany & Co.** and **Coach** meet local and national boutiques such as **Hemline, Standard Style,** and **American Apparel.** Complete with a plush movie theater, numerous restaurants, and a sprawling three-story **Barnes & Noble,** the Plaza pleases everyone from shopaholics to thrifty window-shoppers. Stop in at locally owned **Lattéland** for a healthy dose of caffeine to fuel your shopping adventures. Ample parking, both curbside and in off-street garages, puts you within steps of Plaza shops. Be prepared for crowds in warmer months and during the holidays.

18TH AND WYANDOTTE

Map 2

Within a half-block stretch of downtown you'll find a sassy lingerie boutique, two eclectic apparel shops, a Peruvian boutique, a coffee shop, and a small independent snack shop that add up to create one of the more vibrant, diverse shopping areas in the city. Creative window displays and photo-worthy signage contribute to the outer character of the area, which is one of the more packed stretches of street during the monthly First Fridays gallery walk. For a true taste of Kansas City fashion, head to 18th and Wyandotte; it's a worthwhile stop even if you do manage to leave empty-handed.

HALLS DEPARTMENT STORE

211 Nichols Rd., 816/274-3222, www.halls.com

HOURS: Mon.-Wed. 10 A.M.-6 P.M., Thurs.-Fri. 10 A.M.-8 P.M., Sat. 10 A.M.-6 P.M., Sun. noon-5 P.M.

Map 3

And you thought Hallmark only created greeting cards. Hallmark founder and Kansas City native Joyce C. Hall opened Halls Department Store in 1913 to remain on the cutting edge in the city. What started as a single showcase in a downtown building has evolved into two majestic department stores that offer an alluring mix of clothing (designer and couture), accessories, cosmetics, housewares, and in-house Hallmark Gold Crown boutiques. Halls is known for its extensive china and silver collections, and is a must-see during the holidays when elaborately decorated trees and tables transform the store's interior into a festive escape.

INDEPENDENCE CENTER

2035 Independence Center Dr., 816/795-8600, www.simon.com

HOURS: Mon.-Sat. 10 A.M.-9 P.M., Sun. noon-6 P.M.

Overview Map

One of two indoor malls left in Kansas City, Independence Center has more than 130 stores and is anchored by three department stores: **Dillard's, Macy's,** and **Sears.** About a 20-minute drive from Kansas City, Independence Center is a great stop if you're planning to explore eastern Jackson County, or if you're headed east on I-70 toward central Missouri. Dining and entertainment options around the mall are numerous, including a 20-screen AMC movie theater and adjacent strip malls filled mostly with national chains and big-box stores.

THE LEGENDS AT VILLAGE WEST

1843 Village West Pkwy., Kansas City, Kansas, 913/788-3700, www.legendsshopping.com

HOURS: Mon.-Sat. 10 A.M.-9 P.M., Sun. 11 A.M.-6 P.M.

Overview Map

Theoretically you could spend the entire day at The Legends, a shopping and entertainment district that combines destination restaurants with a collection of mostly outlet stores. Park around the perimeter and make your way by foot through the district, which also serves as a tribute to famous Kansans. Look for sculptures, signs, and even a yellow brick road as you traverse your way through the area. If you're looking for local flavor, stop at the **Kansas City T-Bones** official team store, or dine at **The Legendary Wild Bill's Steakhouse and Saloon**.

OAK PARK MALL

11461 W. 95th St., Overland Park, Kansas, 913/888-4400, www.thenewoakparkmall.com

HOURS: Mon.-Sat. 10 A.M.-9 P.M., Sun. 11 A.M.-6 P.M.

Overview Map

Johnson County has a reputation as a Kansas City–area shopping mecca, thanks in large part to Oak Park Mall. The spacious indoor shopping mall has an upscale flair thanks to retailers like **Nordstrom, Coach, Banana Republic,** and **White House Black Market.** Shop specialty boutiques like Lush, an England-based bath and body retailer that specializes in natural preservative-free products, some of which even require refrigeration. Stop for a snack at the mall's food court, or choose from sit-down eateries like **Panera, Rainforest Cafe,** and **Cheddar's.** I-35 is the easiest way to reach Oak Park Mall from downtown Kansas City; expect a 20-minute drive, traffic permitting.

ONE NINETEEN

119th St. and Roe Ave., Leawood, 913/338-5800, www.onenineteenshopping.com

HOURS: Mon.-Sat. 10 A.M.-9 P.M., Sun. noon-6 P.M.

Overview Map

An upscale collection of boutiques and

© KATY RYAN

One Nineteen, an outdoor shopping area in Johnson County, offers a mix of national retailers and local boutiques, such as Mitzy London's and Habitat Shoe Boutique.

restaurants is one of the newer additions to Johnson County's vast shopping landscape. National retailers like **Crate & Barrel** and the **Apple Store** stand alongside locally owned shops like **Soho 119, Mitzy London's,** and **Habitat Shoe Boutique,** all worth a visit while you're at One Nineteen. Choose from eclectic drinking and dining options like **NoRTH** (Italian) and the second **JP Wine Bar & Coffee House** location, as well as **119 The Restaurant** (located in the back of SoHo 119).

TOWN CENTER PLAZA

5000 W. 119th St., Leawood, 913/498-1111, www.towncenterplaza.com

HOURS: Mon.-Sat. 10 A.M.-9 P.M., Sun. noon-5 P.M.

Overview Map

Take a typical strip mall layout, multiply it by at least 10 and add aesthetically pleasing facades that combine streamlined awnings with brick exteriors. The result is Leawood's Town Center Plaza, an outdoor mall that spans the gamut of stores from **Barnes & Noble** to **Restoration Hardware** and **Express.** Stop in at locally owned **Standard Style Boutique** for men's and women's apparel and accessories. While at Town Center, you're in the heart of Johnson County and surrounded by restaurants that range from casual chains like **On the Border** and **Houlihan's** to locally owned sports bar **810 Zone.**

ZONA ROSA

8640 Dixson Rd., 816/587-8180, www.zonarosa.com

HOURS: Mon.-Thurs. 10 A.M.-9 P.M., Fri.-Sat. 10 A.M.-10 P.M., Sun. noon-6 P.M.

Map 5

Built on the tenets of new urbanism, including mixed-use and walkability, Zona Rosa is a large shopping, dining, and entertainment district modeled after a small town. Mostly national boutiques and restaurants mingle with locally owned favorites like **Swagat Indian Restaurant** and **Bo Ling's.** Be sure to feed the meters here—all money goes to charity. In 2008, Zona Rosa unveiled a sizable addition anchored by a three-story **Dillard's** department store and other retailers, including **Chico's** and **Sephora.**

HOTELS

Kansas City hotels have something to offer every traveler, whether you're vacationing or in town on business. Most of the city's locally owned and boutique hotels are sprinkled throughout downtown, Westport, and the Country Club Plaza—prime locations that put guests within walking distance of shops, restaurants, and area attractions. The hotels in these areas are as eclectic as the neighborhoods themselves—whether you opt to stay in the environmentally conscious Q Hotel or prefer the modern surroundings of the Aladdin, complete with a stylish restaurant and on-site martini bar—you'll probably find something to suit your needs, taste, and budget. Downtown hosts the city's historic properties, some of which are also top choices for Kansas City's most luxurious accommodations. For true Old World glamour, the Savoy Hotel is unmatched; it is an architectural marvel that still boasts many of its original fixtures and decorative accents.

With its numerous festivals and events and some of the city's best shopping, the Plaza is a popular lodging destination. Several chain hotels offer both economical and upscale options, yet the Plaza also hosts hidden gems like the Southmoreland Bed and Breakfast and The Raphael, a European-style boutique hotel that's ideal for a romantic getaway.

COURTESY OF THE KANSAS CITY CONVENTION AND VISITORS ASSOCIATION

HIGHLIGHTS

LOOK FOR ☾ TO FIND RECOMMENDED HOTELS.

☾ **Best Hotel Renovation:** The towering **Hilton President Kansas City** offers 1940s elegance along with contemporary updates (page 141).

☾ **Best Historic Escape:** History meets European elegance in **The Savoy Hotel**'s luxurious decor complete with Victorian-inspired suites (page 142).

☾ **Best View:** One of the hottest accommodations in town is a Plaza-view room at **The InterContinental Kansas City at the Plaza** during the Plaza lighting ceremony on Thanksgiving night (page 144).

☾ **Best Green Retreat:** One of Kansas City's only green hotels, **The Q Hotel and Spa** is an eco-conscious retreat that's as stylish as it is sustainable (page 145).

☾ **Most Romantic Hotel:** Sumptuous rooms and intimate restaurants make **The Raphael** ideal for a romantic getaway. Take an after-dinner stroll on the Plaza for a truly special experience (page 145).

☾ **Best Bed-and-Breakfast:** Distinctively decorated rooms named for famous Kansas Citians make the **Southmoreland Bed and Breakfast** a truly local escape (page 145).

☾ **Best Casino Hotel:** Gambling, dining, plush rooms, and an on-site spa? **Argosy Casino** delivers all these, and puts you just 10 minutes north of downtown Kansas City (page 146).

☾ **Best Chain Hotel:** Contemporary, spacious rooms await at **Hyatt Place.** The appeal is the combination of location, affordability, and the hotel's streamlined aesthetic (page 146).

© KATY RYAN

The InterContinental Kansas City at the Plaza

☾ **Best Modern Decor:** The loft-like surroundings of **Aloft Leawood** are a sumptuous retreat for travelers, and you may leave with a few friends thanks to the hotel's abundant number of chic common spaces (page 147).

☾ **Best Themed Getaway:** The themed rooms of **Chateau Avalon** immerse you in your choice of surroundings, from the luxurious Camelot suite to the Tahitian treehouse suite (page 147).

PRICE KEY

$ Less than $150 per night
$$ $150-250 per night
$$$ More than $250 per night

Further outside the city, newer hotels form pockets of accommodation options around popular business and leisure points of interest, including convention centers and Kansas City International Airport. Although you may tack on extra driving time to get to the heart of the city, many of the suburban-area hotels offer cheaper rates and on-site conveniences that make up for the additional mileage.

CHOOSING YOUR HOTEL

Because Kansas City is spread out over such a large area, it's best to choose your hotel after you have a rough idea of where you're headed, what you're going to see, and what sort of transportation you'll use while you're here. If you want to spend most of your time in the downtown/Westport/Plaza corridor, selecting a hotel within those districts and relying on public transportation or taxis will give you access to most of the city's favorite sights. If you'd prefer an affordable option and don't mind driving, select a hotel by Kansas City International Airport, in Johnson County, or in Wyandotte County. You'll still be close to highways and interstates, putting you within a 20-minute drive of the center of Kansas City and its accompanying destinations.

Should you decide to travel with your pet, Intrigue Park Place and Aloft Leawood welcome four-legged friends for a small non-refundable deposit.

Business travelers doing business in Johnson County might want to stay in hotels around Overland Park's Corporate Woods business park, especially at the Doubletree Hotel Overland Park–Corporate Woods. If proximity to your business meetings and functions isn't a concern, opt to stay near the airport or in downtown Kansas City, where you'll have easy access to dining and nightlife.

River Market and Power and Light District Map 1

ALADDIN HOLIDAY INN $$

1215 Wyandotte St., 877/863-4780, www.holidayinn.com

After a thorough facelift that transformed The Aladdin's historic shell into hip, boutique-style lodging, the hotel received the 2007 Holiday Inn Renovation of the Year. Intricate architecture inside and out channels the art deco style that's so prevalent throughout downtown Kansas City. And in an ideal balance with the hotel's historic roots, The Aladdin offers modern, chic spaces like the Zebra Room Restaurant and the Martini Loft Lounge in which to relax, unwind, and reminisce about the day's adventures. For a truly luxurious experience, book a service in The Aladdin's on-site CitiScape Day Spa. Rooms at the Aladdin have a modern aesthetic complete with brightly colored walls, trendy textiles, and pedestal sinks. For a luxurious retreat, opt for the Greta Garbo or Mickey Mantle suites, named after two of the most famous visitors to the original Aladdin hotel.

CROWNE PLAZA DOWNTOWN KANSAS CITY $$

1301 Wyandotte St., 816/474-6664, www.crowneplaza.com

Night owls and bar flies will love Crowne Plaza's close proximity to Kansas City's Power and Light District, an area filled with restaurants, bars, and clubs. Refresh your body and spirit in the hotel's heated outdoor pool; if you'd prefer a night in, the City Grille and City Bar offer extensive cocktail and dining menus to whet your appetite. Guest rooms and suites offer picturesque views of the surrounding city, while plush beds await to give guests a truly memorable night's sleep. For business travelers, in-room work areas, an on-site business center, and nine state-of-the-art meeting rooms make the Crowne Plaza an ideally located option.

HILTON PRESIDENT KANSAS CITY $$

1329 Baltimore Ave., 816/221-9490, www.hilton.com

Channel 1940s elegance within the Hilton President, located in the heart of the city and billed as "the official hotel of the Power and Light District." An extensive renovation completed in 2008 preserved many of the hotel's historic features while adding updated rooms that make for an aesthetically pleasing contrast. The ornate lobby, complete with velvet-covered chairs, plush rugs, and quietly luxurious accents gives way to guest rooms and suites that embrace simple, clean decor to offer a relaxing respite after a long day of exploring. Two dining options at the Hilton President offer remarkably different experiences. The luxe Walnut Room is a reflection of the hotel's historic charm, while in The Drum Room you'll dine and drink among the ghosts of past performers such as Benny Goodman, Glenn Miller, Frank Sinatra, and Patsy Cline while enjoying live entertainment on Friday and Saturday evenings.

HOTEL PHILLIPS $$$

106 W. 12th St., 816/221-7000, www.hotelphillips.com

After opening in 1931 at a cost of $1.6 million, Hotel Phillips reigned as the tallest and most luxurious hotel in Kansas City. Today, the Hotel Phillips continues a tradition of historic elegance and European luxury in chic, well-appointed rooms complete with a choice of pillows, evening turndown service, and individual climate control. Ideal for lunch, happy hour, and dinner, the adjacent 12 Baltimore Cafe offers a flavorful dining menu, a full bar, and live entertainment on Saturday night featuring jazz, swing, zydeco, and more. If you'd prefer to take advantage of some of the city's most celebrated events along with Hotel Phillips' luxe accommodations, reserve one of the hotel's travel packages that combine lodging, events, and complimentary valet parking.

THE MUEHLEBACH HOTEL $$

200 W. 12th St, 816/421-6800, www.marriott.com

To most Kansas Citians, the Marriott Muehlebach isn't merely known as a quality hotel. Throughout the year, a state-of-the-art LED light display flashes on the hotel's exterior, and during the holiday season the displays change to reflect holiday decor and other seasonal images. If you're staying at the Marriott Muehlebach, don't worry—the lights are designed in a way that they don't interfere with guests' in-room experiences, so you'll still enjoy a relaxing stay. A 2008 renovation refreshed each of the 983 rooms, available in a variety of layouts including guest rooms, parlors, small suites, and presidential suites. Try to get a room with a view of the adjoining Barney Allis Plaza, a greenspace that thrives in the heart of the city. Multiple on-site restaurants allow for varied dining experiences, and the Marriott Muehlebach also features a lobby bar and coffee kiosk stocked with Seattle Roast coffees and the breakfast of champions—Krispy Kreme doughnuts.

THE SAVOY HOTEL $$

219 W. 9th St., 816/842-3575, www.savoyhotel.net

For a more intimate hotel experience, book a room at The Savoy, a European-style bed-and-breakfast known for elegance and luxury since its 1888 opening. Careful preservation has protected some of the hotel's original decorative features including imported marble and tile, brass fixtures, and art nouveau–style stained glass. Choose from a Victorian room, Victorian suite, or deluxe Victorian suite, all of which include a complimentary gourmet breakfast. The well-appointed rooms include claw-footed bathtubs, sitting areas, and pieces of the hotel's original furniture. You can dine at the adjacent Savoy Grill, an upscale restaurant and steakhouse that echoes The Savoy Hotel's historic grandeur.

Crossroads and 18th and Vine

Map 2

FAIRFIELD INN KANSAS CITY DOWNTOWN/UNION HILL $$

3001 Main St., 816/931-5700, www.marriott.com

With a location halfway between downtown and the Plaza, the Fairfield Inn is a prime choice for travelers seeking convenient access to multiple parts of the city. Guest rooms and larger guest rooms are available, all equipped with in-room wireless Internet, luxury bedding, a refrigerator, and a microwave. On-site amenities include a complimentary hot breakfast and dinner delivery from local restaurants

PACKAGE DEALS

Many Kansas City hotels offer packages that combine rooms with additional amenities, or better yet, city tours or access to favorite local venues and events. To get the most bang for your buck, try any of the following package deals or inquire at your hotel of choice about special rates and upgrades. Enjoy a Heavenly Getaway and Escape at **Westin Crown Center** (from $149, 816/474-4400), which offers daily in-room breakfast for two, local paper delivery, and extended check-out as available. Or try the fine dining package, which includes a $100 food credit to the Westin's on-site Benton's Steak and Chophouse, an elegant retreat that combines perfectly cooked steak and live jazz performances. For the ultimate a girls-only escape, try Girlfriend Get-A-Way at the **Residence Inn by Marriott-Country Club Plaza** (from $289, 816/753-0033). A two-bedroom suite that can sleep five comes with a bottle of wine, hot breakfast buffet, and covered parking. You'll also receive a complimentary $50 Plaza gift certificate to jump-start your shopping adventures. Rediscover your romantic side with **The Raphael**'s Romantic Getaway Package (from $271.50, 816/756-3800), a lavish combination that includes a welcome basket, a bottle of wine, French terry monogrammed bathrobes, heart-shaped chocolates, turndown service complete with rose petals, and breakfast in bed. Thrill-seeking families should book the Worlds of Fun package at **Intrigue Park Place** ($229 plus tax, 816/483-9900), which includes a one-night stay, four Worlds of Fun tickets, four water bottles, a Coca-Cola six-pack, free shuttle service to and from the park, and a 25 percent discount on a second night's stay.

COURTESY OF THE KANSAS CITY CONVENTION AND VISITORS ASSOCIATION

The Westin Crown Center is connected to Union Station and Crown Center by an enclosed skywalk that leads visitors over downtown streets.

if you opt to stay in for the evening. Several bars and restaurants are within walking distance in nearby Union Hill, but to get elsewhere in the city, take a taxi or drive.

HYATT REGENCY CROWN CENTER $$

2345 McGee St., 816/421-1234, www.crowncenter.hyatt.com

Towering above Kansas City's Crown Center, the Hyatt Regency is a study in high-rise hotel luxury complete with Hyatt's signature Grand Beds, stunning views of the surrounding city, and eight restaurants and cafés from which to choose. For a truly one-of-a-kind experience, start or end your evening at Skies, the Hyatt's revolving rooftop restaurant and bar that makes one revolution per hour. For the ultimate in accessibility, the Hyatt is adjoined to The Link, a covered walkway that connects with Union Station and Crown Center, open 6 A.M. to midnight daily.

WESTIN CROWN CENTER $$

1 E. Pershing Rd., 816/474-4400, www.starwoodhotels.com/westin

At the Westin Crown Center, all of the high-end hotel amenities await: fully appointed rooms with the hotel's signature Heavenly bed, as well as an on-site health club, beauty salon, and 24-hour business center. Yet the true appeal of the Westin is its afternoon Unwind program, weeknights 5:30–7:30 P.M. at the hotel's Brasserie bar. Relax with the sounds of Kansas City jazz and the tastes of local barbecue, and challenge your mind with trivia—it all adds up to a rejuvenating experience that gives you the best the city has to offer.

Westport, Midtown, and The Plaza Map 3

EMBASSY SUITES $$

220 W. 43rd St., 816/756-1720, www.embassysuites1.hilton.com

For visitors interested in exploring the heart of the city, a good option is the centrally located Embassy Suites, a towering Spanish-inspired property with spacious suites, numerous amenities, and an expansive breakfast buffet. Allow time between the 4 P.M. check-in and your evening excursion to enjoy the hotel's happy hour. Each guest receives drink tickets upon checking in, and the bar is a great place to meet fellow travelers or plan your next activity. If you prefer to set out on foot, Embassy Suites is within walking distance to both Westport and the Plaza, putting guests just steps away from bars, restaurants, and specialty boutiques.

© KATY RYAN

The Spanish-inspired interior of Embassy Suites mimics the architecture of the nearby Country Club Plaza.

HOLIDAY INN EXPRESS $

801 Westport Rd., 816/931-1000, www.ichotelsgroup.com

Just up the street from the bars and restaurants of Westport, this is an excellent hotel for night owls eager for a quick walk back after a night on the town. Start the day with a complimentary buffet or continental breakfast, as well as newspaper delivery. The hotel also includes a fitness center, business services, and same-day dry cleaning. Guest rooms include a television and coffee maker and suites are equipped with microwave ovens and miniature refrigerators.

THE INTERCONTINENTAL KANSAS CITY AT THE PLAZA $$

401 Ward Pkwy., 816/756-1500, www.ichotelsgroup.com

Impeccable service and numerous luxuries await guests of the InterContinental, which overlooks the Plaza. Views from the Plaza-facing rooms are so good, in fact, that the hotel is booked years in advance for the Thanksgiving lighting ceremony. An outdoor pool, also with prime Plaza views, is an ideal place to cool off between Memorial Day and Labor Day. Choose from suites or standard rooms, each with a mini bar, coffee maker, morning newspaper delivery, and in-room safe. On-site dining is available at The Oak Room. Local favorites include the mango-encrusted red snapper and steak served with pine-nut risotto.

MARRIOTT EXECUSTAY THE NEPTUNE $$

333 W. 46th Terr., 913/451-3300, www.execustay.com

Extended-stay business travelers or short-term

residents will find a home at The Neptune, adjacent to both the Plaza and Mill Creek Park. Fully furnished apartments include walk-in closets, a balcony, and a washer-dryer, and some boast picturesque views of the surrounding Plaza area. Choose from a variety of layouts, including studios and one-, two-, and three-bedroom units. Other ExecuStay properties are available throughout Kansas City, including a location minutes away from downtown's Charles B. Wheeler Airport.

THE Q HOTEL AND SPA $$

560 Westport Rd., 816/931-0001, www.quarteragehotel.com

After The Quarterage Hotel changed hands in 2007, a thorough "greenovation" transformed the boutique hotel into The Q, Kansas City's first green hotel and spa. Numerous earth-friendly practices, including water conservation, hotel recycling, and EnergyStar lightbulbs and thermostats significantly reduce the hotel's carbon footprint without compromising luxury and amenities. Several types of rooms are available, including a honeymoon suite, business queen, deluxe double, and a two-room balcony suite that offers panoramic views of the surrounding Westport neighborhood. High-definition flat-screen TVs, in-room MP3 players, Turkish cotton linens, and Aveda bath products complete the relaxing experience.

THE RAPHAEL $$$

325 Ward Pkwy., 800/821-5343, www.raphaelkc.com

Billed as "Kansas City's original boutique hotel," The Raphael is modeled after the small hotels of Europe and features standard rooms, deluxe suites, and Plaza-view suites. In-room amenities include iPod docking stations, a mini-bar, and work areas. An in-house restaurant, Chaz on the Plaza, serves modern cuisine accompanied by a varied wine list. An adjacent lounge hosts live performers. For a true Kansas City experience, The Raphael offers a number of themed travel packages such as Baseball and BBQ, Chiefs Gridiron, and City Shopping that include accommodations, select retailer discounts or event tickets, and complimentary valet parking at the hotel.

SHERATON SUITES $$

770 W. 47th St., 816/931-4400, www.starwoodhotels.com

Stay at Sheraton Suites and you'll be within the heart of the vibrant Plaza district. The crown jewel of the spacious suites, the signature Sheraton Sweet Sleeper bed, is a plush respite after a long day spent exploring the city. In-room coffee makers, microwaves, and refrigerators make Sheraton Suites an ideal choice for both business travelers and those who wish to enjoy meals (or restaurant leftovers) in their rooms. On-site amenities are numerous and include indoor and outdoor heated pools, a complimentary fitness facility, and an indoor whirlpool. Active travelers will enjoy being near tennis courts and a golf course.

SOUTHMORELAND BED AND BREAKFAST $$

116 E. 46th St., 816/531-7979, www.southmoreland.com

Twelve rooms await in this urban inn that also features a luxury suite in the attached carriage house. Each room boasts a special feature such as a whirlpool tub, wood-burning fireplace, or treetop deck. Rooms are named after notable Kansas Citians, and the decor within reflects the namesakes' personal tastes and styles of the era: Stay in the Clara & Russell Stover room and you'll be treated to a two-person whirlpool tub, pastel decor, and a queen-sized brass cannonball bed. Opt for the George Caleb Bingham and you'll be surrounded by copies of Bingham portraits from his home. Step outside and soak in the view from the attached oversized deck, and you might just be inspired to create your own masterpiece. First-floor common areas allow you to mingle with other guests and the Southmoreland's owners.

Northland

Map 5

AMERISTAR CASINO & HOTEL KANSAS CITY $$$

3200 Ameristar Dr., 816/414-7000, www.ameristar.com

Recognized in 2007 as the Best Overall Casino Hotel in Missouri by *Casino Player* magazine, Ameristar's 184 plush, comfortable rooms are a mixture of standard rooms and spacious suites that offer a relaxing escape away from the activity and energy of the adjacent casino. Although Ameristar's hotel is a bit off the beaten path when it comes to exploring the heart of Kansas City, guests will be just minutes away from the city's adjoining amusement parks, Worlds of Fun and Oceans of Fun. Be advised that prices increase dramatically for weekend stays, so booking a room during the week may be a more economical option.

ARGOSY CASINO $$

777 Argosy Pkwy., Riverside, 816/746-3100, www.stayargosy.com

Located just a few minutes north of downtown Kansas City, the hotel at Argosy Casino is a study in luxury accommodations complete with oversized guest rooms, plush beds, and rain showerheads. For the ultimate in relaxation during your stay, book a session at Argosy's on-site spa, including manicures/pedicures, massages, facials, and more. The hotel's proximity to both downtown Kansas City and the airport make this an ideal stop for business travelers and those eager to explore both the northern and central parts of the metro area.

HARRAH'S HOTEL AND CASINO $$$

1 Riverboat Dr., 816/472-7777, www.harrahsnkc.com

If you plan on gambling and/or eating during your stay at Harrah's Hotel and Casino, opt for a Stay & Play package. A two-night getaway includes a food credit that can be used at one or several of the on-site restaurants. Like other casino hotels in Kansas City, Harrah's is a slight drive from downtown Kansas City and points south, making this an ideal lodging option for those who plan on spending some time at the casino. Rates often change between Friday and Saturday nights, so be advised that you may not pay the same rate per night during a weekend stay. Premium and luxury rooms are available with one king bed or two double beds and include a comfortable sitting area and spacious bathrooms.

HYATT PLACE $

7600 NW 97th Terr., 816/891-0871, http://kansascityairport.place.hyatt.com

The loft-style rooms at Hyatt Place are a modern oasis ideal for business travelers or those who prefer their accommodations near Kansas City's airport. Coffee is served all day in the library, and in the afternoon and evening, cocktails are available from Hyatt Place's full bar. Beverages are an additional charge, but a continental breakfast and morning newspaper are included in the price of the room. A complimentary shuttle provides transport to the airport and locations within a three-mile radius, including Zona Rosa, a shopping, dining, and entertainment district that often hosts special events, festivals, and concerts.

INTRIGUE PARK PLACE $$

1601 Universal Ave., 816/483-9900, www.parkplacekc.com

Locally owned and operated, Intrigue Park Place is also one of a few Kansas City hotels that offer pet-friendly rooms, complete with a 35-inch pet pillow, ceramic food and water bowls, and pet treats. A $25 non-refundable pet deposit is required. Newly remodeled rooms include flat-screen televisions, granite countertops, and the hotel's signature Intrigue comfort bedding. Intrigue Park Place is a great choice for those who want to spend time at Worlds of Fun and Oceans of Fun, as the hotel is just over a mile away.

THE PORCH SWING INN $

702 East St., Parkville, 816/587-6282, www.theporchswinginn.com

The quaint, historic rooms of The Porch Swing Inn blend seamlessly with the surrounding Parkville area, a charming small town just 15 minutes north of downtown Kansas City. Choose from the Colonel Park, Molly Brown, Jesse James Hideaway, or Calamity Jane rooms, each of which is fully appointed, some with special features like a balcony. Enjoy a two-course hot breakfast before you set out to explore Parkville and the surrounding Kansas City area. Convenient accessibility to state and interstate highways makes for quick navigation regardless of where you're headed.

Greater Kansas City

Overview Map

ALOFT LEAWOOD $

11620 Ash St., Leawood, 913/345-9430, www.starwoodhotels.com

Airy, high-ceilinged rooms that channel a loft-style aesthetic are the latest offerings from the W Hotels group. Walk-in showers include toiletries from Bliss spa, and the pet-friendly, fully equipped rooms are designed to act as high-tech office and entertainment centers that include an all-in-one connectivity station. Social butterflies will thrive amid Aloft's numerous public spaces including the Re:mix lounge, complete with a pool table, and XYZ bar. At Aloft you'll be in the heart of Johnson County, near several shopping centers, a plethora of restaurants, and the state-of-the-art Overland Park Convention Center.

CHATEAU AVALON $$

701 Village West Pkwy., Kansas City, Kansas, 913/596-6000, www.chateauavalonhotel.com

Whether you want to spend a weekend immersed in Tuscan luxury or nestled among the foliage of the Mayan rain forest, Chateau Avalon awaits with 62 themed rooms and suites. From a Tahitian treehouse suite to a Jesse James escape suite, the elaborate interiors available at Chateau Avalon add a dimension of adventure to your Kansas City vacation. The hotel's location in western Wyandotte County puts visitors next to Kansas Speedway and the Legends at Village West shopping district, but be prepared to drive at least 20 minutes to other must-see attractions such as the Country Club Plaza and downtown Kansas City.

COURTESY OF THE KANSAS CITY CONVENTION AND VISITORS ASSOCIATION

The Great Wolf Lodge is a family-friendly escape complete with an indoor waterpark.

DOUBLETREE HOTEL OVERLAND PARK-CORPORATE WOODS $

10100 College Blvd., Overland Park, Kansas, 913/451-6100, www.doubletree1.hilton.com

Located within Overland Park's bustling business corridor, including Corporate Woods, the Doubletree Hotel is a prime choice for business travelers. An on-site business center includes a notary public, meeting rooms, and equipment rental. With family packages, children's activities, and video rental, the Doubletree is also a great choice for families eager to explore the Kansas side of the metropolitan area, or reach destinations like downtown Kansas City, the Plaza, and the zoo in 20 to 30 minutes. The basic rooms are clean and spacious and the larger suites feature a wet bar, refrigerator, sleeper sofa, two televisions, and two telephones.

GREAT WOLF LODGE $$

10401 Cabela Dr., Kansas City, Kansas, 913/299-7001, www.greatwolf.com

Book a room at the family-friendly Great Wolf Lodge and you might have too much fun to leave the property. Once you've settled on a suite—no easy task when confronted with a variety of layouts, from the family or wolf den to KidCabin and majestic bear—pull on your swimsuit and spend the day at Great Wolf's indoor water park, a splashtacular soak-fest complete with water slides, an activity pool, hot tub, and Fort Mackenzie, a four-story interactive treehouse and water fort. If you prefer to stay dry, Great Wolf offers story time, miniature golf, a fitness room, arcade, and Elements Spa, a peaceful full-service retreat.

SHERATON KANSAS CITY SPORTS COMPLEX $$

9103 E. 39th St., 866/716-8134, www.starwoodhotels.com

Sports enthusiasts, look no further than the Sheraton Kansas City Sports Complex, a short walk away from Arrowhead Stadium and Kauffman Stadium, home of the Chiefs and Royals. Families will love the Sheraton's indoor Coco Key Water Resort, featuring body and tube slides, adventure river, and more. Purchase a day pass for Coco Key, or opt for a package combining a hotel room with access to the water resort. After a long day, sink into Sheraton's signature Sweet Sleeper bed for a relaxing night's sleep.

EXCURSIONS FROM KANSAS CITY

Several destinations within a few hours of Kansas City offer another layer of local culture, history, and heritage that will become an unforgettable part of your Kansas City experience.

Wine and dine in Rocheport, a hamlet along the bluffs of the Missouri River that features Les Bourgeois winery and restaurant and several bed-and-breakfasts, as well as a direct connection to Missouri's famed Katy Trail, a must for hikers and bikers.

For a college-town escape that's much closer to Kansas City, spend a day—or weekend—in Lawrence, Kansas. Sample the food and brews of Free State Brewery, shop the boutiques of Mass Street, and stop at the University of Kansas to pay homage to the site where basketball inventor James Naismith worked for decades. Lawrence is also home to a flourishing arts community, resulting in a number of galleries, museums, and live-music venues that add a healthy dose of culture to your visit. A trip to Lawrence isn't complete without a stop at one of the city's many historic sites, still-standing tributes to Lawrence's turbulent role in the Civil War and other local historical milestones.

Or consider a trip to Omaha, Nebraska, home of the famous Henry Doorly Zoo, for a day trip or a full weekend spent exploring Nebraska's ever-evolving metropolitan center.

COURTESY OF OMAHA CONVENTION AND VISITORS ASSOCIATION

HIGHLIGHTS

LOOK FOR ☾ TO FIND RECOMMENDED SIGHTS, ACTIVITIES, DINING, AND LODGING.

☾ **Best Place to Relive Your College Years:** One of the main thoroughfares of the University of Kansas campus in Lawrence, **Jayhawk Boulevard** offers a scenic stroll and a taste of campus life (page 154).

☾ **Best Shopping:** Boutiques, breweries, and book shops line **Massachusetts Street,** a thoroughfare so appealing it's like a smaller Lawrence-style version of the Magnificent Mile (page 154).

☾ **Best Way to Learn on Vacation:** The interactive exhibits and collection of personal artifacts at the **Robert J. Dole Institute of Politics** in Lawrence make learning about local government and politics anything but dull (page 154).

☾ **Best Architecture:** Built solely for foot traffic, Omaha's cable-stayed **Bob Kerrey Pedestrian Bridge** is an impressive work of architecture, and is even more picturesque when it's illuminated after dark (page 159).

☾ **Best Local Attraction:** Wear comfortable shoes if you want to see all that Omaha's **Henry Doorly Zoo** has to offer in one day. Duck into the IMAX theater to recharge your batteries (page 159).

☾ **Best photo opportunities:** Brick-lined streets, converted warehouses, horse-drawn carriages – the **Old Market** in Omaha is like a picturesque postcard in perpetual motion (page 160).

☾ **Best Recreational Activity:** You won't find any white-water rapids on this river, but the **Missouri River Boating Tour** is an interactive and one-of-a-kind way to see the river and surrounding valleys and bluffs near Rocheport. Get ready for an upper-body workout, and don't forget the sunscreen (page 164).

☾ **Best Blast from the Past:** The building may be small, but the **Friends of Rocheport Historical Museum** boasts an extensive display of local memorabilia that makes for an interesting – and educational – stop (page 165).

COURTESY OF OMAHA CONVENTION AND VISITORS ASSOCIATION

The Henry Doorly Zoo features the world's largest indoor desert within the Desert Dome.

☾ **Best Reason to Rent a Bike:** Even if you don't want to bike the **Katy Trail**'s full 225-mile length, heading out from Rocheport for a quick five-mile ride is still a great way to experience the historic trail and enjoy prime views of the Missouri River (page 165).

☾ **Best Spot for Souvenirs:** Stock up on old-fashioned candy, lye soap, and other nostalgic favorites at the **Rocheport General Store,** also a great spot for a game of checkers or a live music performance (page 165).

An appealing, eclectic mix of shops, bars, and restaurants makes Omaha's Old Market hard to leave, and it's best to keep your camera out and ready as you walk the brick-paved streets through an area oozing with charm and character. Pry yourself away and you'll be rewarded with worthy stops like the Bob Kerrey pedestrian bridge and the Omaha push pins, an inventive sculpture system that's part public art installation and part giant guidebook.

PLANNING YOUR TIME

Because each of the proposed day trips are within reasonable drives of Kansas City, you could opt to spend a day at each location, or a weekend if you'd prefer more time to explore and get a feel for some of the surrounding areas. All three drives are easy to navigate: take I-70 west to Lawrence or east to Rocheport, or head north on I-29 to reach Omaha.

Lawrence, a college town, may be crowded and difficult to navigate during fall football season and Jayhawk home games. The summer months and late December/early January leave Lawrence a bit emptier as many students opt to go home for holiday and summer breaks. Omaha and Rocheport tend to be more crowded during special events and festivals, but the excess foot traffic shouldn't have a detrimental impact on your excursion.

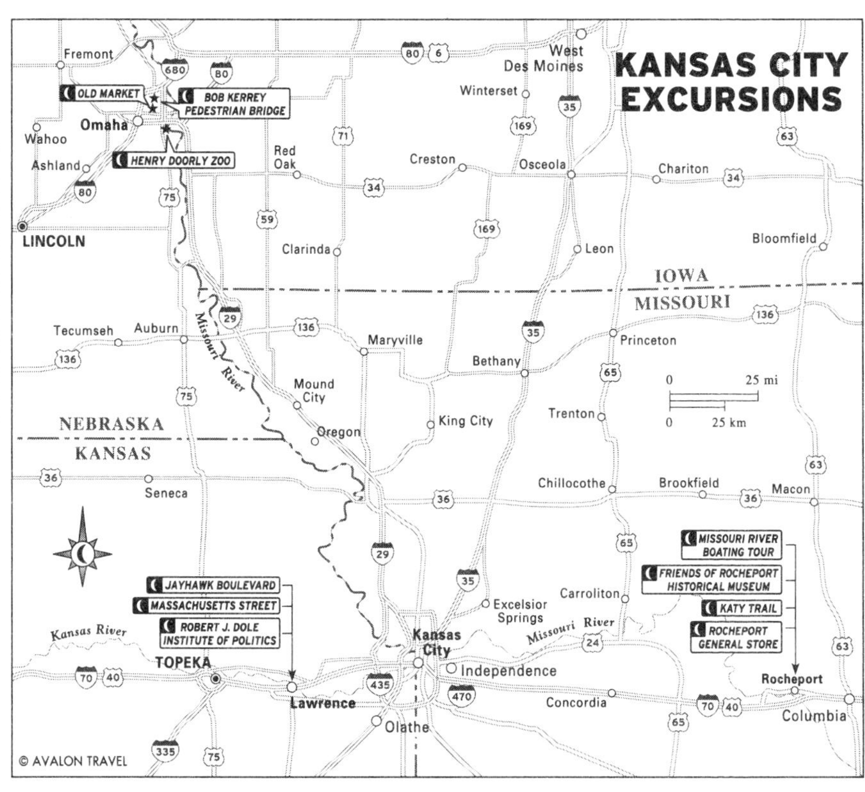

Lawrence, Kansas

Born during a time of intense civil conflict, Lawrence was founded by a group of abolitionist explorers from Massachusetts. After the Civil War took the country in its bloody grip, Kansas chose to enter the Union as a free state, a move that fueled violent fighting between Lawrence's "Jayhawkers" and Missouri's proslavery "Bushwhackers." The most infamous encounter occurred August 21, 1863, when raider William Quantrill sped into Lawrence, accompanied by 400 of his men. After several gruesome hours, hundreds of Lawrence residents had been killed and many of its buildings engulfed by fire. Instead of retreating into hiding, Lawrence residents banded together to rebuild the town, and today many of the buildings from that time period are still in use.

Now the sixth-largest city in the state of Kansas, Lawrence is home to the University of Kansas (founded in 1865) and enjoys a reputation as a bustling, liberal college town that hosts eclectic boutiques, delicious eateries, two microbreweries, and a wealth of museums, art galleries, and local historical sights.

Because Lawrence is a relatively quick 40-minute drive from Kansas City, it's an ideal setting in which to spend the entire day or, if you're pressed for time, a few hours. Stop in at the Lawrence Visitors Center for maps and other pertinent literature; you can also download iPod tours for several local highlights including Quantrill's Raid, the historic cemeteries of Lawrence, Old East Lawrence, and the Underground Railroad. After you've stocked up on sightseeing materials, head to the heart of downtown Lawrence, Massachusetts Street. With a wealth of coffee shops and restaurants, Mass Street is a great place to grab breakfast, coffee, or lunch while you plan the rest of the day. Spend some time shopping, then head to your car and make tracks to some of Lawrence's strongholds of local culture, history, and heritage such as the Hobbs Park Memorial, Jayhawk Boulevard, and the Robert J. Dole Institute of Politics.

HISTORY OF THE KANSAS JAYHAWK

The official University of Kansas mascot, the Kansas Jayhawk is an easily recognizable red and blue bird. Named for the city's early anti-slavery pioneers, the Jayhawk is said to be a combination of two common types of birds: the blue jay and the hawk.

The word took on new meaning during the Civil War, according to the Lawrence Convention and Visitors Bureau, when the term Jayhawk "became associated with the spirit of comradeship and the courageous fighting qualities associated with efforts to keep Kansas a free state. Following the war, most Kansans were proud to be called Jayhawkers."

In 1901, the university's yearbook became known as the Jayhawk, and in the 1950s KU student Hal Sandy created the smiling bird mascot still used by the University today.

SIGHTS

Hobbs Park Memorial

In a tribute to Lawrence's significance throughout the Civil War conflict, the Hobbs Park Memorial (10th and Delaware Sts., 785/749-7394, www.hobbsparkmemorial.org, 11 A.M.–7 P.M. Sat.–Mon., free) features the Murphy-Bromelsick house, a masonry home that dates back to the town's rebuilding period following the devastating raid and massacre by William Quantrill. The carefully preserved home, which was at one time slated for demolition, now serves as a museum and is surrounded by various markers explaining the park land's significance during the mid- to late-1860s. The home of newspaper publisher John Speer, a vehement free-stater, Hobbs Park was the site of tragedy during Quantrill's raid when Speer's two eldest sons were murdered by raiders. The Murphy-Bromelsick house is also said to represent a style of "working-class architecture," prevalent in buildings constructed by Lawrence citizens in the months following Quantrill's raid.

Jayhawk Boulevard

Now the main thoroughfare that winds through the University of Kansas campus, Jayhawk Boulevard once served as a connective ridge along which explorers and families climbed in their quest to reach the Oregon Trail. Although erosion has erased the wagon wheel ruts that once criss-crossed the path, Jayhawk Boulevard is now home to 16 campus buildings that include classrooms, auditoriums, a chapel, museums, and laboratories. A self-guided tour of Jayhawk Boulevard is available at the Lawrence Visitors Center, a great way to explore both the boulevard's past and its university-centered present.

Massachusetts Street

Named for the home state of the abolitionists who founded Lawrence, Massachusetts Street (U.S. 40 to 14th Street) is the colorful, vibrant core of downtown Lawrence and the city's first thoroughfare. Peppered with boutiques, national chain stores, restaurants, galleries, bars, coffee shops, and more, Mass Street is the place to soak up Lawrence culture and a taste of college life. The lengthy boulevard is also home to historic sites like the gracious Eldridge Hotel and the aptly named Free State Brewery, as well as favorite annual events like the St. Patrick's Day Parade (Mar. 17) and Sidewalk Sales (mid-July).

Old West Lawrence

Once the home of Lawrence's elite, Old West Lawrence (bounded by Tennessee Street to the east, Indiana Street to the west, Sixth Street to the north and Eighth Street to the south) became a prime target for Quantrill's vicious raiders. Many homes were destroyed but several remained, and now the neighborhood has garnered several accolades including a listing on the National Register of Historic Places, as well as being a finalist in the nationwide "America's Prettiest Painted Places" competition. The stately homes are an enduring testament to Lawrence history, and worth a picturesque stroll accompanied by a self-guided tour, available at the Lawrence Visitors Center.

Robert J. Dole Institute of Politics

Dedicated in 2003, the Robert J. Dole Institute of Politics (2350 Petefish Dr., KU's West Campus, 785/864-4900, www.doleinstitute.org, 9 A.M.–5 P.M. Mon.–Sat., noon–5 P.M. Sun., free) houses Senator Dole's complete 35-year collection of congressional papers, along with several displays and exhibits dedicated to the life of the Kansas senator and presidential candidate. Located on the KU campus, the institute also serves as a research nucleus designed for visitors and students alike. The Dole Institute hosts the presidential lecture series, during which prominent political figures and authors present lectures on a variety of topics. Additional highlights of the institute include a September 11 memorial complete with the world's largest stained-glass American flag, and a video tour that explains the inner workings of Congress and the legislative process.

RESTAURANTS

An eclectic, flavorful array of restaurants has evolved Lawrence into a local culinary destination, often enticing Kansas Citians to make the drive for a memorable meal. I tend to always make a beeline for **Free State Brewing Company** (636 Massachusetts St., 785/843-4555, www.freestatebrewing.com, 11 A.M.–midnight Mon.–Sat., noon–11 P.M. Sun., $7.75–17.45) for a sizable menu that includes the batterless, flavorful Copperhead Chicken Tenders—oh, and locally brewed beers, too. Wheat State Golden and Copperhead Pale Ale rank as favorites among area beer snobs. Burger enthusiasts have two very delicious, very different options. Nationally acclaimed **Local Burger** (7th and Vermont Sts., 785/856-7827, www.localburger.com, 11 A.M.–9 P.M. Mon.–Sat., 11 A.M.–8 P.M. Sun., $4–11.75) is an organic fast-food restaurant that uses grass-fed beef, elk, and bison to create rich, mouthwatering burgers that are environmentally responsible. Vegetarians, don't fret—you've got a gluten- and dairy-free veggie burger that ranks high on taste. Conventional gourmet burgers take center stage at **Dempsey's Pub** (623 Vermont St., 785/856-5460, 11 A.M.–2 A.M. daily, $7–9 for burgers, $2–4 for sides), including the Kobe burger, an incredibly rich concoction featuring a top-shelf blend of sirloin and Kobe beef topped with a healthy dollop of truffle butter, pickled onions, and greens. Add a side of genuine duck-fat fries for a truly indulgent experience. Sushi rules within the stylishly cavernous surroundings of **Yokohama** (811 New Hampshire St., 785/856-8862, 11 A.M.–9 P.M. Mon.–Wed., 11 A.M.–1:30 A.M. Thurs.–Sat., $4.50–18), which boasts an extensive sushi menu of traditional favorites and one-of-a-kind house specialties. Don't leave without sampling the Crunchy Munchy roll, one of my personal addictions. Whether for breakfast or lunch, **WheatFields Bakery & Cafe** (904 Vermont St., 785/841-5553, www.wheatfieldsbakery.com, 6:30 A.M.–8 P.M. Mon.–Fri., 6:30 A.M.–6:30 P.M. Sat., 7:30 A.M.–4 P.M. Sun., $3.25–7.95) is an inviting retreat that offers sandwiches and baked goods, some of which feature "Turkey" variety heirloom wheat, a hearty grain grown in Decatur County. A dining experience awaits at **Pachamama's** (800 New Hampshire St., 785/841-0990, www.pachamamas.com, 11 A.M.–2 P.M. and 5–9:30 P.M. Tues.–Sat., until 10 P.M. Fri.–Sat., $7–28) as chefs create edible works of art using fresh, flavorful ingredients. Stop in their modern Star Bar, complete with an imbedded solar system, for cocktails and conversation.

NIGHTLIFE

A college town without a hopping nightlife scene is a near impossibility, and Lawrence is no exception. The city also has a reputation as a local music stronghold, so it's more than likely you'll catch a live show or three while you visit. The spacious, architecturally intricate interior of **Abe and Jake's Landing** (8 E. Sixth St., 785/841-5855, www.abejakes.com, 9 P.M.–2 A.M. Thurs.–Fri.) is not to be missed. Named for two local fishermen who caught record-breaking blue catfish, Abe and Jake's is now a multilevel nightlife destination that often hosts live music performances. As part of The Eldridge Hotel's renovations in

2005, **The Jayhawker** (701 Massachusetts St., 785/749-5011, 7 A.M.–midnight Sun.–Wed., 7 A.M.–2 A.M. Thurs.–Sat.) was expanded and revitalized. The wraparound bar is a great place to unwind if you're staying at The Eldridge, or an ideal opportunity to scout out the hotel's historic surroundings if you're staying elsewhere. Lawrence boasts a lively music scene, and **The Granada** (1020 Massachusetts St., 785/842-1390, hours vary), originally a 1920s vaudeville theater, is a high-energy place in which to catch a show. Admission varies based on the performer, but be prepared to shell out between $8 and $20 for most shows. Said by some to be the best bar in Lawrence, **The Sandbar** (117 E. Eighth St., 785/842-0111, www.thesandbar.com, 3 P.M.–2 A.M. Mon.–Fri., 2 P.M.–2 A.M. Sat., 5 P.M.–2 A.M. Sun.) is big on beach-inspired fun, tropical drinks, and a bar specially made for dancing.

THE ARTS

Museums and Galleries

With a thriving college population and an atmosphere conducive to the greater creative community, Lawrence boasts a lively arts scene complete with regular exhibits and arts-related events. Artist-run **DotDotDot ArtSpace** (1910 Haskell, www.dotdotdotartspace.wordpress.com, 2–8 P.M. Thurs.–Fri., 4 –6 P.M. Sat.) is a contemporary art gallery that also serves as the weekly meeting site of the Fresh Produce Art Collective (6 P.M. Tues.), a group of artists who unite to plan new projects, shows, and parties. The community-centric space at **Lawrence Arts Center** (940 New Hampshire St., 785/843-2787, www.lawrenceartscenter.com, 9 A.M.–5 P.M. Mon.–Sat.) hosts classes, special programs, and 13–16 arts exhibitions annually. After you've finished browsing current displays, head to the Lawrence Arts Center Gallery Shop to pick up fine arts and crafts created by local artisans. Part art gallery, part screen-printing house, and part merchandise retailer complete with DIY goods and zines, **Wonder Fair: Art Gallery and How!** (803 Massachusetts St., 406/360-5875, www.wonderfair.com, noon–6 P.M. Thurs.–Sat.) is a celebration of contemporary works that evoke a comfortable viability reflective of the Lawrence arts community. Formerly a flood-damaged basement, Wonder Fair is now a multifaceted arts space that's a must-see in Lawrence. Nationally known artists, group shows, and individual artists that focus on "compelling concepts" are the focus at **6 Gallery** (716 1/2 Massachusetts St., 785/856-6480, www.6gallery.net, noon–5 P.M. Thurs.–Sun., and by appointment), which hosts exhibits created in a variety of media, from paintings and prints to mixed media and book arts. Director Sally Piller also offers personalized art shopping services if you're interested in starting—or adding to—a collection. Peruse works that span European and American art histories at the **Spencer Museum of Art** (1301 Mississippi St., 785/864-4710, www.spencerart.ku.edu, 10 A.M.–4 P.M. Tues.–Sat., until 8 P.M. Thurs., noon–4 P.M. Sun., free), a museum that began when Kansas City art collector Sallie Casey Thayer donated her entire 7,500-piece collection to start an on-campus art museum. Today, the neoclassical structure also hosts an extensive digital library collection, as well as temporary exhibits and children's programming.

Performing Arts

Check the performance schedule of the **Lied Center of Kansas** (1600 Stewart Dr., 785/864-2787, www.lied.ku.edu, prices vary) to see if your trip coincides with any of the center's performances, which range from dance and singing to musicals and orchestral ensembles. Or try **Liberty Hall** (644 Massachusetts St., 785/749-1972, www.libertyhall.net, prices vary) a historic former opera house that now hosts music concerts and independent movies in a majestic setting. A true stronghold of local history, the **Watkins Community Museum of History** (1047 Massachusetts St., 785/841-4109, www.watkinsmuseum.org, 10 A.M.–4 P.M. Tues.–Sat., until 8 P.M. Thurs., free) dates back to 1887 and now hosts a variety of exhibits, memorabilia and more dedicated to preserving Lawrence's often-turbulent history. The Watkins Museum also hosts an on-site research room, as well as Miss Lizzie's Gifts, the perfect place to find your Lawrence souvenir.

SHOPS

An eclectic mix of boutiques and specialty shops makes shopping in Lawrence a daylong excursion in itself. Stop in to **Joe College** (734 Massachusetts St., 785/856-4563, www.joecollege.com, 11 A.M.–7 P.M. Mon.–Wed. and Fri., 11 A.M.–8 P.M. Thurs., 10 A.M.–7 P.M. Sat., noon–5 P.M. Sun.) for a wide selection of snarky, irreverent, and unlicensed T-shirts and other collegiate apparel. For authentic British food and gifts, stop into **Brits** (929 Massachusetts St., 785/843-2288, www.britsusa.com, 10 A.M.–6 P.M. Mon.–Wed., 10 A.M.–8 P.M. Thurs.–Fri., 10 A.M.–6 P.M. Sat., noon–5 P.M. Sun.) Pick up a box of Twinings tea and shortbread, or browse Brits' housewares section for tea accessories and baking tools. **Blackbird Trading Post** (8 W. 9th St., 785/841-1498, 11 A.M.–6 P.M. Wed.–Mon.) is a consignment shop filled with brand-name clothing, accessories, and shoes. It takes a little patience to dig through the racks, but you just may be rewarded with a one-of-a-kind find, and at a reduced price, no less! **Waxman Candles** (609 Massachusetts St., 785/843-8593, www.waxmancandles.com, 9:30 A.M.–7 P.M. Mon.–Sat., noon–5 P.M. Sun.) is a veritable candle emporium, stocked floor-to-ceiling with columns, tapers, votives, and every other candle imaginable. The handmade candles come in a variety of scents, from floral or fresh to sugary and seasonal. Several Kansas souvenir candles are available, including a Jayhawk and sunflower silhouettes. Duck into the **Dusty Bookshelf** (708 Massachusetts St., 785/539-2839, www.thedustybookshelf.com, 10 A.M.–8 P.M. Mon.–Thurs., 10 A.M.–10 P.M. Fri.–Sat., noon–6 P.M. Sun.) and browse an impressive array of new and second-hand books on subjects ranging from comic books and communications to history and travel.

HOTELS

If you decide to extend your Lawrence day trip into a weekend excursion, severally locally owned hotels await that add additional local flavor to your trip. Book a room at the historic **Eldridge Hotel** (701 Massachusetts St., 800/527-0909, www.eldridgehotel.com, $145–159), a stately hotel that still stands despite being burned and raided several times during the town's early (and turbulent) history. Spacious suites are a quietly modern contrast to the hotel's carefully preserved lobby, and an on-site restaurant and bar are great places to unwind if you opt to stay in.

The Halcyon House Bed and Breakfast (1000 Ohio St., 785/841-0314, www.thehalcyonhouse.com, $55–99) features nine distinct rooms, including the luxurious master suite and Cozy Nooks and Crannies room, and homemade breakfasts. Despite the bed-and-breakfast's 100-year-old setting, it's fully equipped with a fax machine, high-speed Internet, and voicemail.

PRACTICALITIES

Tourist Office

The **Lawrence Convention and Visitors Bureau** (402 N. 2nd St., 785/865-4499, www.visitlawrence.com) is a great source for city maps, self-guided tour information, and other materials that can help you plan your time in Lawrence.

Media

The *Lawrence Journal-World* (www2.ljworld.com) is Lawrence's daily newspaper that offers news, sports, business, arts, and other pertinent local information. The *Journal-World* operates an information-packed, easy-to-navigate website with great information about local businesses and upcoming events that may assist you in trip-planning. If you're on the University of Kansas campus, pick up a *University Daily Kansan* for a print guide to student life. You can also find the *Kansas City Star's Ink* magazine throughout Lawrence, a good source for nightlife and event calendars.

Tune your radio to Kansas Public Radio (91.5 FM, www.kansaspublicradio.org) for NPR news and shows and jazz and classical music.

Getting There

Lawrence is an easy 45-minute drive on I-70 west out of Kansas City. Although Lawrence has a great public transportation system, it would be difficult—and pricey—to get to Lawrence from Kansas City by any means other than driving. Bring a couple of dollars in cash with you for the tollway, which you'll have to pay as you cross into Lawrence. Exit U.S. 59 south and turn left on 2nd Street to get to downtown Lawrence and Massachusetts Street, an ideal spot to start your journey.

Getting Around

If you opt to stay in and around downtown Lawrence, you'll find the college town walkable (although be sure to wear comfortable shoes). Look for long-term parking lots near places like the Lawrence Public Library (707 Vermont St., www.lawrence.lib.ks.us); the parking meter patrol are particularly active in Lawrence, and it's best to avoid running back to your car every hour or two to refresh the meter.

The Lawrence Transit System (www.lawrencetransit.org) runs routes throughout the city on "The T." Buses are a great way to get from downtown to the KU campus and points in between, if you'd prefer to see more of the city. You can download a route map before you go, or visit the Lawrence Chamber of Commerce (734 Vermont St.), Lawrence Public Library, or Lawrence Visitors Center to pick up maps.

Omaha, Nebraska

Omaha and Kansas City share many similarities, and you'll find much to do and see in Kansas City's cousin to the north. Although smaller than Kansas City, Omaha still packs a tourism punch thanks to concentrated efforts to make the city a regional destination. Founded in 1854, Omaha is also a railroad city and was home to stockyards, making Omaha at one time, according to historians, "the fastest growing city in America."

Head to Omaha, and you'll be in good company. Famous natives include president Gerald Ford, Malcom X, Fred Astaire, Marlon Brando, and Warren Buffett. The nation's 42nd-largest city offers an appealing array of shopping, dining, and must-see sights, as well as a variety of annual events like the **River City Roundup,** the **Summer Arts Festival,** and the **Holiday Lights Festival.**

COURTESY OF OMAHA CONVENTION AND VISITORS ASSOCIATION

View tropical animals in their native habitat within the Henry Doorly Zoo's Lied Jungle, the world's largest indoor rainforest.

Omaha is home to the award-winning **Henry Doorly Zoo,** and in the heart of downtown Omaha you'll find the vibrant must-see **Old Market** area, a shopping, dining, and entertainment zone so scenic you'll have a hard time putting your camera away.

Although Omaha has experienced the same outward growth as Kansas City, you'll still get a feel for the city's soul if you confine your trip to the downtown area and the immediately surrounding attractions, like the **Bob Kerrey pedestrian bridge.** If you're feeling adventurous, however, hop on I-80 west for a quick 10-minute drive to the behemoth **Nebraska Furniture Mart** headquarters that encompasses—no kidding—more than a city block.

SIGHTS

Bob Kerrey Pedestrian Bridge

This stunning architectural example is the only pedestrian bridge in the United States to link two states (Council Bluffs, Iowa, is on the other side). The Bob Kerrey pedestrian bridge (705 Riverfront Dr., 402/444-5900, www.ci.omaha.ne.us/parks) is a 3,000-foot cable-stayed bridge that connects to 150 miles of hiking and biking trails on either side. Although the bridge is magnificent at any time of day, it's an especially breathtaking adventure at night, when you'll be afforded a glittering view of Omaha's skyline, as well as of the lighted bridge itself, suspended 60 feet above the river.

Henry Doorly Zoo

Renowned as one of the premier zoos in the Midwest, Omaha's Henry Doorly Zoo (3701 S. 10th St., 402/738-2088, www.omahazoo.com, 9:30 A.M.–5 P.M. daily, $11.50 adult, $10 senior, $7.75 child) is a huge zoological park complete with exhibitions like Desert Dome, the world's largest indoor desert. Or travel into the dark depths of Kingdoms of the Night, the world's largest nocturnal exhibit. Because day-night cycles are reversed, you can view nocturnal animals like naked mole rats, bats, and freshwater crocodiles in their natural habitat. The zoo is also home to the Lozier IMAX theater, which hosts educational and animal-related 3-D movies with stunning sound and clarity. Check the zoo's website for an updated list of shows and showtimes.

Old Market

Feel the pulse of the city within Omaha's historic Old Market (www.oldmarket.com), a shopping, dining, and entertainment district bounded by Farnam to the north, 10th Street to the east, 13th Street to the west, and Leavenworth Road to the south. Formerly the city's vibrant wholesale district, the light industrial and warehouse buildings have since been renovated into a diverse mix of boutiques, restaurants, and bars connected by charming brick-paved streets. Explore the Old Market in a horse-drawn carriage, or let your feet lead you through the quaint streets often filled with street performers and impromptu music concerts. Historic building facades combined with lush landscaping, including rooftop flower boxes that line most of Old Market's spaces, make the area ripe with photo opportunities. Be sure to seek out the Old Market passageway, a covered thoroughfare that offers a different—and photogenic—view of several Old Market shops and restaurants.

Omaha Push Pins

It's an ingenious idea—enterprising minds thought to put giant blue push pins at important sights throughout the city, and if you pick up a corresponding map at the Omaha Visitors Center or any Omaha hotel, you can spend several hours on a self-guided tour through some of the city's premier attractions. To get you started, I'll give you a hint—there's a push pin in the Old Market. If you don't immediately see it, you can't miss the crowds of people standing around to have their picture taken in front of what is both a brilliant marketing campaign and an unusual public art installation. You can download the push-pin map before you go at www.visitomaha.com/includes/media/docs/GO-ElectronicMap2.pdf.

RESTAURANTS

Come to Omaha hungry, and your stomach won't be sorry. Lunch on the patio at **Stokes Grill** (12th and Howard Sts., 402/408-9000, www.restaurantsinc.net, 11 A.M.–10 P.M. Mon.–Thurs., 11 A.M.–11 P.M. Fri.–Sat., 10 A.M.–9 P.M. Sun., $6.45–27.95) is a relaxing setting for Southwestern cuisine. Take my word for it and order Sharon's almost-famous chicken enchiladas washed down with any of the bar's signature cocktails, like a raspberry mojito. If you're in the mood for American food and locally brewed beer, the **Upstream Brewery** (514 S. 11th St., 402/344-0200, www.upstreambrewing.com, 11 A.M.–11 P.M. Mon.–Thurs., 11 A.M.–midnight Fri.–Sat., 2 P.M.–midnight Sun., $7.50–36.50) awaits with pizza, salad, and perfectly cooked steak—including an Omaha Steaks filet mignon—that pair well with Upstream's house-made brews. If you crave a laid-back atmosphere and simple, filling fare, head to **Lisa's Radial Cafe** (817 N. 40th St., 402/551-2176, 7 A.M.–2 P.M. daily, $3.99–8.99), an Omaha institution in the Cathedral District that serves one of the best breakfasts in the city. And when you're finished, pop over to nearby **Sweet Magnolias Bakery** (813 N. 40th St., 402/934-6427, 7 A.M.–2 P.M. Mon.–Sat., less than $5) for oversized cupcakes, cherry scones, and iced cinnamon rolls, perfect to satisfy an immediate sweet-tooth craving or to save later for snacks. For dinner, head back to Old Market for pasta and salad at family-friendly **Spaghetti Works** (502 S. 11th St., 402/422-0770, www.spagworks.com, 11 A.M.–9 P.M. Mon.–Thurs. and Sun., 11 A.M.–10 P.M. Fri.–Sat., $5.99–14.49), which lets you pick the sauce, noodles, and additional toppings for a truly customized—and bottomless—pasta dish. And all entrées come with a salad bar, a seemingly lost art in today's restaurant world. If you're looking for something more intimate, **Vivace** (1108 Howard St., 402/342-2050, www.vivaceomaha.com, 11 A.M.–11 P.M. Mon.–Thurs., 11 A.M.–midnight Fri.–Sat., 5 P.M.–10 P.M. Sun., $8.95–14.95) serves up traditional Italian favorites with a side of ambience. The covered patio beckons with relaxing visions of enjoying wine and bread while people-watching, although if you plan to go on a Friday or Saturday night, make a reservation or be prepared to wait an hour or more. If you decide to explore the more outlying areas of the city, look for an outpost of **Runza** (www.runza.com, 10:30 A.M.–10 P.M. Mon.–Sat., 10:30 A.M.–9 P.M. Sun., $4.95–8.95) while you drive. The favorite fast-food joint, consistently voted as having Omaha's best french fries, carries the city's signature stuffed sandwiches (think Hot Pockets, but way better) with combinations like swiss mushroom or the original.

NIGHTLIFE

As with Omaha's shopping scene, much of the city's nightlife is concentrated within the Old Market District. And because most spots offer a casual environment, you can explore the city all day and still make plans for a nightcap without a wardrobe change. If you're in the mood to dance, head below to **The Underground** (1017 Howard St., 402/341-3547, 7 P.M.–1 A.M. daily), a three-room bar and dance club that welcomes area DJs in a cavernous environment complete with stone walls. For something more laid-back—and less loud—try the **Old Market Tavern** (514 S. 10th St., 402/341-1091, 4 P.M.–1 A.M. Mon.–Sat., 6 P.M.–1 A.M. Sun.), which serves up a variety of cocktails and Kansas City's Boulevard beer in no-fuss surroundings. To perfect the art of the cocktail, **Myth** (1105 Howard St., 402/884-6985, www.mytholdmarket.com, 7 P.M.–1 A.M. Tues.–Wed., 5 P.M.–1 A.M. Thurs.–Sat.) awaits with a sophisticated lounge-style interior and a cocktail menu that just might make you drool. The 2009 sapphire dragon, a refreshing mix of muddled cucumber and watermelon, Bombay Sapphire Gin, and a splash of Simply Limeade, was a regional award-winner. For a similar lounge-style atmosphere, the **Sake Bombers Lounge** (416 S. 12th St., 402/408-5566, www.bluesushisakegrill.com, 11 A.M.–10 P.M. Mon.–Thurs., 11 A.M.–midnight Fri.–Sat., noon–9 P.M. Sun.) awaits with an extensive sake menu, fish-bowl drinks, and plush seating prime for relaxing or people-watching. Wine enthusiasts, make tracks to **Urban Wine Company** (1037 Jones St., 402/934-0005, www.urbanwinecompany.com, 3–11 P.M. Tues.–Wed., 3 P.M.–1 A.M. Thurs.–Fri., 11 A.M.–1 A.M. Sat., noon–9 P.M. Sun.), a wine bar that also serves flavorful small bites as well as meat and cheese flights, the perfect accompaniment to the Urban Wine Company's more than 40 boutique wines served by the glass or 200 served by the bottle.

SHOPS

For the best in locally owned boutiques, the Old Market is the place to be. **City Limits** (1120 1/2 Howard St., 402/345-3570, 10:30 A.M.–8 P.M.

Mon.–Thurs., 10:30 A.M.–9 P.M. Fri.–Sat., 11 A.M.–5 P.M. Sun.) is a quirky shop filled with gifts and novelty items like pulp novel postcards, bacon mints, kitschy cards, art prints, and a surprisingly large selection of magnets. If you'd prefer to shop for your home, **Room** (421 S. 11th St., 402/342-7666, www.roomomaha.com, 11 A.M.–7 P.M. Mon.–Sat.) is a contemporary haven filled with furniture and accessories, and is also a FLOR distributor. The shop carries several gifts from the Metropolitan Museum of Art's gift store, so if you can't make it to New York in the near future, a visit to Room might be the next best thing. It's Christmas year-round in **Tannenbaum Christmas Store** (1007 Howard St., 402/345-9627, www.otannenbaum.com, 11 A.M.–5 P.M. Mon.–Thurs., 11 A.M.–7 P.M. Fri.–Sat., noon–3 P.M. Sun.), where you'll find decorations, ornaments, and other Christmas novelties whether you're visiting Omaha during the holidays or you like Christmas in July. The aptly named **Pulp** (1026 Howard St., 402/319-7857, www.p-u-l-p.com, 11 A.M.–7 P.M. Tues.–Fri., noon–6 P.M. Sat.) is an upscale paper shop that doubles as a paper arts gallery space. Browse letterpress and other cards, decorative papers from PaperSource, and a small but impressive array of art books on a variety of subjects. If fashion is what you seek, head to **Nouvelle Eve** (1102 Howard St., 402/345-4811, www.nouvelleeve.com, 11 A.M.–8 P.M. Mon., 11 A.M.–9 P.M. Tues.–Sat., noon–5 P.M. Sun.), a spacious boutique crammed with apparel, accessories, and lingerie in pretty, feminine surroundings that beg "girl's day out!" Owned by a former *InStyle* accessories editor, **Trocadero** (1208 1/2 Howard St., 402/934-8389, www.shoptrocadero.com, 11 A.M.–6 P.M. Mon. and Wed., 11 A.M.–7 P.M. Thurs.–Sat., noon–5 P.M. Sun.) is a must-see filled with designer shoes, handbags, accessories, and a diverse array of New York– and Paris–inspired merchandise including vintage maps, Diptyque candles, and guidebooks. And for more home furnishings, **Niche** (1112 Howard St., 402/344-4399, www.nichegifts.com, 10 A.M.–9 P.M. Mon.–Thurs., 10 A.M.–10 P.M. Fri.–Sat., noon–6 P.M. Sun.) is a well-stocked interiors haven that offers furniture and accessories artfully arranged on shelves and in, well, niches scattered throughout the boutique.

EXCURSIONS

HOTELS

Hotels are located throughout Omaha, especially near prime venues like the Qwest Center and the newly finished convention center. If you plan to spend most of your time in and around the Old Market, the **Courtyard by Marriott Omaha Downtown** (101 S. 10th St., 402/346-2200, www.marriott.com, $99–229) puts you less than three blocks away from the Old Market District, as well as across the street from the Omaha Visitors Center. A little more off the beaten path, **The Cornerstone Mansion** (140 N. 39th St., 402/558-7600, www.cornerstonemansion.com, rates vary) is an elegant inn operated by Mark J. O'Leary and Julie K. Mierau that includes authentically furnished rooms complete with claw-footed bathtubs, canopy beds, and fireplaces, depending on the room. Sophisticated, modern surroundings make you feel instantly welcome at **The Magnolia Hotel** (1615 Howard St., 402/341-2500, www.magnoliahotelomaha.com, $134–149), complete with hot breakfast, a nighttime cookie buffet, and plush club lounges that encourage interaction with other hotel guests.

PRACTICALITIES

Tourist Office

The **Omaha Convention and Visitors Bureau** (1001 Farnam St., 866/937-6624, www.visit

COURTESY OF THE MAGNOLIA HOTEL OMAHA

The Magnolia Hotel

omaha.com) includes a wealth of city literature, as well as a gift shop for all of your Omaha souvenir needs. Before you head out to explore the city, stop at the bureau's coffee shop for a beverage and a chat with knowledgeable baristas who can help you plan the rest of your day.

Media

The *Omaha World-Herald* (www.omaha.com) is the largest daily newspaper in Nebraska and is available at newsstands and distribution boxes throughout the city. Also look for *The Reader* (www.thereader.com), Omaha's news weekly that's an invaluable source for local event calendars, nightlife information, and profiles of notable Omaha residents.

Tune into KKAR (1290 AM) for local news, talk, sports, and community events. Omaha Public Radio (91.5 KIOS-FM, www.kios.org) hosts regular NPR news updates and afternoon and evening jazz shows ranging from blues to experimental and groove-oriented jazz.

Getting There

Driving is the best and most economical way to get to the southeast corner of Nebraska from Kansas City. At just under three hours, the drive is a relatively straight shot north on I-29. Merge onto I-80 to head into the city; the 13th Street exit will take you to the Henry Doorly Zoo as well as into the heart of downtown Omaha.

Getting Around

Omaha is a fairly walkable city, especially if you're planning to spend most of your time in and around the Old Market. Street parking is ample although sometimes hard to find, especially during the Saturday-morning farmers market.

Omaha's **MAT public transit system** (www.metroareatransit.com) offers routes throughout Omaha's downtown and outlying areas, including numerous routes that take riders directly to the Bob Kerrey pedestrian bridge.

Rocheport, Missouri

Formerly a trading post for area settlers and Native Americans, Rocheport (pronounced "roach-port") dates back to the 1830s. Increased steamboat travel along the Missouri River contributed to Rocheport's 19th-century growth. The small town boasts a population of just over 200, but Rocheport's prime location along the bluffs of the Missouri River and the Katy Trail have made it a favorite historical escape for travelers eager to explore the past. Celebrated Native American author William Least Heat Moon is a Rocheport native.

The town of Rocheport is located 10 minutes west of Columbia, Missouri, on I-70, approximately a one hour, 40-minute drive from Kansas City. Because Rocheport is small, you can easily see it in a day and head back to Kansas City, or continue on to Columbia to explore the home of the University of Missouri–Columbia. To take advantage of the wealth of recreational options like biking on the Katy Trail or canoeing on the Missouri River, however, you may opt to spend more time in Rocheport and book a room at one of the town's charmingly quaint bed-and-breakfasts.

SIGHTS

Missouri River Boating Tour

Enjoy the glory of Big Muddy with a guided Missouri River tour from **Drew's Guide Service** (573/881-6160, $125–350 one–two people, cost increases for larger groups), which welcomes guests into 17-foot handmade, motorized lorry boats. Choose from a variety of cruises like sunset or sunrise viewings, all-day

© ALLISON SMYTHE

Perched on a bluff overlooking the Missouri River, Rocheport is a scenic community 10 minutes west of Columbia, Missouri.

and all-night fishing expeditions, and bird-watching or sightseeing tours. Drew is also happy to create customized tours for small groups depending on your interests. Meals are discussed at the time of tour bookings. For the ultimate souvenir, talk to Drew about Missouri Boatworks, his custom boat-building business. Crafted out of wood, the boats are available in a variety of styles, from dinghies to race boats.

Friends of Rocheport Historical Museum

Although its hours are a bit limited, the Friends of Rocheport Historical Museum (First and Moniteau Sts., 1–4 P.M. Sat.–Sun. May–Oct.) provides a fascinating glimpse into local history. The volunteer-staffed museum contains carefully preserved artifacts and historical documents from the town's rich history as a former trading post and river and railroad town. The town of Rocheport was near one of Lewis and Clark's stops as they made their way west on their infamous early-1800s journey.

Katy Trail

The Katy Trail is a 225-mile bike path that crosses most of Missouri and winds through several cities and towns including Rocheport, Sedalia, Columbia, state capital Jefferson City, and St. Charles. While you're in Rocheport, stop at the Trailside Cafe and Bike Shop to rent a bike and head out for your own trail exploring. Bicycling enthusiasts will want to check in with the Missouri Department of Natural Resources (www.dnr.mo.gov) for updated information on the annual end-to-end trail ride, held in June. Formerly the route of the MKT (Missouri–Kansas–Texas) rail line, the Katy Trail remains an homage to railroad history with several restored train cars and depots that can be seen along the trail. If you're interested in spending more time on the trail, visit www.bikekatytrail.com and order the *Katy Trail Guidebook,* an invaluable source of information on trail towns, camping, wineries, bicycling tips, and more.

TUNNEL VISION

While you're in Rocheport, a visit to the Katy Trail is mandatory. Formerly the site of the MKT (Missouri-Kansas-Texas) Railroad, the Katy Trail now traverses 225 miles of scenic Missouri countryside, often navigating a path through towns and cities that are picturesque retreats in their own right – not to mention welcome havens for tired bikers ready for a meal and a good night's sleep.

At mile marker 178.9 in Rocheport, you'll pass through the only tunnel to be built on the MKT line. Constructed in 1893, the 243-foot stone structure is arch-shaped to allow for passing trains, and now serves as a shaded thoroughfare for passing bikers, walkers, and joggers.

Just past Rocheport on the trail, stop to admire the stunning bluffs that tower over the Missouri River. You won't be the first to notice the staggering natural beauty; research suggests that explorers Lewis and Clark described the view in their travel journals as they headed west on their infamous exploration.

Rocheport General Store

Stepping into the Rocheport General Store (202 Central St., 573/698-2282, www.rocheportgeneralstore.com, 7 A.M.–10 P.M. Wed.–Sat., 8 A.M.–6 P.M. Sun.) is as close to getting in a time machine as you can get. Owners Dan and Sherrie Ingram remain committed to preserving the store's history and offer a variety of nostalgic goods, including old-fashioned candy and gifts that make you yearn for days

© ALLISON SMYTHE

Step back in time at the Rocheport General Store and stock up on old-fashioned goods and candies.

gone by. A favorite town gathering place, the Rocheport General Store also serves meals and welcomes special events like live music performances, as well as town-wide events like the September Wine Stroll. Pull up a chair to one of the tables and test your skill at one of the store's board games. If you're feeling especially adventurous, challenge a local to a match and you may end up learning about Rocheport from a first-hand source.

Les Bourgeois Winery

Wine enthusiasts from around Missouri flock to Rocheport's celebrated winery, Les Bourgeois (12847 W. Highway BB, 800/690-1830, www.missouriwine.com, 11 A.M.–9 P.M. Tues.–Sat., 11 A.M.–3 P.M. Sun., $6–24), for flavorful red, white, and blush varieties made entirely on-site. Before you relax with a glass (or bottle) at one of the bluff-top tables overlooking the Missouri River, get a glimpse of the wine-making process with a guided tour and complimentary tasting (1, 2, and 3 P.M. Sat. and Sun.). An adjacent understated yet stylish bistro is a picturesque place to enjoy a meal against the backdrop of the Missouri River. Try a sandwich with locally grown tomatoes, portobello mushrooms, and arugula; for dinner, you can't go wrong with the indulgent buttermilk-marinated, cornflake-baked chicken breast. Stop at the gift shop on your way out to pick up gift baskets, bottles of your favorite Les Bourgeois wine, and other wine-centric souvenirs.

RESTAURANTS

You'll work up quite an appetite exploring Rocheport and biking the Katy Trail, and Rocheport restaurants offer quite the culinary variety. Try **Abigail's** (206 Central St., 573/698-3000, 11 A.M.–2 P.M. and 5–9 P.M.

Wed.–Sat., $8–30) for filling fare and a menu that changes daily, although you'll want to make a reservation for dinner. Head to the **Trailside Cafe and Bike Shop** (700 First St., 573/698-2702, www.trailsidecafebike.com, 9 A.M.–6 P.M. Mon.–Tues., 9 A.M.–7 P.M. Thurs.–Fri., 8 A.M.–7 P.M. Sat., $5–10) to fill up before you hit the Katy Trail. Sandwiches (try the reuben special) and sides are simple yet satisfying, and you can take your pick from indoor or outdoor seating.

SHOPS

Take home a taste of Missouri when you shop at **Flavors of the Heartland/Rocheport Gallery** (204 Second St., 573/698-2088, 11 A.M.–5 P.M. Wed.–Sat., noon–5 P.M. Sun.), a charming boutique that stocks Missouri-made gourmet food products. Try infused vinegars, or for a taste of fall, freshly made pumpkin and apple butters. Or opt for a Boone County ham and, because you're never too far from Kansas City's barbecue aura, a bottle of barbecue sauce. There's no better place to shop for antiques than in a historic town, and at **White Horse Antiques** (505 Third St., 573/698-2088, 10 A.M.–5 P.M. Wed.–Sat., noon–5 P.M. Sun.) you'll find antique furniture, decorative country quilts, and modern interior accessories should your tastes run more toward contemporary. You may have a hard time getting them home, but the more than 1,500 varieties of annuals, tropicals, and roses at **Vintage Hill Nursery** (5643 Hwy. 87, Franklin, 660/848-2373, www.vintagehill.com, 9 A.M.–5 P.M. daily) still make for beautiful and fragrant browsing.

HOTELS

Bed-and-breakfasts rule in Rocheport, and they offer the perfect way to end a day spent exploring, hiking, biking, and boating. Try my personal favorite, the **School House Bed and Breakfast** (504 Third St., 573/698-2022, www.schoolhousebb.com, $149–260), for cozy rooms named for schoolhouse themes like The Prose, Dick & Jane's Room, and The Schoolmarm. **The Katy Trail Bed and Bikefest** (101 Lewis St., 573/698-2453, www.katytrailbbb.com, $70–200), a renovated 1880s home that's a secluded retreat for bikers and guests. Choose from the Attic Suite, the Katy View Room, or the Jefferson Suite, or for large groups, inquire about renting the Tree House. The Queen Anne Victorian–style **Amber House Bed and Breakfast** (705 Third St., 573/698-2028, www.amberhousebb.com, $149–249) is a luxurious retreat that offers packages to coincide with various local events. Satisfy your inner foodie with the Amber House Cooking School Culinary Getaway, a two-night stay that includes a demonstration cooking class for 6–8 people (from $30/person plus the cost of room).

PRACTICALITIES

Tourist Office

Rocheport doesn't offer a visitors center, but you can find a comprehensive guide to Rocheport at www.rocheport.com, including a PDF version of the visitors guide that will help you navigate the historic town. Business owners and residents are friendly, so don't hesitate to stop and ask for directions, recommendations, or opinions about the weather.

Media

Because Rocheport is located just outside of Columbia, Missouri, the town is served by the daily *Columbia Tribune* newspaper and Columbia/Jefferson City news stations including Channel 8 (NBC affiliate), Channel 13 (CBS affiliate), and Channel 17 (ABC affiliate).

Getting There

Head east from Kansas City on I-70, and after an hour and 40-minute drive take the Rocheport exit and turn left to head into town. If you want to start your day with a winery tour or glass of Riverboat Red on a patio perched atop a river bluff, Les Bourgeois Winery is just to the north of I-70.

Getting Around

You can plan to park and explore Rocheport on foot—the town's small size allows for the shops, restaurants, and sights to be clustered fairly close together. Hikers are welcome on the Katy Trail, but to cover the most amount of ground in the least amount of time, bike rental is the best option.

BACKGROUND

The Setting

GEOGRAPHY AND CLIMATE

Kansas City's location on the southern banks of the Missouri River lends itself to a gently rolling terrain throughout the area. It's a geography that's a pleasing hybrid of the expansive prairies of Kansas and the hillier terrain that's a signature of Missouri's Ozarks region. Weather-wise, Kansas City knows how to introduce each of the four seasons. A modified continental climate often leads to dramatic temperature changes, especially in early spring and again in late fall. Winters can be cold and snowy, with average temperatures that hover around the freezing mark. Summers are a marked contrast, with average temperatures in the mid-70s. During July and August, however, the weather can be hot; add a high degree of humidity, and you've got a recipe for swampy days best spent inside or in close proximity to a swimming pool. Spring and fall are favorite weather times in Kansas City, when mild temperatures and abundant sunshine entice residents and visitors outside, whether for a picnic, a nap, or a leisurely stroll. Pack an umbrella, even if the advanced forecast doesn't indicate rain. Weather changes

COURTESY OF THE KANSAS CITY CONVENTION AND VISITORS ASSOCIATION

CITY BEAUTIFUL

Kansas City has long exuded a strong sense of civic spirit, seen even in the city's early history as the rail, industrial, and stockyard capital clawed its way to Midwestern dominance. As a direct response to the profitable yet unsightly railroads, stockyards, and bleak industrial buildings, city leaders united in the late 1800s to launch the City Beautiful project, spearheaded by *Kansas City Star* founder William Rockhill Nelson.

German immigrant George Kessler had arrived in Kansas City and finished a design for a Merriam-based railroad excursion park. Nelson was so impressed with the design that he asked Kessler to sketch ideas for a crumbling area of bluffs overlooking the West Bottoms. The drawings were a success, and Kessler was soon asked to create an ambitious citywide plan, launched in the early 1900s, that would create an expansive boulevard system that not only traveled throughout the city but also linked a series of lush greenspaces meant to provide an aesthetically pleasing respite for travelers and area residents, most notably the wealthy population that built grandiose mansions in neighborhoods surrounding the then-downtown area.

Kessler's impressive work remains visible today as you travel down scenic Ward Parkway or Brookside Boulevard, both of which are multilaned thoroughfares lined with trees and dotted with grassy sculpted medians and majestic fountains.

© FRANK ROMEO/WWW.123RFC.OM

Kansas City skyline

quickly in Kansas City, thanks to fast-moving weather systems that propel eastward across Kansas and northward from the Gulf of Mexico. Skies can quickly cloud, causing a sudden change in temperatures. In the spring and summer months, severe thunderstorms are prevalent, a by-product of the city's location in the heart of Tornado Alley. In the winter, snow and ice storms can be difficult to predict and pinpoint. On average, the city receives just over 20 inches of snowfall each winter, most of which is concentrated during a few winter storms that range from moderate to severe in terms of precipitation generated and travel difficulties posed.

FLORA AND FAUNA

Because Kansas City straddles Missouri and Kansas, visitors have an ideal opportunity to see foliage and wildlife common to both states. Wildflowers and grasses are common sites along the city's interstates and highways, although be aware that picking these plants is illegal. While you're out and about, look for these 10 common native plants that thrive amid the city's weather conditions: bluestar, blue false indigo, willowleaf sunflower, smooth hydrangea, spicebush, cardinal flower, ninebark, fringe tree, christmas fern, and sourgum. The Missouri state tree, the dogwood, and the Kansas state tree, the cottonwood, are both prevalent throughout Kansas City, as are Bradford pears and several varieties of oak trees.

Arguably the most common animal sighting in the Kansas City area is deer, often subjected to overcrowding because of habitat loss. In fact, deer have become so prevalent in some of the outlying parks that city councils have approved the controlled hunting of deer in an effort to thin out the population.

ENVIRONMENTAL ISSUES

A gradual outward growth that began in the mid-1900s has created an overwhelming reliance on the automobile, a practice that has had hazardous effects on Kansas City's environment and air quality. Ground-level ozone, produced by emissions generated from vehicles, lawn mowers, power plants, and industries, can become a problem during the summer months, when hot temperatures and high humidity create a blanket conducive to trapping ozone emissions at or near ground-level. Local media outlets publish daily SkyCasts, which rate the following day's air quality on a scale from good (green) to red alert. When an orange or red ozone alert is issued, the Kansas City Area Transportation Authority issues fare discounts on the Metro, the Jo, and Unified Government Transit as a way to entice people to rely less on cars and instead opt for public transportation. Motorists are also encouraged to fuel up during afternoon and evening hours, a practice that results in a decrease of potentially harmful emissions.

City-wide expansion has also led to a concern about producing sustainable structures that have less of an environmental impact. A proliferation of mixed-use districts indicates the city's commitment to creating walkable areas that give residents a place to live, work, and play all within a short radius. More and more Kansas City buildings are being built to LEED standards, indicating a use of responsible construction materials; energy-efficient wiring, HVAC, and lighting systems; and other green qualifications.

History

THE FOUNDING OF KANSAS CITY

Gazing out at today's sizable metropolitan area, it's difficult to believe that Kansas City started as two mere trading posts in the early 1800s, one on the Missouri River (the Town of Kansas) and one located several miles away, known as Westport. Enterprising fur trader Francois Chouteau and entrepreneur John Calvin McCoy worked in the towns of Kansas and Westport, respectively, to provide goods to those passing through on various trails headed for points west like Santa Fe and Oregon. Upon its incorporation by Missouri on February 22, 1853, the town became known as the City of Kansas, a name shortened in 1889 to Kansas City.

Looking back on Kansas City's early history, it's almost as if a perfect storm formed over the flourishing city in order to give it an advantage over regional neighbors (such as Omaha, Chicago, and St. Louis)—and those cities close by, such as St. Joseph and Leavenworth. Historian W. H. Miller attributes Kansas City's explosive early development to several characteristics: "In the first place, it was the junction of the Missouri and Kansas rivers at this point that induced the early French traders and trappers to locate here. The junction of the Missouri and Kansas rivers, therefore, afforded them this facility in a much more extended area of country than any other point in the west. Steamboat navigation on the Missouri being begun almost simultaneously with that trade, afforded cheaper transportation than by wagons; hence it was employed to this, the nearest point to Santa Fe."

In the mid-1850s, Kansas City vied with Leavenworth, Kansas, and St. Joseph, Missouri, for the role of metropolis of the West, a struggle for regional dominance that became more difficult following the economic devastation of the Civil War, a national conflict that hit close to home thanks to vicious fighting among pro- and anti-slavery supporters that culminated in the Battle of Westport. In *Kansas City: An American Story,* authors Rick Montgomery and

THE SHOTS HEARD 'ROUND KANSAS CITY

The morning of June 17, 1933, dawned like any other. Convicted robber Frank Nash, who had escaped from the U.S. Penitentiary in Leavenworth, was recaptured in Hot Springs, Arkansas, and was being brought by train back to Kansas City. Both federal and local law enforcement anxiously awaited his arrival to escort him back to Leavenworth.

After Nash's train pulled into Union Station, officers led him in handcuffs through the building and out into the parking lot. They were intercepted by a car carrying three Nash supporters, one of whom was rumored to be infamous gangster Charles "Pretty Boy" Floyd. A vicious gun battle ensued in the parking lot, leaving Nash, a federal agent, two Kansas City police officers, and an Oklahoma police chief dead.

Nash's rescuers sped away, and federal officials quickly launched a full-scale investigation into the day's events. Adam Richetti would later be executed as a result of the investigation, which also uncovered the activities of several Kansas City crime bosses in harboring and aiding conspirators. J. Edgar Hoover led the investigation, and gained such momentum during that time that he would eventually evolve his investigatory agency into what we now know as the Federal Bureau of Investigation, or FBI.

Shirl Kasper published an account from William Sidney Shepherd, a participant in the battle, as he recalled the day's events in later years: "The day of the battle 'was warm, warm from the sun, the burning grass and haycocks and the excitement of roaring cannon and rifle fire. The church bells did not ring, although it was Sunday. People of Westport were too busy serving Union soldiers and worrying whether the Confederates would win and sack the town. On that day Kansas City was besieged. What now is the Country Club Plaza was peppered with cannon balls.'"

After the gruesome battle, known as the "Gettysburg of the West," peace settled over the area, bringing with it "a new and strangely altered west, and for Kansas City, the beginning of a period of uninterrupted growth," according to Frank H. Gille's *The Encyclopedia of Missouri*.

The first stockyards were built in 1870, a move that would forever shape Kansas City's future economic growth. In just two decades, Kansas City usurped Texas as the largest cattle handler in the region. And in 1874, agriculture arrived as Kansas City growers began shipping corn to the west and wheat to the east.

The late 1800s found Kansas City prosperous but filthy, an unsightly conglomeration of roads, buildings, and an increasing number of automobiles. Influential city residents including Col. Thomas H. Swope and newspaper editor William Rockhill Nelson identified the need for a parks and boulevard reform system and enlisted the help of talented German architect George Kessler. His first creation, Hyde Park, "converted an ugly shantytown into a beauty spot," according to Wilda Sandy's *Here Lies Kansas City*. After just a few years, Kansas City housed several lush parks and wide, tree-lined boulevards that not only improved the flow of traffic, but also created a picturesque drive for travelers.

Even during difficult times like World War I, the Great Depression, and World War II, Kansas City prospered thanks to its immense stockyards and agricultural output, as well as railroads that criss-crossed the city in order to transport cattle, goods, and people.

Kansas City's jazz culture blossomed in the period from the 1920s through the 1940s, when the city's musically significant 18th and Vine District helped earn Kansas City the title Paris of the Plains, a testament to the city's rollicking atmosphere, created by a plethora of saloons and music clubs.

WHO'S THE BOSS?

Although many people played a defining role in Kansas City's early growth and development, one name is synonymous with the city: Tom Pendergast, Kansas City's political boss, credited with the rise of Harry S. Truman to the presidency. Political machines were common in the 1920s and '30s, yet Pendergast stood out from the crowd thanks to a propensity for gambling, a deep and unabashed love for the city, and an unexpected compassion for Kansas City's poor.

On the second floor of a two-story yellow brick building at 1908 Main Street, Pendergast ruled the city—although, ironically enough, he never held an elected position. He used voter fraud and intimidation to fix local elections and personally selected most of the police officers, a move that resulted in law enforcement's turning a blind eye to alcohol and gambling, even during the Prohibition era. Pendergast was involved in several city development projects, including the Power and Light Building, Fidelity Bank and Trust Building, and Municipal Auditorium as part of the city's Ten Year Plan, an ambitiously detailed plan that sought to increase public works projects in a direct attempt to assuage the debilitating effects of unemployment and poverty inflicted throughout the Great Depression.

In the late 1930s, Pendergast's gambling addiction finally caught up with him and he was convicted of income tax evasion. He served a 15-month prison sentence at the U.S. Penitentiary in Leavenworth, after which he returned home and lived a quiet life as a divorcé with no money until his death in 1945.

MOB MAYHEM

At one time Kansas City boasted a Mafia so far-reaching it was even mentioned in Martin Scorsese's iconic movie *Casino:* "Now, that suitcase was goin' straight to one place: right to Kansas City, which was as close to Las Vegas as the Midwest bosses could go without gettin' themselves arrested."

In his book *The Mafia and the Machine,* author Frank Hayde succinctly describes Kansas City's Mob impact. "Kansas City is key in the history of organized crime. This conflict is rooted in the century-old struggle between the Pendergast family, with their permissive political machine, and publishing magnate William Rockhill Nelson and his crusading *Kansas City Star.* But to omit the Mob's role in the city's history is a denial to the power and influence of organized crime here and in the nation as a whole."

Added Hayde, "What's remarkable is how unremarkable the local Mafia is to Kansas Citians. For generations, the local Mob was a simple fact of everyday life, something almost as old as the city itself, and something so enmeshed in business and politics that it was taken for granted as an inevitable part of city life." Credited as being more politically involved than most American Mafia families, the Kansas City Mafia flourished in the early 20th century in Kansas City's Little Italy neighborhood, a mostly Sicilian district where crimes went unpunished thanks to a strict adherence to omertà, or code of silence.

Kansas City was the setting for notoriously corrupt and violent elections. As Tom Pendergast rose to power at the beginning of Prohibition, he partnered with Kansas City Mafia boss Johnny Lazia in the 1930s to enact a takeover of the local police department. Ex-cons and corrupt officers began patrolling the streets, a pivotal move that would later lead to the infamous Union Station massacre and the creation of J. Edgar Hoover's Federal Bureau of Investigation. Lazia, as the unofficial chief of police, made Kansas City a safe haven for criminals, but he met a bloody end during a 1934 gun battle; his funeral is said to have been the largest ever in Kansas City.

Post-Lazia, Charley "The Wop" Carollo took over briefly as front man but was sent to prison thanks to a federal probe that ensnared both him and Pendergast in 1939. Charlie Binaggio assumed leadership and quickly launched a political coup to open the entire state of Missouri to police-protected gambling and vice—essentially a state-sized Las Vegas. "With a friendly statehouse and Harry Truman in the White House, the KC [Kansas City] Family seemed poised to leap ahead of Cleveland to claim the number three spot behind NY [New York] and Chicago," Hayde writes. Yet Binaggio and Charlie Gargotta were murdered on Truman Road, having fallen short of statewide dominance.

The Mafia continued to play a role in Kansas City; by the 1970s, they were skimming cash from several Las Vegas casinos that they owned, and sharing the riches with the families in Chicago, Cleveland, and Milwaukee. As Hayde describes, "It was a sweet deal for the modern mob; a hands-off, mostly non-violent, white-collar conspiracy that delivered cash from the counting rooms by charter jet. It represented the new, relatively clean way of doing things. Unfortunately for Nick Civella, a Mafia member who rose to prominence in the 1950s, a messy mob was brewing on the streets of Kansas City. Adding to the pressure was the Kansas City Organized Crime Strike Force, which was patiently bugging businesses and building cases."

Kansas City's River Quay (pronounced "key"), now known as the River Market, became a Mafia stronghold in the 1970s. Conflict sprung up over land and building use in the area, resulting in a violent series of bombings, arson, and shootings that left the once-picturesque district resembling a war zone by the late '70s. In 1978, three masked men invaded the Virginian Tavern east of downtown Kansas City in an attempt to pull off what was called the most aggressive gangland hit since the Union Station massacre. The targets were the three Spero brothers, who were ensconced in a booth eating a late dinner. A letter later identified the possible suspects as Carl DeLuna, Joe Ragusa, and Charles Moretina; while listening in on a meeting between DeLuna and Carl "Cork" Civella (Nick Civella's older brother), organized-crime agents instead picked up incriminating conversation regarding the Teamsters union, the Chicago outfit, and someone called "genius." The evidence was eventually compiled into the Strawman case, which would later be popularized in the film *Casino,* an adaptation of Nick Pellegi's book. The Strawman case shed light on the operation to skim cash from Las Vegas casinos, and after two major trials in Kansas City the Mob's grip over Cowtown loosened considerably.

ARCHITECTURAL IMPACT

In the present day, Kansas City is celebrated for an architecturally diverse landscape that embraces several styles, most notably art deco. Notable structures also remain from the city's early history, as the city's downtown slowly rose out of the dirt in the 19th century. According to the *American Institute of Architects Guide to Kansas City Architecture and Public Art,* "During the late 1860s, [downtown] began to interest merchants and residents when Kersey Coates, a real estate speculator, began investing in and developing the land around what is now 10th Street. South of the original center of commerce, the Riverfront District, the Coates Addition was platted. The new development attracted wealthy families to build mansions on the bluffs overlooking the river."

Construction continued at a heightened pace throughout the late 1800s as builders sought to keep the pace of demand set by incoming employees and business owners eager to cash in on Kansas City's growing reputation as an agricultural, railroad, and industrial force. The AIA guide continues, "In the 1880s, Kansas City's population more than doubled and the city stretched to 13 square miles. Imposing structures such as the New England Building and the New York Life Building, the city's first high-rise, were designed by prestigious architectural firms and constructed during this time." Celebrated early architects included Mary Elizabeth Colter, Louis Curtiss, Mary Rockwell Hook, George Kessler, Clarence Kivett, Nelle Nichols Peters, Edward Tanner, and Henry Van Brunt.

Prominent examples of historic architecture in downtown Kansas City include Delaware Street from 2nd to 5th Streets, defined by the AIA guide as "one of the few remaining commercial streetscapes from the late 19th century." Significant features include Romanesque arches, intricate cornice brickwork, cast-iron columns, and stained glass. The Cathedral of the Immaculate Conception (411 W. 10th St.) was built in 1882. During a 1960 renovation, 23-karat gold leaf was applied to the original copper dome and spire to prevent deterioration. The result is an eye-catching exterior that's become a luminescent part of Kansas City's skyline. The historic Savoy Hotel (219 W. 9th St.) retains several of its original features including imported marble and tile, claw-footed tubs, brass fixtures, stained-glass windows, and a magnificent art nouveau skylight in the hotel's lobby. The New York Life Building is a 10-story Renaissance Revival building that stands at 20 West 9th Street. Look for terracotta ornamentation and brickwork, as well as an exterior eagle sculpture created by Louis Saint-Gaudens. Interior tile work is said to have been completed by Russian immigrants. Formerly a fire station, the Central Exchange (1020 Central St.) is described by the AIA as "a Mannerist interpretation of a classical facade, an unusual design for a fire station." A few blocks away, the towering Kansas City Power and Light Company Building (1330 Baltimore St.) was one of the first Kansas City high-rises to embody architectural modernism. Art deco building features include dramatic stepbacks and stylized geometric surface description, and this building, along with Municipal Auditorium and Jackson County Courthouse, are said by many architectural experts to be three of the nation's art deco treasures. Municipal Auditorium was built during the Depression to the tune of $6.5 million, part of the city's Ten Year Plan.

Although singular examples of superior architecture still define Kansas City as an architectural haven, researchers from the Kansas City Public Library identify two events in the city's early history as having such a far-reaching impact that they continue to influence the city's present-day construction: "The development of an extensive park and boulevard system designed by George Kessler...and the plan of real estate developer Jesse Clyde Nichols to create 'a high-class district on scientific lines' later known as the Country Club District."

THE REBIRTH OF KANSAS CITY

Although the Civil War had initially proved devastating to the Kansas City area, World War I had an opposite effect. Increased demand for horses, mules, and cattle caused the local economy to skyrocket, and in the first two decades of the 20th century, Kansas City welcomed auto assembly plants, a development that further expanded the city's industrial reach.

After struggling through the Great Depression and World War II, however, the mid-1900s were, simply put, a desolate time for Kansas City. After desegregation laws were approved, outward movement from downtown left an empty shell where once there had been a bustling, vibrant city core. A devastating 1951 flood destroyed much of downtown Kansas City, washing away the decay that had begun to plague the area. In a startling contrast, Kansas City's suburbs thrived, continuing an outward growth in all directions even while the city's center sat abandoned except for a handful of businesses. Conditions worsened as the city's highway system was carved out of the ground, an ambitious network of thoroughfares that began with Southwest Trafficway in 1950. With the addition of several interstates, a loop was created around downtown Kansas City, one that improved outward accessibility yet left the heart of the city an island, cut off from the surrounding area and increasingly abandoned as residents sped outward on the newly constructed highways. As

Montgomery and Kasper write in *Kansas City: An American Story,* "They did what the planners envisioned—making car traffic easier into and around the city. But they also made it easier for travelers to leave the central city, helping the metro area sprawl outward. Today the Kansas City area has far more freeway miles per person than any other major U.S. city." Additionally, according to Montgomery and Kasper, "In a time when Americans cheered freeway construction as a sign of progress, more than 125 buildings came tumbling down with barely a hint of regret: the former Lyric Theater at 622 Main Street; the red-brick Washington public school, Kansas City's first, at Independence Avenue and Cherry Street; and the faro hall at No. 3 Missouri Avenue, owned by the gambler Bob Potee, who had fitted the place with mirrors, carpets and a glittering bar." In 1962 a gaping hole at Truman Road and Walnut Street signaled the beginning of the Crosstown Freeway, a so-called "depressed highway" that required removing all the buildings in its path. Some called the new Interstate Highway System "the greatest construction project in the history of man."

In the 1970s, city leaders pushed for a comprehensive urban renewal plan and Kansas City saw a number of architectural accomplishments throughout the city, including the completion of the 4,700-acre Kansas City International Airport (1972), the nation's first adjoining sports stadiums Arrowhead and Kauffman Stadiums (1972), Kemper Arena (1974), and H. Roe Bartle Exposition Hall (1976).

Additional industries helped continue Kansas City's reputation as a regional leader in areas like foreign trade zones, underground storage, and automobile plants. Kansas City remained an agricultural giant, a role that would later serve the city as it evolved into an animal health and life science stronghold in a research corridor that stretches from Columbia, Missouri, to Manhattan, Kansas.

In the 1980s and '90s, development started to turn inward, focusing on a city core that, although long-neglected, still had life left beneath a layer of grit.

KANSAS CITY TODAY

In a sharp contrast to the outward annexation made popular in the 1950s and '60s, the Kansas City of today has returned to its roots to focus a multibillion-dollar redevelopment renaissance on the city's downtown. New landmarks like the Power and Light District, H&R Block World Headquarters, the Sprint Center, and the *Kansas City Star*'s state-of-the-art printing plant stand alongside downtown's historic buildings in a seamless blend of past and present. Downtown activists like the Downtown Council and various neighborhood associations have become a vocal, energetic part of the redevelopment process, working tirelessly to attract new business, residents, and, in the future, a downtown school.

Historically significant districts like 18th and Vine are undergoing their own makeovers, adding attractions and businesses like the American Jazz Museum and Negro Leagues Baseball Museum to enhance the district's existing appeal and pay tribute to the rich history that defined these districts and their residents. In Kansas City's outlying areas, expansion continues as developers spread outward in search of land and opportunities. Possibly one of the most dramatic metro case studies, the development of western Wyandotte County is a true Cinderella story. Anchored by Kansas Speedway, Schlitterbahn Vacation Village, the Legends at Village West, and a supersized Nebraska Furniture Mart, along with hotels, restaurants, and strip malls, the western half of Kansas's most population-dense county has become a true tourism destination for the Kansas City area, and a much-needed source of revenue for Kansas City, Kansas. The overall transformation of Kansas City is one that's been well-received and documented in various national news and travel publications, many of which name Kansas City as a city to watch now and in the coming years. It's a fanfare the city deserves after overcoming so much hardship, a return to an unadulterated joy reminiscent of Kansas City's early decades when the city rapidly rose to regional prominence. Kansas City has made its triumphant return on a journey expected to become only more impressive with each year.

Government and Economy

GOVERNMENT

Prior to the formation of Kansas City's government, Independence was named the Jackson County seat in 1826. In the beginning, Independence was little more than a tree and a spring. But as travelers passed through to intersect with several trails, Independence's role as a trading post helped the city rise to the role of Queen City of the Trails.

The Civil War brought a great deal of strife to Independence and Jackson County, most notably because of General Ewing's Order No. 11, which mandated that all persons living along the state line between the Missouri and Osage Rivers leave their farms. Artist George Caleb Bingham captured on canvas much of the misery provoked by the order. After the war ended, Jackson County residents returned to rebuild their lives—and their government. In 1970, Jackson County became only the second county in Missouri to adopt a home-rule charter. Executive power in the county is held by the county executive, a full-time salaried position. The general population of Jackson County elects the county executive for a four-year term. In addition, a county legislature passes ordinances and other similar documents, a body comprised of nine members: six elected from smaller districts within the county and three elected at large by voters of the whole county. Terms are four years and begin on January 1.

In 1889, a Kansas City charter established a city council comprised of 14 at-large aldermen in an "upper house" to serve four-year terms, and 14 ward alderman in a "lower house" to serve two-year terms. The local legislative system worked as a fairly harmonious and effective unit, yet in 1925 a sweeping political change was enacted that would forever change Kansas City's governmental landscape. By a 4:1 ratio, Kansas Citians voted to throw out the previous model and instead replace it with a nine-member, non-partisan council. The mayor would be one part of the council, have no veto, and would appoint a city manager, an expert to hire and fire city employees based solely on performance. Political scientists were thrilled with the new model, and predicted that not only would the new system eliminate pesky political patronage but would also leave Kansas City in the fate of nonpartisan managers, eliminating the partisan bickering and squabbling that had clouded so many other governmental bodies.

But "Boss" Tom Pendergast, one of the biggest political bosses of the early 20th century, would not be deterred by the new governmental body. Instead, he saw it easier to befriend a smaller group of councilpeople and quickly ushered handpicked candidates into five of the nine seats. It was a rapid and sweeping domination that would leave Pendergast the new political dominator of the city, and the true winner within the city's newly instated political system.

Today, Kansas City is governed by a 13-member city council that includes the mayor. The city is divided into six council districts, with the mayor and six councilmembers elected at-large. The remaining six councilmembers are elected by voters within their respective districts. Kansas City's current mayor, Mark Funkhouser, has received an overwhelming amount of negative publicity thanks to near-constant skirmishes with the city council over a variety of topics, including the status of his wife, Gloria Squitiro, as a city volunteer. In a time when Kansas City is facing massive budget shortfalls, prevalent crime and pressing civic issues like road improvements, a number of citizens have become increasingly impatient with what they see as a lack of leadership on many levels. In the summer of 2009, concerned citizens launched a recall campaign against Mayor Funkhouser, an effort that fell short by a few hundred petition signatures.

Previous to Mayor Funkhouser, mayor Kay Barnes served two terms in Kansas City and is largely credited with overseeing the necessary logistical and financial concerns that led to the early stages of downtown Kansas City's development renaissance, most notably the Sprint Center.

ECONOMY

Captain of Industry

Built on livestock-packed stockyards and the iron backbone of the railroad, Kansas City is rooted in industry and continues to be one of the nation's leading producers of agricultural products. The Missouri Pacific railroad arrived in 1865, and after Kansas City defeated Leavenworth to secure the Hannibal & St. Joseph bridge over the Missouri River, the city's population quadrupled in a mere five decades.

Kansas City's prime central location and proximity to railroads helped the city become a regional leader in the cattle industry, rivaling only Chicago for stockyard output. The booming success of the city's stockyards led to the affectionate nickname "Cowtown," still in use today to refer to Kansas City's livestock roots and a continued passion for barbecue.

After the devastating floods of 1951, Kansas City's stockyards were mostly destroyed and never fully rebuilt. The city continued to thrive as an agricultural powerhouse, producing grain, corn, and wheat that was later shipped around the country. The Kansas City Board of Trade reports that more than 10 billion bushels of wheat change hands during one year on the exchange, and producers worldwide look to Kansas City for the fair price of hard red winter wheat, used primarily in creating most of the world's bread supply.

Today, Kansas City maintains success in several industries, including architecture and engineering, creative services, entrepreneurship, financial services, life sciences and biotech, technology, and telecommunications.

Health Care and Biosciences

In 2004, city leaders met to examine ways in which to take Kansas City's fledgling life science economy in a new direction, one that could eventually have global significance. After an evaluation, six "hot zones" were identified that make Kansas City a regional bioscience leader, including health-care knowledge and personalized medicine; animal health and research; new bio-pharma drug discovery pathways; oncology research, discovery, and treatment; cardiovascular research; and tissue engineering and neuroscience.

Life sciences and animal health in Kansas City date back to 1863, when Bayer Healthcare AG was established. Today, leading life sciences companies like Cerner, IVX Animal Health, Quintiles, and the Stower's Institute for Medical Research all call Kansas City home.

After Kansas governor Kathleen Sebelius signed the Kansas Economic Growth Act in 2004, the state's commitment to bioscience advancement was solidified. Over the next several years, more than $500 million is expected to be invested in ways that will ensure bioscience progress. To date, public and private research spending exceeds $1.8 billion; as the location for more than 200 bio-tech companies, Kansas City has already carved out a niche as a bio-industry front-runner not just in the region, but also nationwide.

People and Culture

The Kansas City area not only boasts a low cost of living but also one of the fastest-growing job markets in the region. Modest home prices that rank below Albuquerque, Richmond, Tampa, and Denver make Kansas City an attractive choice for first-time homeowners, and a high concentration of colleges and universities in and around Kansas City has resulted in an increasingly large population of young professionals eager for the amenities of a large city but without the high costs generally associated with sizable metropolitan areas.

Kansas City's population of two million people is comprised of a variety of ethnic groups that each contribute to the city's rich heritage. African, Irish, Italian, and Croatian immigrants provided the majority of the manpower and labor that built Kansas City from two small trading posts to a sprawling metropolis. The city still clings tightly to its ethnic roots with annual celebrations like the St. Patrick's Day Parade, Irish Fest, Festa Italiana, and Rhythm and Ribs, each designed to pay homage to the tastes, sounds, and cultures of some of the city's significant populations.

Thanks to large Irish and Italian populations, Kansas City is a predominantly Catholic city, with ornate churches a common sight throughout most neighborhoods and districts. The *Kansas City Star*'s Saturday Faith section is a great resource for places of worship and faith-based stories.

The city's largest minority group is African-American, comprising 31.2 percent of the population according to 2000 U.S. census data. Although cultural divides aren't as apparent as they are in larger cities, Kansas City is home to several neighborhoods built around a certain ethnicity or heritage. Downtown's Columbus Park is predominantly Italian, but also hosts a growing number of Vietnamese and Asian specialty stores. The Westside neighborhood, as well as Kansas City's across-the-river neighbor, Kansas City, Kansas, are home to a flourishing Latino population, in addition to young professionals eager to be near downtown Kansas City while enjoying lower home prices often found in both areas. They're sometimes criticized for a lack of diversity, but Kansas City's suburbs retain a mostly Caucasian population that dates back to the white flight of the 1950s. Other cultures are slowly carving a niche for themselves,

FAMOUS KANSAS CITIANS

In addition to producing mouthwatering barbecue and breathtaking fountains, the Kansas City area is home to a number of celebrities past and present. They include:

- **Count Basie,** jazz musician (1904-1984)
- **Don Cheadle,** actor (1964-)
- **Walt Disney,** animator and creator of the Disney company (1907-1966)
- **Joyce C. Hall,** founder of Hallmark Cards (1891-1982)
- **Thomas Hart Benton,** artist (1887-1975)
- **Jesse James,** famed outlaw (1847-1865)
- **Charlie "Yardbird" Parker,** jazz musician (1920-1955)
- **Ginger Rogers,** actress (1911-1995)
- **Paul Rudd,** actor (1969-)
- **Russell Stover** (1888-1954) and **Clara Stover** (1882-1975), founders of Russell Stover's candies
- **Jason Sudeikis,** actor/comedian (1975-)
- **Calvin Trillin,** columnist/author (1935-)
- **Harry S. Truman,** former president (1884-1972)

especially in Johnson County, which hosts sizable Jewish and Indian populations.

Kansas City boasts a productive, educated population that earns an annual average per-household income of $53,500. Nearly 91 percent of Kansas City residents have a high school education, and nearly 32 percent hold a college degree.

The Arts

ON STAGE

Kansas City has long been a regional arts and culture capital, a city filled with the sounds of symphony, the sights of graceful ballet dancers, and the lyrically haunting voices of opera singers. In 2011, the opening of the state-of-the-art Kauffman Center for the Performing Arts will boost the city's reputation as a regional performing arts leader in a 285,000-square-foot space said to rival the world-renowned Walt Disney Concert Hall in L.A. A 1,800-seat proscenium theater and 1,600-seat concert hall are separated by a surrounding acoustic joint that allows for simultaneous performances with no sound interruption. The Lyric Opera and Kansas City Symphony will relocate to the Kauffman Center for the Performing Arts upon its 2011 completion. The Kansas City Ballet will also perform at the Kauffman Center, and, in 2011, they will move to their new permanent home, the Bolender Center for Dance and Creativity.

Plays, dance, and performance art also thrive on Kansas City's smaller stages. From the University of Missouri–Kansas City's Repertory Theatre to Union Station's H&R Block City Stage and the Quality Hill Playhouse, Kansas City offers any number of opportunities to catch a live performance or musical review while you're in town. You'll even find impromptu street performances during events like First Fridays, or one-person plays acted out on stages that double as empty

THE ORIGINAL MICKEY MOUSE

Born in Chicago, Walt Disney moved to Kansas City at the age of nine and, while he was in elementary school, took weekend drawing classes at the Kansas City Art Institute. Disney worked overseas in World War I, but later returned to Kansas City and was hired at an ad agency. In 1920, Disney joined his mentor, Ub Iwerks, to produce animated cartoons they called Laugh-O-Grams. They produced these cartoons for local theaters at their Kansas City studio (1127 E. 31st St.).

While Disney worked at his Laugh-O-Gram studio, a mouse reportedly took up residence in one of his desk drawers and is said to have influenced the creation of Mickey Mouse, one of the most recognizable cartoon characters in history.

After Laugh-O-Gram studios went bankrupt in 1923, Disney relocated to Los Angeles to work with his brother and was joined by Iwerks as well as several other artists. Disney would go on to create one of the biggest entertainment companies ever, along with a stable of instantly recognizable cartoon characters that remain beloved by kids both young and young at heart.

storefronts. And for a city-wide celebration of performing arts and master playwright William Shakespeare, don't miss the annual Heart of America Shakespeare Festival in July.

PUBLIC ARTS INITIATIVES

As the city continues to make lengthy strides in shaking its old Cowtown image, public arts initiatives have become an increasingly important part of downtown architecture, a movement that has extended its creative reach to some of the city's outlying areas.

Art in the Loop is a nonprofit organization that commissions permanent art exhibitions in public spaces throughout downtown Kansas City. A partnership between the Downtown Council, the Greater Kansas City Community Foundation, the Kansas City Art Institute, and the Kansas City Municipal Art Commission, Art in the Loop also works to introduce artistic and educational opportunities for artists affiliated with the Kansas City Art Institute. Several Art in the Loop exhibitions can be seen throughout downtown, including *Celestial Flyaways* (Oppenstein Brothers Memorial Park, 12th and Walnut Sts.), *ARTwall* (Town Pavilion Parking Garage, 13th St. and Grand Blvd.), and *Uplifted Arms* (Transit Plaza, 10th and Main Sts.).

The Charlotte Street Foundation, founded in the mid-1990s, is a multifaceted organization that assists with artist needs as well as fulfills a role as a creative, social, and economic resource for Kansas City. Charlotte Street's services are numerous and include the gift of annual cash awards to visual and generative performing artists, the supply of free studio space, coordination of public exposure, and the facilitation of educational and professional development opportunities. The Urban Culture Project, part of Charlotte Street, is one of the foundation's more significant accomplishments and works to repurpose vacant storefronts and downtown buildings into gallery and exhibition spaces. La Esquina, Paragraph, and Project Space host a variety of events, including video screenings, performance art, and exhibits, in street-level spaces that can be viewed from both inside and outside the building.

Although public art has become an undeniably important part of Kansas City's appearance and culture, the installation of such works has not been without controversy, especially in earlier decades. The sculpted shuttlecocks carefully perched around the Nelson-Atkins Museum of Art caused an unbelievable amount of outrage when plans for the commissioned works were announced, yet now the playful creations have become an iconic image for the city and a photo backdrop used for everything from local weddings and events to magazine covers and advertising campaigns. Another project, "Wrapped Walk Ways," brought almost as much controversy to Kansas City in the 1970s. Bulgarian native and world-renowned contemporary artist Christo wanted to cover Loose Park's walking paths with a huge continuous sheet of gold nylon. He had completed similar projects before, such as "Valley Curtain," a sheet of orange fabric that was hung across a valley in the Colorado Rockies. Once Christo arrived, parks officials reluctantly gave their support, although the Municipal Art Commission did not. On October 2, 1978, art students and workers joined to staple the fabric over the walkways, resulting in a public art installation that stretched nearly three miles. Just over two weeks later, the fabric was removed at the exhibit's conclusion and left in Starlight Theater's parking lot for those who wanted to snip off a piece of artistic memorabilia.

WRITERS

Kansas City has borne its fair share of writers who have gone on to local and even national prominence. Yet no local writer is perhaps as famous as Ernest Hemingway, a literary icon whose works have left a lasting impression on all who read his extraordinary works.

Few know that Ernest Hemingway began his career at the *Kansas City Star,* 18 years old and fresh out of high school. He spent six and a half months pounding the pavement in search of stories, and left on April 30, 1918, to join the Red Cross ambulance service as World War I ravaged parts of the globe. Hemingway covered a variety of topics for the *Star,* including a human-interest piece on a soldiers' dance. The lead reads as follows: "Outside a woman walked along the wet street lamp-lit sidewalk through the sleet and snow. Inside in the Fine Arts Institute on the sixth floor of the YWCA Building, 1020 McGee Street, a merry crowd of soldiers from Camp Funston and Fort Leavenworth fox trotted and one-stepped with girls from the Fine Arts School while a sober-faced young man pounded out the latest jazz music as he watched the moving figures. In a corner a private in the signal corps was discussing Whistler with a black haired girl who heartily agreed with him. The private had been a member of the art colony at Chicago before the war was declared."

Kansas City–influenced scenes are said to appear in several Hemingway works, including *For Whom The Bell Tolls, The Sun Also Rises,* and *Across the River and into the Trees.*

Notable contemporary writers are numerous in Kansas City. In 2009, three authors were honored with the Thorpe Menn Award, sponsored by the Kansas City Branch of the American Association of University Women, is distributed annually to a local author who exhibits literary excellence. Honorees included John Mark Eberhart for his poetry collection *Broken Time,* Matthew Eck for his debut novel *The Farther Shore,* and Donna Trussell's poetry debut *What's Right About What's Wrong: Poems.*

Other notable local writers include Charles Gusewelle, a *Kansas City Star* columnist and essayist who has published several books; Joel Goldman, an attorney and author of Kansas City-based crime fiction; and Whitney Terrell, whose debut novel *The Huntsman* was named a notable book by *The New York Times* and the best book of 2005 by *The Christian Science Monitor.*

ESSENTIALS

Getting There

BY AIR

Kansas City International Airport (816/243-5237, www.flykci.com) welcomes travelers with a straightforward, no-fuss layout divided into three C-shaped terminals: A, B, and C. Midwest and Southwest Airlines are two of the busiest at KCI since the demise of TWA, Kansas City's primary airline. Accommodations around the airport are plentiful, but the airport is just 20 minutes north of downtown; arrange for shuttle transportation or car rental to your final destination, more economical options than taxis, which could run $50 and higher. Several kiosks located throughout each terminal provide direct connections to nearby hotels, as well as shuttle and car rental services like Hertz, Avis, and Budget Rent-A-Car. Public transportation also runs between KCI and downtown Kansas City, a convenient and inexpensive option if you're staying downtown. Exact change is required for bus tickets; updated fare information and route maps are available at www.kcata.org. KCI includes several casual eateries and coffee shops, but if you're departing in the late evening, stop for food on the way. Most shops and kiosks close by 8 P.M. or earlier.

COURTESY OF THE KANSAS CITY CONVENTION AND VISITORS ASSOCIATION

COURTESY OF THE KANSAS CITY CONVENTION AND VISITORS ASSOCIATION

Southwest Airlines is one of several carriers that operates out of Kansas City International Airport.

BY TRAIN

Although prone to delays, **Amtrak** (816/842-0749, www.amtrak.com) operates numerous regional and national routes on the Missouri River Runner and Southwest Chief. An especially popular choice for those coming from Chicago, St. Louis, and points in between, Amtrak operates out of Kansas City's Union Station (Amtrak abbreviation "KCY," 30 W. Pershing Rd., www.unionstation.org), putting travelers in the heart of downtown upon arrival. Taxis, often waiting outside the main entrance, are a good bet if you're staying in downtown, Westport, and the Plaza, and most rides average $5–15. Or ride the Metro, Kansas City's bus system, which stops throughout the day at Union Station. Bus schedules and fare information are available at the Metro stop located outside the front entrance.

BY BUS

Greyhound runs bus service to and from Kansas City out of its main terminal (1101 Troost Ave., 816/221-2835, www.greyhound.com), which is in the heart of downtown. If you will arrive during the evening, arrange for transportation from the bus station prior to your arrival, as it's not recommended to walk to downtown hotels.

An increasingly popular bus option, the **MegaBus** (877/462-6342, www.megabus.com), travels across Missouri and to Chicago, sometimes with fares as low as $1 per seat. You'll arrive at the Kansas City Transportation Authority's 3rd and Grand MetroCenter, in the heart of the River Market. You'll want to secure additional transportation to your hotel, as those located in the River Market and Power and Light District are quite a hike from the bus station.

© KATY RYAN

The Metro and the MAX are express transit buses that make fewer stops.

Getting Around

DRIVING

Because Kansas City's core spreads out over four counties and the greater Kansas City area encompasses 18 counties, driving is the best option in order to see as much of Kansas City as possible. Only one of five U.S. cities connected by three interstates, Kansas City's wealth of highway access makes getting to outlying areas a (relatively) quick drive. The average commute time is 20.7 minutes; if possible, avoid major interstates and highways during the week's morning (7:30 to 9 A.M.) and evening (4:30 to 6 P.M.) rush hours. I-435 forms one giant loop around the city; although it would take several hours to make the whole loop, staying on I-435 will eventually get you where you need to go. I-70 is the major east–west thoroughfare that connects Kansas City's main county, Jackson, with its Kansas counterpart, Wyandotte, and also leads to two of the suggested day trips: Rocheport to the east and Lawrence to the west. I-35 is the bridge between the Northland and Johnson County, and these three highways, in addition to I-670, I-29, U.S. 71, U.S. 24, U.S. 40, and U.S. 169, form a multi-highway loop that encircles downtown before branching out in various directions.

BIKING

Although city leaders are working to add more bike paths and lanes, most bicyclists agree that Kansas City is not a terribly bike-friendly city. Bicycling through downtown, Westport, and the Plaza offers great views of the city, but navigating traffic and city buses can be difficult. If you're eager to experience a road ride while you're in Kansas City, get in touch with one of several bicycling clubs including Kansas City Bike Club, Earth Riders, and Johnson County Bike Club for information about group rides and other bicycling-related events. For trail rides, try the Mid-America Regional Council's MetroGreen, an interconnected system of public and private greenways and trails that winds over 1,144 miles throughout the metropolitan area. MetroGreen is a modern take on Kansas City's parks and boulevard system that began in the early 1900s and "identifies more than 75 separate corridors that will form a regional network to connect many of the area's most valuable natural assets," according to MARC. Visit their website (www.marc.org/metrogreen) to download a PDF map of the complete MetroGreen trail system.

Downtown Westport and the Country Club Plaza are the best areas to hail a taxi.

TAXIS

For the most part, taxis are prevalent throughout downtown, Midtown, Westport, and the Plaza. Sporadically located taxi stands are an ideal place to hail a cab, especially Thursday, Friday, and Saturday evenings. Your hotel concierge will be happy to arrange taxi transportation, or if you'd prefer to make your own reservation, call any of the following cab companies and a car will meet you within 10 to 20 minutes, depending on call volume. Try **Yellow Cab of Kansas City** (1300 Lydia Ave., 816/471-5000, www.kctg.com), **Atlas Cab Company** (303 Broadway Ave., 816/421-2999), or **Crosstown Cab Company** (1001 Spruce Ave., 816/241-6500).

PUBLIC TRANSPORTATION

An ongoing debate swirls around Kansas City's public transportation and, in some opinions, lack thereof. Light rail is consistently a hot-button issue, with proposals that tout a light rail line from the Kansas City Zoo to the Northland. The debilitating expense of, and planning flaws related to, the light rail continue to prevent any forward movement, although local champions are reluctant to give up the fight.

The Kansas City Area Transportation Authority operates several bus lines that run throughout the metro area on more than 70 routes. If you're riding through downtown, Midtown, Westport, and the Plaza, look for **Metro** stations or opt to use the Park & Ride Metro Center (3rd and Grand Sts.) in the City Market, from which you can access several bus routes. KCATA also operates **MAX,** the city's first bus rapid-transit system that uses fewer stops in order to guarantee faster arrival times. MAX serves downtown, Crown Center, Midtown, and the Plaza, and the glass stations are easily recognizable. Exact change is required for both the Metro and MAX bus services, although bus tickets can be purchased online. The regular bus fare is $1.50. Visitors can also purchase a three-day pass for $10 that's good for unlimited rides on three consecutive days. Visit www.kcata.org for a complete set of route maps, schedules, updated fares, and pertinent rider bulletins.

DISABLED ACCESS

Kansas City International Airport offers curbside terminal assistance, including wheelchair reservations, that are arranged through the airline. KCI buses that provide shuttle service to and from the various parking lots are equipped with wheelchair lifts and kneeling capability, and all high-traffic areas of KCI can be accessed by elevators, located near the escalators. KCI also offers TTY at all pay phone locations, Braille signage, and visual paging monitors with taxi and security alert information.

All KCATA Metro buses are equipped with wheelchair lifts or low-floor ramps. Service animals are permitted on buses, and priority seating is available at the front of the bus. Disabled persons also qualify for reduced bus fare with either a Metro Reduced Farecard or a reduced fare monthly pass. For information, call 816/221-0660.

For disabled passengers who cannot ride wheelchair-accessible buses, KCATA offers comparable paratransit that provides door-to-door service with vans or cabs. To qualify, the passenger must be certified as ADA Eligible. For more information and to schedule a ride, call Share-A-Fare in Kansas City at 816/346-0810. In Wyandotte County, including Kansas City, Kansas, contact Dial-A-Ride at 913/573-8351.

Tips for Travelers

TRAVELING WITH CHILDREN

With plenty of museums, parks, and activities, Kansas City is definitely a kid-friendly destination for those interested in a family getaway. One of the best local kids hang-outs is Crown Center, which hosts the Crayola Cafe and Kaleidoscope, an interactive arts environment that encourages creativity. During the summer months, head outside Crown Center to a fountain playplace that evokes shrieks and giggles from kids of all ages. Traveling in winter? Make tracks to Crown Center's ice terrace, an outdoor skating rink with a prime view of the surrounding area and Mayor's Christmas Tree.

A short walk away, Union Station houses Science City, an interactive museum where kids can dig fossils, participate in a newsroom, and learn about the inner workings of a crime lab. And in the center of downtown, big and little kids alike will have a blast at the College Basketball Experience, a basketball-themed museum that puts you at center court, or behind the sports anchor desk—your choice.

Kansas City's parks are also great places for family-friendly entertainment. The lawn surrounding the Nelson-Atkins Museum of Art is also a sculpture garden, and a popular weekend spot for Frisbee, picnics, and other outdoor activities. Swope Park is an all-in-one destination complete with ample greenspace and play equipment and is also home to the Kansas City Zoo and Starlight Theater.

For a more action-packed adventure, head to Kansas City's side-by-side amusement and water parks, Worlds of Fun and Oceans of Fun. Both offer plenty of kid-friendly rides and attractions like Worlds of Fun's Camp Snoopy or Oceans of Fun for kids. If you're headed

WHAT TO TAKE

Maybe it's the city's roots as an industrial and agricultural powerhouse, or perhaps it's simply the laid-back Midwestern attitude that permeates the majority of interactions within the city. Whatever the reason, Kansas City is hardly a formal metropolis, so feel free to pack casual attire for your trip.

However, as in most cities, a few exceptions exist to the casual dress code. If you plan to thoroughly explore Kansas City's nightlife, especially at places in the Power and Light District and lounges like Blonde, "dress to impress" codes are strictly enforced. For these your best bet, male or female, is to bring dressy pants and shoes along with an equally dressy top or button-down. Ties, jackets, and gowns are worn at only the most formal of occasions.

You may also want to do a quick bit of research regarding the restaurants in which you plan to dine. The overwhelming majority of Kansas City restaurants welcome diners in casual attire, but there are a few fine-dining establishments that prefer to see guests arrive in dressier – yet still not formal – clothing.

If you're traveling to Kansas City for business, you'll want to bring a few suits and business-casual outfits. Kansas City professionals, both local and out-of-towners, are often in suits or something equally as dressy at bars and restaurants throughout downtown and the Plaza for lunch and dinner meetings.

Also be sure to pack a light rain jacket or an umbrella. Kansas City weather is as unpredictable as it comes, and what starts as a brilliantly sunny day could end in rain showers – or vice versa. In fact, I've seen it rain when there's not a cloud in the sky, a phenomenon I haven't quite been able to explain. If you're traveling during the spring or fall, you may also consider a heavier sweater or jacket to slip on during the cooler evening hours, especially if you plan on spending a lot of time outside. If you're traveling during winter, make sure to bring several layers. Consider long johns or similar undergarments layered under a long-sleeved T-shirt and sweater. If you'll be in and out of buildings, opt for fewer layers and instead stay warm with a heavy coat, scarf, gloves, and a hat. If you expect snow while you're in town, a pair of boots makes walking more comfortable.

to the west side of the city, spend a day at the Schlitterbahn Vacation Village Waterpark, a tropical paradise complete with slides, swimming pools, and other watery rides.

A sampling of kid-friendly itineraries is available at www.visitkc.com, the official site of the Kansas City Convention and Visitors Association.

GAY AND LESBIAN TRAVELERS

Midwestern hospitality, a signature of the Kansas City area, extends to all travelers. The annual gay pride festival (early June) and other events like the Kansas City AIDS Walk (April) are well attended by both gay and straight celebrants.

Visit the website of **Lesbian and Gay Community Center of Kansas City** (www.lgcc-kc.org) for more information on upcoming events, support groups, and radio broadcasts. While you're out on the town, look for a free copy of *Camp,* "Kansas City's voice for the LGBT and allied communities," online at www.campkc.com.

TRAVELING WITH PETS

Several pet-friendly hotels, including Intrigue Park Place and Aloft Leawood, make traveling in Kansas City with pets relatively easy. Treat your four-legged friend with a trip to one of the city's dog parks, including **Penn Valley Park Off-Leash Dog Park** (Pershing Rd. and

Main St.) or **Wayside Waifs Bark Park** (3901 Martha Truman Rd., 816/761-8151, www.waysidewaifs.org, $3 daily access). If you'd prefer to leave your pet in caring hands while you explore the city, consider one of several pet boarding and play services like **Citydog** (4706 1/2 Holly St., 816/561-4504, www.citydogwalking.com, $25 for one hour of park time, $20 for one dog visit), **Dog's World of Fun** (1220 W. 31st St., 816/931-5822, www.dogsworldoffun.com, $11/day for daycare), or **Kate's Canine Resort** (2823 Main St., 816/753-4188, www.katescanineresort.com, $15/day for daycare), all of which are centrally located near downtown Kansas City.

SMOKING

In 2008, the Kansas City city council passed a no-smoking ban intended for businesses, restaurants, and other commercial buildings except for casino gaming floors. Although decried by some who worried about a negative economic impact as a result of the ban, it's a move that's largely been supported by residents and visitors alike. Smoking is still permitted outdoors, and hotels are currently allowed to designate up to 25 percent of their rooms as smoking rooms.

Health and Safety

HOSPITALS

Should you need emergency treatment while you're in Kansas City, you'll have several choices for care. **Saint Luke's Hospital** (4400 Wornall Rd., 816/932-2000, www.saintlukeshealthsystem.org) is located between Westport and the Plaza and offers a comprehensive array of medical services in a faith-based environment. Located five minutes north of downtown, **North Kansas City Hospital** (2800 Clay Edwards Dr., 816/691-2030, www.nkch.org) is an acute-care facility recognized as a leader in health-care technology. The child-friendly surroundings of **Children's Mercy Hospital** (2401 Gillham Rd., 816/234-3000, www.childrens-mercy.org) have made the hospital a local favorite when seeking pediatric care and specialty services.

For comprehensive health services, the **University of Kansas Hospital** (3901 Rainbow Blvd., 913/588-1227, www.kumed.com) is located a short drive from Midtown in Kansas City, Kansas, and specializes in heart and cancer care. The hospital adjoins **KU Medical Center,** a comprehensive research facility that examines cutting-edge treatments and equipment.

The University of Kansas Hospital also operates several urgent-care facilities throughout the greater metro area, including Creekwood (5601 NE Antioch Rd., Ste. 12, 816/505-5050) and KU MedWest (7405 Renner Rd., 913/588-8450).

PHARMACIES

Pharmacies are abundant throughout Kansas City; for directions to the closest location, consult your hotel's concierge. **CVS** operates a pharmacy in the heart of downtown Kansas City (921 Main St., 816/842-2514) as well as a Midtown location (3902 Main St., 816/931-5452). **Walgreens** also operates several pharmacies in the area, including a 24-hour Midtown location (3845 Broadway Blvd., 816/561-7620). If you prefer natural remedies, try the **Wild Oats Natural Marketplace** (4301

TORNADO SAFETY

Tornadoes are prevalent in Kansas City from late spring to late fall. Kansas averages 56 tornadoes annually, while Missouri averages 67 tornadoes annually.

If you find yourself visiting during a severe storm and have access to a television, tune in to one of the local networks (channels 4, 5, 9 or 13) for up-to-date information on watches, warnings, and precautionary measures.

Because the Kansas City metropolitan area is so large, tornadoes rarely cross more than one county. If a tornado is spotted, a citywide warning system is activated, which includes a siren warning. Sirens will not be sounded in more than one county simultaneously unless the tornado is predicted to affect several areas during its lifespan. If you hear a siren, it's best to immediately take cover. If you're driving, pull off the road and seek safety under an overpass.

Weather experts advise to never try and outrun a tornado. If you're outside at an event, organizers should direct you to the nearest safe location, such as a restroom. As you take cover, be sure to duck down and protect your head from flying debris if the tornado is in close proximity to you.

Main St., 816/931-1873, www.wholefoodsmarket.com) for vitamins, supplements, and other health products.

EMERGENCY SERVICES

During a medical or fire emergency, or to immediately reach local police in an emergency situation, dial 911. To reach the **Kansas City Police Department** in a non-emergency situation, dial 816/234-5000. A **24-hour poison control hotline,** operated by the University of Kansas Hospital, is available at 800/222-1222.

The **Kansas City Crime Stoppers Tips Hotline** can be reached at 816/474-8477 or via text message to "CRIMES" (274637). Begin your message with "TIP452."

Visit the **Prepare Metro KC** website (www.preparemetrokc.org) to access emergency preparedness guides on local emergency operations and the tornado outdoor warning siren system.

Information and Services

MAPS AND TOURIST INFORMATION

The **Kansas City Convention and Visitors Association** (11th and Main Sts., Ste. 2200, 816/221-5242, www.visitkc.com, 8:30 A.M.–5 P.M. Mon.–Fri.) is an informative one-stop resource for local literature, maps, and other guides. Most bookstores, both locally owned and national chains, carry a wide range of foldout maps and heftier atlases.

The **Kansas Travel and Tourism Division** (www.travelks.com) and **Missouri Division of Tourism** (www.visitmo.com) also provide helpful information on Kansas City, as well as other statewide attractions and destinations. Before you go, request free guides to help in your advance trip planning.

LIBRARIES

The **Kansas City Public Library** (www.kclibrary.org) system operates 12 branches throughout the city, including downtown's central branch (14 W. 10th St., 816/701-3400, www.kclibrary.org, 9 A.M.–9 P.M. Mon.–Wed., 9 A.M.–6 P.M. Thurs., 9 A.M.–5 P.M. Fri., 10 A.M.–5 P.M. Sat., 1–5 P.M. Sun.) located in the heart of the Library District.

EDUCATION

The University of Missouri-Kansas City (816/235-1000, www.umkc.edu) welcomed its first class in 1933 and has since expanded to Kansas City's largest university. Three campuses—Volker, Hospital Hill, and Northland—offer more than 50 majors or programs. UMKC is celebrated for its dental, business, and urban planning programs, as well as its quarterly Communiversity series, a variety of classes and instructional workshops open to the public. Prominent alumni include James B. Steele, *Vanity Fair* contributing editor and Pulitzer Prize–winning journalist; Kay Waldo Barnes, Kansas City's first female mayor; Harry S. Truman, 33rd president of the United States; Brett L. Ferguson, the first black oral surgeon to graduate from UMKC; and Tom Condon, former Kansas City Chiefs right guard and current sports agent representing 75 active NFL players.

Other prominent higher education institutions include **Avila University** (800/462-8452, www.avila.edu), a small Catholic university; **Park University** (816/741-2000, www.park.edu), which specializes in continuing education; and **Rockhurst University** (816/501-4000, www.rockhurst.edu), a Jesuit institution.

The **University of Kansas** (785/864-5823, www.ku.edu) operates several satellite campuses throughout Kansas City, including the Edwards Campus (12600 Quivira Rd., Overland Park, Kansas, 785/864-4790, www.continuinged.ku.edu) and the University of Kansas Medical Center (3901 Rainbow Blvd., 913/588-4488, www.continuinged.ku.edu).

COMMUNICATION AND MEDIA

Phones and Area Codes

Two area codes serve Kansas City, and you'll know which one to use depending on which state you're in. Kansas City, Missouri, numbers all begin with 816, while all numbers on the Kansas side use 913. Dial the complete area code and number when you make a call, as some outlying areas that fall into the two area codes are still considered long-distance.

Internet Services

Wi-Fi hotspots are available throughout Kansas City, including at the Convention and Visitors Center, the Kansas City Public Library, and most coffee shops. More restaurants are also offering Wi-Fi access, and most places post signs detailing connectivity details such as passwords or IP addresses. Check with your hotel regarding online usage; although most hotels offer Wi-Fi, some charge for access, whether hourly or daily.

Mail Services

Each Kansas City neighborhood or district has its own post office, with the centralmost location being downtown's Union Station (30 W. Pershing Rd., 816/460-2020). Free parking is available for postal customers. Another option is the post office in Westport (200 Westport Rd.)

For other mailing services, there's a Fed-Ex Office on the Country Club Plaza (612 W. 47th St., 816/960-2030) that offers a variety of packing, shipping, and copying needs. Or try the UPS Store (4741 Central St., 816/561-7411) for printing, mailing, and packing services.

Newspapers and Periodicals

Kansas City's major metropolitan daily

COURTESY OF THE KANSAS CITY CONVENTION AND VISITORS ASSOCIATION

The *Kansas City Star* is printed in an eye-catching facility.

newspaper, the *Kansas City Star* (www.kansascity.com) is the city's go-to source for news, sports, business, and arts and culture. Although many Kansas Citians enjoy a love-hate relationship with the *Star,* a news organization that's suffered massive layoffs since 2008, the newspaper is still a favorite source for local information. The *Star*'s younger sibling, *Ink* (www.inkkc.com), is a newsprint magazine targeted to the city's young professionals and is published on Wednesdays. Look for the bright green distribution boxes located throughout the city for event calendars, local profiles, happy-hour guides, and more.

Pitch Weekly, a product of the larger Village Voice Media, is Kansas City's original alt-weekly (www.pitch.com). Distinctive red boxes house free copies of the *Pitch,* published on Thursdays. Although its longer features are often criticized for their controversial content, the *Pitch* is an unparalleled source of nightlife, event, and concert calendars. Check online for a database of restaurant reviews.

For a moderate-sized metropolitan area, Kansas City is home to a surprisingly large—and diverse—amount of print media. While you're in town, check area newsstands for *KC Magazine,* an upscale monthly publication that covers local dining, fashion, arts and culture, and other lifestyle topics, including September's often-anticipated "Best Of Kansas City" issue. *Spaces* magazine, produced by Grand Communications, a division of the *Star,* is a favorite choice for home decor and interior design enthusiasts. *KC Parent* is a colorful magazine filled with articles and local events geared toward families, and is available for free throughout the city. Arts enthusiasts should pick up a copy of *Review* magazine, a visual arts publication that offers one of the most comprehensive guides to local arts events. Check downtown galleries and coffee shops, as well as the Nelson-Atkins Museum of Art, for copies. An informative and versatile resource for city-wide events and information is online-only *Present* magazine (www.presentmagazine .com), which covers arts, design, business, food and drink, and music. Consult the calendar for upcoming events—it's a great source as you're planning your trip's itinerary. Look for other publications in drop boxes around Kansas City, as well as the travel and regional sections of bookstore newsstands.

Radio and Television

Billed as Kansas City's "local source for NPR news," **KCUR** (89.3 FM, www.kcur.org) is a university-run station home to hourly NPR news reports and several news and music shows. Tune in at 10 A.M. for *The Walt Bodine Show,* a local favorite that explores a variety of local, national, and international topics. Throughout the evening, programming switches to the musical variety with shows hosted by various KCUR disc jockeys.

Kansas City Community Radio, KKFI (90.1 FM, www.kkfi.org), is an independent nonprofit station that offers a mix of eclectic talk and music programming hosted by local on-air talent, as well as numerous syndicated shows that play throughout the day.

Local all-talk stations include **KCMO Talk Radio 710** (710 AM), the Fox News affiliate. Or try right-leaning **News Radio 980 KMBZ** (980 AM, www.kmbz.com), with shows from Glenn Beck, Rush Limbaugh, and local talent Darla Jaye. For all sports, all the time, tune to **Sports Radio 810 WHB** (810 AM, www.810whb.com), after which Kansas City's 810 Zone sports bars were named. Most Kansas City stations can be heard about an hour outside the city, although some stations broadcast on smaller frequencies that suffer quicker signal interruptions.

Kansas City Public Television (www.kcpt.org) on channel 19 offers a mix of local and national programming including Ruckus, a round-table discussion focused on the largest of Kansas City's community issues. Other local stations include **channel 4** (Fox affiliate), **channel 5** (CBS affiliate), **channel 9** (ABC affiliate), and **channel 41** (NBC affiliate).

RESOURCES

Suggested Reading

HISTORY AND GENERAL INFORMATION

Dodd, Monroe. *Kansas City: Then and Now.* 1st ed. Kansas City: Kansas City Star Books, 2000. Explore the past and present of Kansas City with side-by-side photographs that detail the city's gradual transformation.

Driggs, Frank, and Chuck Haddix. *Kansas City Jazz: From Ragtime to Bebop—A History.* 1st ed. New York: Oxford University Press, 2006. Explore the golden age of Kansas City jazz, a musical tradition so rich it made the city one of four national capitals of jazz beside New Orleans, Chicago, and New York.

Haskell, Harry. *Boss-busters and Sin Hounds: Kansas City and its Star.* 1st ed. Columbia: University of Missouri Press, 2007. Former *Kansas City Star* music critic Harry Haskell details the *Star*'s rise to prominence as a scandal-uncovering newspaper and later a target in one of the most significant antitrust actions to be brought against an American daily newspaper.

Hayde, Frank R. *The Mafia and The Machine: The Story of the Kansas City Mob.* 1st ed. Fort Lee: Barricade Books, 2008. A comprehensive and entertaining look at Kansas City's illustrious Mafia family and its impact on local history.

Janicke, Tim. *City of Art: Kansas City's Public Art.* 1st ed. Kansas City: Kansas City Star Books, 2001. Follow a stunningly visual tour of some of the city's greatest public art installations, including the *Shuttlecocks, Thinker,* and *Sky Stations.*

Larsen, Lawrence H., and Nancy J. Hulston. *Pendergast!* 1st ed. Columbia: University of Missouri Press, 1997. An informative look at the life of infamous Kansas City political boss Tom Pendergast.

Maxwell, H. James, Bob Sullivan Jr., and Anne Marie Hunter. *Hometown Beer: A History of Kansas City's Breweries.* 1st ed. Kansas City: Omega Innovative Marketing, 1999. Complete with vintage photographs and illustrations, this book traces the history of Kansas City's breweries from the mid-1800s to present-day, including those out-of-town breweries that, pre-Prohibition, did business in Kansas City.

Million, Stacey. *The American Institute of Architects Guide to Kansas City Architecture &*

Public Art. 2nd ed. Kansas City: Highwater Editions, 2000. Arranged by 12 geographic districts, this comprehensive guide to Kansas City architecture and public art details designers, completion dates, and other pertinent information, as well as maps and an overview of each district.

Montgomery, Rick, and Shirl Kasper. *Kansas City: An American Story.* 1st ed. Kansas City: Kansas City Star Books, 1999. A dense yet immensely readable book that details Kansas City history from its founding through the 1990s. Text is supplemented with vibrant illustrations, easy-to-read infographics, and quirky sidebars that present a complete and informative look at the city.

O'Neill, Pat. *From the Bottom Up: The Story of the Irish in Kansas City.* 1st ed. Kansas City: Seat O' The Pants Publishing, 1999. Trace the colorful history of Kansas City's largest immigrant group and discover the defining role the Irish played in Kansas City's early history.

Shortridge, James R. *Cities on the Plains: The Evolution of Urban Kansas.* 1st ed. Lawrence: University Press of Kansas, 2004. Follow a detailed history of Kansas's larger communities, including Kansas City, from the 1850s to the present and how various industries, movements, and decisions shaped these cities into their present-day formations.

Unger, Robert. *The Union Station Massacre: The Original Sin of J. Edgar Hoover's FBI.* 1st ed. Kansas City: Kansas City Star Books, 2005. After a bloody shoot-out at Union Station, FBI founder J. Edgar Hoover launched a manhunt under false pretenses for "Pretty Boy" Floyd and Adam Richetti. Discover the truth about the massacre and how it changed the opinion of Hoover and the FBI.

Worley, William S. *J. C. Nichols and the Shaping of Kansas City: Innovation in Planned Residential Communities.* 1st ed. Columbia: University of Missouri Press, 1993. The story of J. C. Nichols, one of Kansas City's most influential developers and the founder of the Country Club Plaza, still studied as a forerunner in walkable, mixed-use districts.

TRAVEL

Eddy, William, and Richard Ballentine. *Hiking Kansas City.* 5th ed. Rocheport: Pebble Publications, 2007. Explore Kansas City through a wealth of off-the-road hiking trails in a variety of conditions, from flat and paved to remote and forested.

Internet Resources

ArtKC365
www.artkc365.com
Artist, former AP writer, and arts enthusiast Steve Brisendine tirelessly combs the Kansas City area to post pictures and information about daily art openings. In January 2010, Brisendine transitioned the website from an independent site to a collaborative endeavor hosted by *Review*, a visual arts publication.

Back To Rockville
www.backtorockville.typepad.com
Kansas City Star music guru Tim Finn blogs thoroughly about the Kansas City music scene, presenting a look at upcoming shows, reviews, music news, and more. Back to Rockville also features a concise venue list, as well as "Give a Listen," a regularly updated section with reader-recommended tracks, streaming radio, and sound equipment.

Blog KC
http://blogkc.com
Discussions on community issues and summaries of prominent local media stories make this a condensed, entertaining guide to all things Kansas City.

City of Kansas City
www.kcmo.org
The official site of the city's government, this is a great place to explore visitor services, receive construction and other updates, and access a complete phone list for all city departments. The parks and recreation and transportation sections are especially helpful for those eager to navigate the city and explore its wealth of green spaces.

The Downtown Council
www.downtownkc.org
Search up-to-date information regarding downtown news, shops, and new businesses from the independent 280-member Downtown Council, a group dedicated to the betterment of Kansas City's urban core.

Fat City
http://blogs.pitch.com/fatcity
From the witty writers of *Pitch Weekly* comes Fat City, a daily look at local and national food culture. Keep up with restaurant openings (and closings), as well as information on other food-related events.

Kansas City Area Development Council
www.thinkkc.com
KCADC is dedicated to the economic development and business recruitment of the greater Kansas City area. Visit the website for fact sheets about the city, including top industries and local statistics, or peruse the "Living and Working" section for entertainment and arts and culture suggestions.

Kansas City Convention and Visitors Association
www.visitkc.com
If you're going to bookmark only one Kansas City site, this should be it. The CVA is a comprehensive, constantly updated guide that offers individual venue profiles, as well as suggested itineraries and themed compilations such as Kansas City's fountains or favorite barbecue spots. Check the annual reader's favorites awards for restaurants, clubs, shops, and events that other KC visitors have ranked

high on the list of must-sees for any visit. Also look for information about seasonal rate specials, city coupon packs, and other discount-oriented materials.

Kansas Couture: A Midwestern Fashion Perspective by Katy Seibel
www.kansascouture.com
Lawrence resident and style guru Katy Seibel diligently photographs her funky, mostly thrifted outfits and provides tips for getting the most out of your own closet. Seibel's style know-how landed her in the pages of *Lucky* magazine in 2009.

KC Beer Blog
www.kcbeerblog.blogspot.com
Beer is an undeniable part of the local culture, and the KC Beer Blog is a refreshing source for beer-related events, news, and even tips on beer-making and yeast brewing. Be sure to check out the blog's local beer feeds list, a comprehensive guide to other local beer- and food-related blogs.

Index

K

L

M

NO

P

QR

Restaurants Index

Nightlife Index

Shops Index

Hotels Index

Acknowledgments

They say it takes a village to raise a child, and it certainly takes the expertise and support of many to write a book. Many thanks to everyone at Avalon Travel, including acquisitions director, Grace Fujimoto, and senior editor, Erin Raber, the dream team that made *Moon Kansas City* a reality and kept me on task while answering my virtual avalanche of questions. Thanks also to map editor, Albert Angulo, a great email pal and cartography whiz, and graphics coordinator extraordinaire, Tabitha Lahr, for creating a visually pleasing final product and guiding me through the process.

Closer to home, I send my heartfelt gratitude to the many people who helped me along the way, including the Kansas City Convention and Visitors Association (especially Derek Klaus, for kindly providing numerous photos), Jasmyn LeFlore and the rest of the staff at the Omaha Convention and Visitors Bureau, the Lawrence Convention and Visitors Bureau, Randy Attwood of The Nelson-Atkins Museum of Art, and Allison Smythe of Ars Graphica for submitting Rocheport photos. Alicia Ahlvers, Kevin Bundy, Casey Carlson, Dee Clark, and Jason Preu responded to various email queries and provided their expertise on various areas and activities in the city. To those who work at the Kansas City Public Library's downtown location, especially the Missouri Valley Room, as well as the Plaza Lattéland on 47th Street, thank you for allowing me to spend many, many hours in your establishment plugging away on the manuscript. And to Kelley Walker-Chance and Ashley of Marsh of Kelley Photo + Design and Katie Snustead of Mink Artistry, I could not have taken such a wonderful headshot without you!

Before this book existed, my family and friends helped nurture my dream to be a writer. To Jamie Young, Dana Hill, and Laine Baker-Alter, you made me feel at home in Kansas City, and now I can't imagine living anywhere else. And to Mom, Dad, Lisa, Len, Adam, Danielle, and Grammy, I would, simply put, not be where I am today without you. Last, but certainly never least, to Rob Schamberger, an artist, fellow writer, and my husband-to-be. From road-tripping to proofreading to offering limitless encouragement and perspective, you helped make this possible and for that I am eternally grateful.

www.moon.com

DESTINATIONS | ACTIVITIES | BLOGS | MAPS | BOOKS

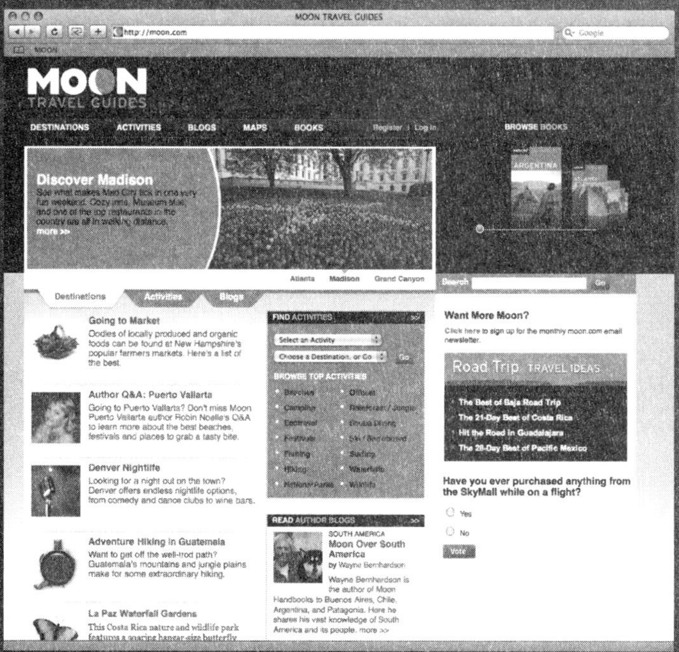

MOON.COM is ready to help plan your next trip! Filled with fresh trip ideas and strategies, author interviews, informative travel blogs, a detailed map library, and descriptions of all the Moon guidebooks, Moon.com is all you need to get out and explore the world—or even places in your own backyard. While at Moon.com, sign up for our monthly e-newsletter for updates on new releases, travel tips, and expert advice from our on-the-go Moon authors. As always, when you travel with Moon, expect an experience that is uncommon and truly unique.

MOON IS ON FACEBOOK—BECOME A FAN!

JOIN THE MOON PHOTO GROUP ON FLICKR

MAP SYMBOLS

- Expressway
- Primary Road
- Secondary Road
- Unpaved Road
- Trail
- Ferry
- Railroad
- Pedestrian Walkway
- Stairs
- Highlight
- City/Town
- State Capital
- National Capital
- Point of Interest
- Accommodation
- Restaurant/Bar
- Other Location
- Campground
- Airfield
- Airport
- Mountain
- Unique Natural Feature
- Waterfall
- Park
- Trailhead
- Skiing Area
- Golf Course
- Parking Area
- Archaeological Site
- Church
- Gas Station
- Glacier
- Mangrove
- Reef
- Swamp

CONVERSION TABLES

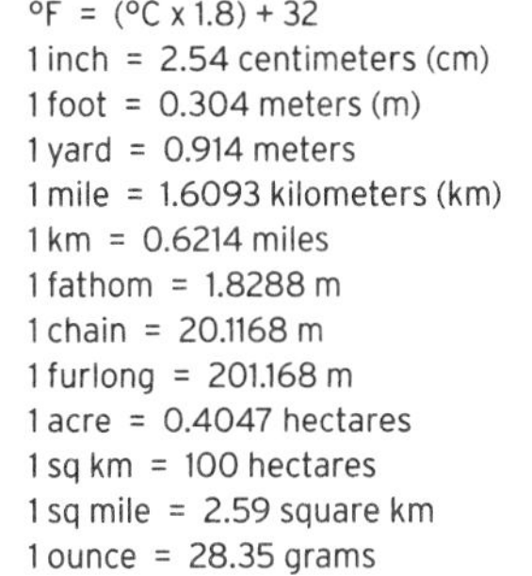

°C = (°F - 32) / 1.8
°F = (°C x 1.8) + 32
1 inch = 2.54 centimeters (cm)
1 foot = 0.304 meters (m)
1 yard = 0.914 meters
1 mile = 1.6093 kilometers (km)
1 km = 0.6214 miles
1 fathom = 1.8288 m
1 chain = 20.1168 m
1 furlong = 201.168 m
1 acre = 0.4047 hectares
1 sq km = 100 hectares

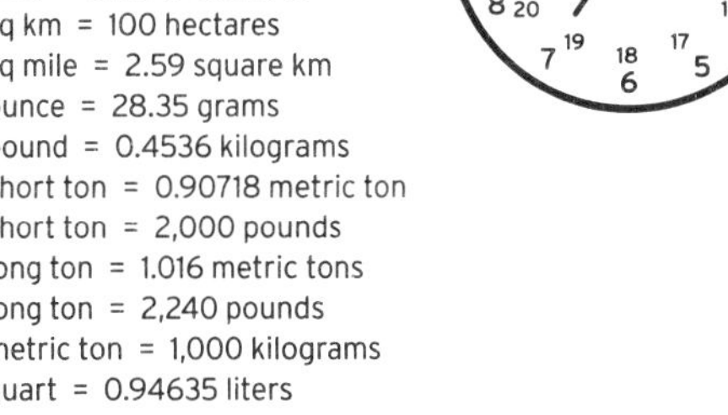

1 sq mile = 2.59 square km
1 ounce = 28.35 grams
1 pound = 0.4536 kilograms
1 short ton = 0.90718 metric ton
1 short ton = 2,000 pounds
1 long ton = 1.016 metric tons
1 long ton = 2,240 pounds
1 metric ton = 1,000 kilograms
1 quart = 0.94635 liters
1 US gallon = 3.7854 liters
1 Imperial gallon = 4.5459 liters
1 nautical mile = 1.852 km

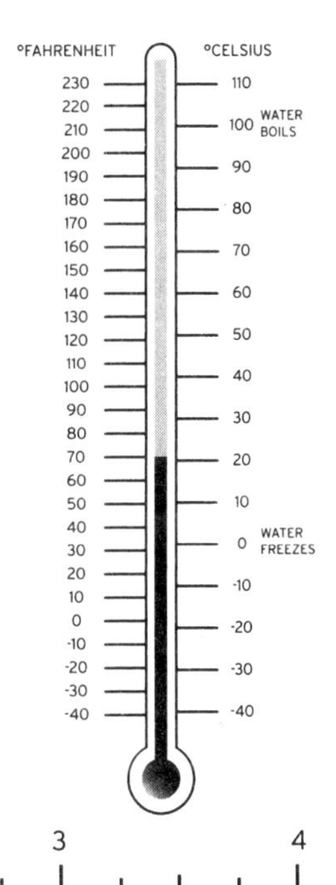

MOON KANSAS CITY
Avalon Travel
a member of the Perseus Books Group
1700 Fourth Street
Berkeley, CA 94710, USA
www.moon.com

Editor and Series Manager: Erin Raber
Copy Editor: Amy Scott
Graphics and Production Coordinator: Tabitha Lahr
Cover Designer: Tabitha Lahr
Map Editor: Albert Angulo
Cartographers: Lohnes & Wright, Brice Ticen, Kat Bennett, Chris Markiewicz, Michelle Trame

ISBN-13: 978-1-59880-362-4
ISSN: 2153-2672

Printing History
1st Edition – April 2010
5 4 3 2 1

Front cover photo: The rearing *Bronco Buster* greets visitors to Barney Allis Plaza. Commissioned in 1980, the 10-foot bronze sculpture was created by Ken Clark as an enlargement of Frederick Remington's *Bronco Buster* statue, first created in 1895 and celebrated as Remington's most well-known sculpture. Photo © Michael Snell/Alamy.
Interior color photos: Courtesy of the Kansas City Convention and Visitors Association - page 1, the River Market; page 10, Country Club Plaza; page 11 (icon), The Patriot rollercoaster; page 11 (bottom right) The Plaza's Spanish-style architecture; page 13, Arrowhead Stadium; page 14, The Hilton President hotel; page 15, the Kansas City Zoo; page 16, Boulevard Brewing Co.;
© Katy Ryan - page 11 (bottom left), Country Club Plaza;
© Rob Schamberger - page 12, City Market

Printed in Canada by Friesens

KEEPING CURRENT

If you have a favorite gem you'd like to see included in the next edition, or see anything that needs updating, clarification, or correction, please drop us a line. Send your comments via email to feedback@moon.com, or use the address above.